LUFTWAFFE EAGLE

LUFTWAFFE EAGLE

A WWII German Airman's Story

ERICH SOMMER

Edited and expanded by J Richard Smith

GRUB STREET • LONDON

Published by
Grub Street
4 Rainham Close
London
SW11 6SS

Copyright © Grub Street 2018
Copyright text © J Richard Smith / Erich Sommer 2018

A CIP record for this title is available from the British Library

ISBN-13: 978-1-910690-54-3

Book design by Daniele Roa

Printed and bound by Finidr, Czech Republic

CONTENTS

PREFACE

Erich in 1990 with his favourite cat, Pussy. He was always a great animal lover.

I began to write down recollections of my family and my past in Germany in March 1979. At that time, I typed them directly into my typewriter with two fingers. My initial accounts were disjointed as I found free time and as memories returned. It was an unplanned and haphazard attempt to leave an account of how we came through those turbulent and, for the whole world, historically important times. I tried to cover the period from the late nineteenth century to the end of the Second World War. At this time, I was sixty-six years old and lived in Bedford Park, South Australia, together with my wife Elfriede (Friedl), sixty, and our daughters Irene and Renate. We had emigrated to Australia in September 1954 and finally settled in this southern suburb of Adelaide in 1960. Although our house is not luxurious it is comfortably situated on the western slopes of the Adelaide hills below Flinders University. We designed and built the house ourselves as we then had our own building business.

We had just celebrated our twenty-fifth year in Australia with the whole family, which included Irene's new husband John Carrig, and Renate. Although Friedl sometimes had a longing for our country of birth and its climate (who wouldn't have that occasionally?) we were well content with the style and ways of our life here in Australia. In 1969 I had retired from the highly competitive life of a builder, finally selling the firm in 1975, after building three flats to generate a little income three years earlier.

My retirement didn't mean that we weren't busy. The garden, too big for our age with vegetable plots and many fruit trees, gave Friedl lots to do, whereas I had to keep the water in the pool crystal clear and look after all the technical items in house and flats as well as maintaining our two cars which no outside tradesman touched – ever. We also had our hobbies – the collecting and preparing of mineral specimens. Friedl cut and polished the opal pieces we mined and collected during our travels and also dabbled in silver work. Another of her hobbies was to design and make lead glass panels which then adorned our rear garden, in addition to mosaic works. I did some faceting, some photography and now and then gliding at the local club near Gawler.

Interest in my past experiences have lately led to historians in Germany, England, Italy and the United States corresponding with me regarding my flying past. Locally I meet pretty regularly with people of the same past and present aeronautical interests. For example, I became friendly with a Royal Australian Air Force Spitfire pilot.

But visitors to our home are now mostly our children, after both returned from two-year working visits to the Continent, Irene 'Bobby' in 1971-73 and Renate in 1976-77 and occasionally old acquaintances of our times from when we arrived in Australia. But both my old Luftwaffe friends here, Martin Widmann and Walter Tietjens have already died and our contact with German families ceased with them.

In 1976 I travelled to Germany and Europe with Renate and managed to collect more details of the events in which I was involved. Most important was that I was able to copy my friend Horst Götz's logbooks, which had survived. I felt my memories refreshed and so felt confident enough to begin writing. The only one in our immediate family who had written anything previously about our family was my uncle, Heinrich Jolas, in his book *Kampf mit dem Alter* (Battles with Aging) which encompasses the times from 1933 to November 1946.

Despite all this, my writings lay in a cupboard until 1993. Then my daughter Renate began to take an interest in them and, with the assistance of her business computer, began to bring order into what was then a pretty incoherent story. I partly rewrote things and added photos to my account.

Many events have changed the world and our family since. Irene now has three children, Angela (fifteen), Mark (eleven) and Justin (seven) who live in Belair in the leafy hill above the city in their roomy house of their own design. Renate is still single but lives happily south of here in her own house in Happy Valley. With me living between them there is a good contact between all of us.

For myself the most fateful event was the death of my beloved Friedl in September 1989, shortly before her seventy-first birthday, which left me living alone here in Bedford Park. Friedl and I were in Germany together last in 1986 visiting many family members and old friends, but not crossing into the then DDR for political reasons. This caused Friedl much pain and many tears as she had been born in Demmin in that country. It was her homeland which was dominating her mind in her last days before she succumbed to cancer after fifteen months of suffering.

It is to her memory that I dedicate this part of our family's story.

Erich Sommer
Bedford Park, Australia,
October 1993

INTRODUCTION

During the summer of 1975 I was surprised and delighted to receive a letter from Erich in which he asked if I could supply him more details of the Ar 234 Kommando which was mentioned in *German Aircraft of the Second World War,* a book I had co-written. I was able to tell him that our information came from a number of German documents, copies of which I sent on. This exchange led us to establish regular correspondence between England and Australia where Erich was then living. He was able to give me detailed information on his life with the Luftwaffe and put me and my co-author, Eddie Creek, in touch with several of his contemporaries, not least of which was Horst Götz.

As Erich mentioned, he travelled to Europe during the summer of 1976, and stayed with us in England for a few days. During this time, we were able to talk in detail about his wartime experiences and we established a great friendship. After he returned to Australia we continued to correspond and I think that Eddie and I helped him with his wartime recollections. Not long before he died, he kindly sent me a copy of his wartime memories which his daughter Renate had typed. Although it proved a fascinating read, it stayed on my bookshelf for several years.

Then, in 2015, I realised that his experiences were something that should be shared with the wider public and I began to edit his writings, adding sections from his letters and background information where necessary.

Richard's meeting with Erich during the summer of 1976.

I was then able to contact his daughter Renate who was kind enough to lend her support to the project and to send me the earlier part of Erich's memoirs which were just as interesting. They gave an impression of what it was like to live in pre-Second World War Germany and how it became almost impossible to avoid joining a Nazi organisation even though he had no sympathy with Hitler and his monstrous plans for Europe.

This photograph (of poor quality) was taken during the meeting between Horst (left) and Erich in Adelaide in September 1991.

During 2005 Erich was confined to a nursing home where he sadly died that year, but I shall always remember him as a charming man with an impish sense of humour. He had little time for some journalists and how they often distorted history in the interests of sensationalism. One of the things which I will always remember is that in my early writings I talked about 'a Nazi pilot' to which Erich said indignantly: 'how do you *know* he was a Nazi?' I quickly changed my words to 'a German pilot'.

Erich's philosophy was neatly summed up in an interview with him in an Australian newspaper, the *Adelaide Advertiser,* following a meeting in September 1991 with Horst Götz. He said:

> 'War is a political instrument – history is a political instrument too. Much has been said about the war which is not true. We never hated the Allied pilots – not during the war – not after the war. They wanted to stay alive too. There was no heroism – just survival.'

I hope this book will bring some joy to his daughters Renate and Irene and her husband and grandchildren.

J Richard Smith
Malvern, England,
September 2017

ACKNOWLEDGEMENTS

As mentioned previously, I would like to thank Erich's daughter, Renate Sommer, not only for giving her blessing and advice but also for helping with proofreading. It was her wish to see her father's story in print that further encouraged me to edit his writings. Thanks too to my good friend Robert Forsyth for giving his advice and suggestions. To my friend of over fifty years, Eddie Creek, I also wish to extend my sincere thanks. During those many years Eddie and I have co-authored a number of books on German aviation of the Second World War. Although he has not been directly concerned with the editing of this book, he has contributed his skills in photo editing and added a number of photographs from his vast collection. Like me, Eddie knew Erich well and was also able to meet Horst Götz, a privilege which I never managed. Eddie's meeting with Horst was to have far-reaching consequences in his personal life. Finally my thanks to my wife, Joan, for putting up with days of relative solitude while I was engrossed in Erich's story.

CHAPTER 1

CHILDHOOD AND SCHOOL YEARS

My grandfather Karl Sommer began his career as a notary in Rockenhausen under the Donnersberg mountain where my father was born in 1868. His parents, my great-grandparents, were Elias and Karoline Sommer. Elias was born in Frankenthal in the Palatinate in 1804 when it was under Napoleonic rule. When I went to the registry in Frankenthal I found out that my great-grandfather Elias was born to and registered by a merchant 'Moses Levi et son Epouse Jeanette demeurant a Frankenthal'. This must have been where the rumours originated that we had Jewish ancestors within the family. I won-

Father and mother with my brothers Walter and Helmuth. They are pictured at Griesbach just before I was born.

dered how my father could have passed through the rigid Arian laws as a judge during the Third Reich with a father who was half Jewish. In fact, both my great-grandfather and Elias were Protestants who had adopted that faith in 1834.

My father, Emil Sommer, studied law at München [Munich] University and as a student, joined the *Deutsch ÖsterReichische Alpenverein* [German Austrian Alpine Society], becoming a competent mountaineer. From 1903 he served as a law student in Landsberg/Lech and, three years later he was appointed to the district court at Griesbach/Rottal, a small but wealthy market town of 1,500 souls in Lower Bavaria.

He married my mother, Sophie Renner, in November 1907 and their first two children were Walter, born on 26 December 1908, and Helmuth born on 5 July 1911. I followed on 12 December 1912 and was the first to come into the world in the newly built *Amtsgericht* [district court] house which stood like a three-storey mansion at the edge of the escarpment

Grandmother Jakobine with (from left) Paul, me, Helmuth and Walter in 1916.

opposite the old castle, with a view far across the plain, below to the east. Father was of a quiet disposition, loving music and reading and browsing through art periodicals to which he subscribed to keep himself up to date in the cultural wilderness of the Bavarian peasantry. My mother, who was a devout Catholic, was more outgoing, enthusiastically organising the social life of the area.

Living with us at the time was my paternal grandmother, Jakobine 'Binchen' Sommer, who was still relatively well off. Father told me once that in 1919 there were still 40,000 Gold Marks in her accounts which were of course completely wiped out in the disastrous inflation of 1923-24, after which she was penniless, supported by my father. On 3 March 1916 my youngest brother, Paul, was born. He was the last of the *'Rotte Cora'*, a description given us four active boys by the *Bezirksamtmann*[1] Herr von Braun who resided in the castle and sometimes found an apple or two missing from his trees. He was fond of using biblical expressions.

With the outbreak of the war in 1914 we came to see more of my father's relatives who visited during the leaner times from Berlin or Munich to have their holidays in Griesbach which was conveniently located in a rich agricultural part of Germany with above-average food stocks. We seldom saw my mother's relatives as Grandfather Renner was a master baker of high repute in Landsberg/Lech, but died in 1916, eight years after his wife Magdalena. When we went there at the end of the war the business was being run by his son Karl,

---

1. Local government official.

who had returned from the front badly injured, and my two aunts, Therese and Leni. I still can smell the fragrance of freshly baked bread and buns when we entered the narrow warm passage to the bakery.

Near to us lived the district veterinary surgeon who drove around the countryside in his Brennabor motor car with high winged mudguards and steam puffs coming from the radiator cap. Sometimes he took me with him but they were pretty rough rides as there was no rubber available for tyres during the war and the wheels of the car had wide steel rims supported all around by steel springs for cushioning. During a visit to Passau I remember seeing a platoon of soldiers riding on pushbikes along the cobblestone promenade by the River Danube making a dreadful noise as their bike wheels had no pneumatics and with steel springs around like women's hair curlers.

Brother Helmuth and I often hung around the post office from where the impressive motor omnibuses left for the Karpfham railway station about five kilometres away. They were beautifully painted and shiny with the driver sitting high in the glassed-in cabin and sounding the emperor tune with his long brassy horn. As we were friends with the drivers, we often hitched a free ride to the station and back. Then, one day, the buses disappeared, requisitioned by the army for war service. They were replaced by horse-drawn carriages.

A shortage of metal for the war effort resulted in the churches being asked to give their bells. It was quite something to see the big bell from our parish church being lowered to the ground. The small bell of our cemetery church was not so lucky, however. A large piece of it broke away when it hit the ground. We boys were so impressed with this that we later re-enacted it. One of us, Bauhuber Schorschl, found a fair-sized brass cow bell and we pushed it off a board laid over the wrought iron handrail of our balcony. As it failed to crack the first time we repeated the procedure and were gratified when it hit a metal manhole cover and shattered. There was great satisfaction as we picked up the pieces, but this quickly changed when we heard Schorschl's grandmother shouting black curses over the neighbouring hedge. As for the parish church bell, it was returned undamaged after the war.

In November 1918 the war ended and the soldiers returned, marching proudly with flowers in their rifle barrels. They brought their equipment with them which was lined up in a big courtyard of the *Bezirksamt* across the hill, guns and gun carriers with gas masks still with them. We managed to pinch some of their hard biscuits, disregarding the loss of teeth and the mouldy taste. The soldiers sat around idly, smoking and smoking because that was all they had to appease their hunger. Shortly afterwards the buses reappeared, now

The Residenz at Eichstätt in 1926 where the Sommer family lived from the early part of the decade.

battered and drably painted with iron tyres, their brass klaxons replaced by rubber bulb hooters which only squeaked. The drivers were now rough fellows, no longer friends of ours. An era had ended.

Our school teacher at the time was Herr Aubele, a muscular middle-aged man and a strict disciplinarian – a retired war veteran. He instilled in us a respect for the arts and for himself by hitting us hard over the knuckles and even on the bare bottom. "He was a 'Red'," we said, "a socialist and he doesn't like us because our father is a judge." Revolution was in the air. Our first taste of politics. Despite this Helmuth and I were into childish pursuits, finding out how to raise butterflies and keeping green frogs in mama's fruit jars.

By 1920, when I was eight years old, my father was due for promotion. Consequently, he was given the position of *Amtsgerichtsrat* and *Amtsvorstand* [chief justice] at Eichstätt. The move to a larger town held great prospects for all of us. At that time my oldest brother, Walter, was in high school at Landshut as a boarder and it had been intended that Helmuth would soon join him. The move meant that both brothers could attend the local *Gymnasium* and I would follow. For father it was a big step up in the promotional ladder and, for mother, it was a widening of her social horizons.

Eichstätt was a totally baroque town as earlier buildings had been destroyed by the Swedes around 1625 and rebuilt by the bishops in the seventeenth and eighteenth centuries. It had almost no industry other than some limestone quarries. It was a white collar town, with schools and a large Roman Catholic church. A place for introverts – and there were plenty of them.

Primary education for all was provided by the *Volkschule* but Helmuth and myself went to a so-called preparatory school for teachers in which there was only limited room for secondary school aspirants. It was of a higher quality, but the spanking was just the same!

The political unrest in Germany following the First World War did not affect us initially but soon after we had established friendships, we did become involved. It was the time of the *Freikorps*[2] fighting the revolutionary *Räterepublic* – the 'Reds' – and due to our conservative upbringing and that of all of our friends we were of course on the side of the *Freikorps*. We detested the Reds and they hated us and there was no compromise.

Swastikas began to appear with the *Freikorps* and became a symbol of the honourable resurrection of a nation. That's the way we boys saw it and everybody around us. Then a chap named Adolf Hitler appeared giving political directions in a maelstrom of conservative opinion. The political right split into the more radical under the swastika and the softer royal bourgeoisie. The latter won out during the Hitler Putsch in November 1924 when the *Landespolizei* [semi-military police] shot the Nazi marchers to bits. The self-made swastikas which we wore clandestinely in class under our lapels were confiscated when detected by our teachers and we began to lose all interest in active politics, keeping aloof from the later fights of the Nazis against Communists. In 1982 Cousin Gerhard Böhm told me that his father, who was a lieutenant in the *Landespolizei,* was accused in 1933 of having said that "the Nazis should be shot down like dogs" something he claimed he had never said, but then it was a tough job to absent himself from this accusation.

It was around 1923 that we were first confronted with anti-Semitism. One winter's night black swastikas with paint running down were splashed on the walls of houses where Jews lived. I remember that the sight horrified me, though I couldn't understand why at the time. For the first time I became aware that there were different people amongst us, like the draper Gutman on the *Dom-Platz*. The Nazis said they were traitors and parasites after Kurt Eisner, who led the appeasing *Räterepublic* government, was assassinated. It was a stigma that stuck in our juvenile minds, although we were never anti-Semitic and subsequently had Jewish friends. From then, however, we distrusted the older Jewish generation just as they naturally distrusted us following the experience of centuries of persecution in a Christian society. At this time Jews played no role whatsoever in Eichstätt's bourgeois society and kept to themselves; as no children of theirs were our age we had no contact with them.

---

2. The *Freikorps* was a paramilitary organisation which sprang up around German soldiers returning from their defeat during the First World War. Its aims were to crush the many Communist uprisings around Germany that followed. Numerous future leaders of the Nazi Party served in the *Freikorps*, including Heinrich Himmler and Ernst Röhm.

The other problem to shake us out of our bourgeois tranquillity was the deteriorating of the value of the Reichsmark. The long war followed by the harsh conditions imposed by the Treaty of Versailles, meant low production. This was because constant political unrest had eliminated any solid base for our currency. Soon the banknote printing presses were running full steam to put out

Me, Helmuth and Paul in 1928.

currency of ever higher denominations. Inflation got worse, so on one occasion father exclaimed in mock despair after little Paul failed to bring back any of the money from his school excursion to Buchenail: *"Versauft der Kerl a halbe Million"* – "Look at this chap – he boozed away half a million." (That's what he had paid for a lemonade.) By 1923 the currency was stabilised at ten billion Reichsmarks to one Renten-Mark. Anyone with any paper money left had nothing. Grandmother Binchen was one of them.

Meanwhile, Walter had been introduced to the new invention of radio and he began to build his own set. Helmuth and I attempted to join him: there was always something going on. We also became involved with chemical experiments which caused lots of anxiety with explosions and acrid smells, but nobody got hurt, apart from slight burns and scalds. But mama had reason to complain about ruined hankies, clothes and towels. This situation improved only somewhat when we shifted more and more to photography, but the towels still suffered. All four of us never stopped taking photographs all our lives.

In addition, there was always music in our house. Father played the violin and viola and had two very good instruments. Of his brothers, Karl played the cello, which he handed over to Helmuth. Not long after we had moved to Eichstätt a string quartet was established and performed on a weekly basis. The ladies came with them and mama prepared fine things for refreshment, like *Zwetschgenkuchen* or anchovy-butter toast. Of us boys, Walter played the piano. This he did with an earnestness which was sometimes frustrating, while Helmuth took up the cello, and Paul and me the violin.

There was a lot of talent in this little town of 8,000 people and much ecclesiastical music was required for religious celebrations, high mass and so on and there was of course a musical section within the Catholic faculty. Its leader, Kapellmeister Widmann, was a little man with a white billowing beard and a rasping voice. We saw a lot of him on his bike in his not always clean black habit, when he was on his way to tune the new church bells or organs within the diocese. A symphony orchestra was formed under him and father, Helmuth and I joined. In my time we played the first movement of Beethoven's First and Mozart's Haffner Symphony.

On a beautiful autumn afternoon Helmuth and I decided that the weather was better spent playing on the *Residenzplatz* than going to the clergyman's singing class. A girl was sent for us and we told her that we were not going to spend our day in 'that stinking hole'. Later that day, Walter returned home to tell us of an event which puzzled him greatly. As he was walking in the fading light along a path down on the *Residenzplatz* he overtook our old conductor who was seemingly deeply involved reading his breviary when, all of a sudden, he felt a kick in the behind and a rasping voice croaked: "I will show you a stinking hole." Hearing this, Helmuth and I slunk away, pretending ignorance.

In 1927 Helmuth began studying architecture at the *Technische Hochschule* in Stuttgart and Helmuth went to the *Oberrealschule* in Würzburg as a boarder and I was to follow him a year later, while brother Paul struggled on at the *Realschule* in Eichstätt. A year later I joined Helmuth at Würzburg which had a similar cultural background to Eichstätt. We both joined the local *Akademische Ruderclub* [school rowing club] and this became the centre of our lives for two years. At this time, I wanted to become a motor engineer. I liked drawing, drew all sorts of motor cars and collected books of drawings and specifications.

By 1929 the Great Depression had engulfed the globe and made things difficult for everybody, including our father struggling with his fixed salary and tightening budget. Politically Germany was in turmoil; the Nazis and Socialists fighting one another fiercely, verbally and physically. There was no respected governmental authority, many people were out of work and there was no future for an engineer at all as manufacturing industry closed. Only the very best could expect a job in government offices. For the rest the future looked bleak.

During the spring of 1930 father had been promoted to district court judge at Ingolstadt/Donau, a prosperous town just 30 km to the south of Eichstätt. At Ingolstadt my new school was near the river, just outside the ring of inner fortifications. It was of medium size, my class having only about fifteen pupils. In spite of having not too good a record I did better than expected, my low point being German again. Of course I joined the local rowing club immediately and trained in the fours and eights for regatta events. My classmates were quite pleasant chaps, from the township and near countryside, and we got on well, with some of them joining the rowing club.

During the summer Uncle Karl Renner, a former brewery director in Havana, Cuba, who was semi-retired and living in Karlsfeld near Munich, told us of his past and praised his profession. This pricked my interest. Later, when I discussed the matter with father, we came to the conclusion that the idea of me becoming a brewery engineer was not bad at all. Firstly, there was no future to be seen within the automotive industry at the time [1931]. Secondly, preparation before studies lasted about four years in practical work in breweries by which time my older brothers would be out of university and earning. Thirdly, there was the good prospect of an immediate job in a brewery.

Although his stories continued to interest me in becoming a brewery engineer, Uncle Karl was already anxious to leave Germany. He saw a black cloud coming with the rise of the Nazis. He was disillusioned as a cosmopolitan by their narrow-minded attitude which promised only disaster. Finally, in 1935, he and his family left for Shanghai.

1931 was my last year at school and I finished my *Abitur* [school certificate] without much difficulty. There was the usual school ball and other celebrations during which we wore our school colours. I still have the cap with the signatures of my classmates inside, now worn around the garden by grandson Mark. There are some quite famous names amongst them, including Ludwig Kraus, Audi's technical director, and Walter Heini, who was in nuclear physics under Professor Sommerfeld in Munich.

CHAPTER 2

THE BREWERY YEARS

Emil Sommer in his Niederlander *society garb.*

For many years my father had been a member of the *'Niederlander'* society which took in the academics with an interest in music and had its annual meeting in Pappenheim. They used old Dutch customs in speech and attire. At his Ingolstadt club he met Herr Yehle, a director of the *Bürgerliche Brauhaus Ingolstadt,* a jovial, one-eyed fellow, who helped me get a position as an apprentice in his brewery, just opposite where we lived. I had now two years of apprenticeship ahead of me during which I had to work in every department for some weeks to gain experience and become a master brewer. As remuneration I got some money of which I was proud and *'Biermarken'* tokens. A small amount of money was deducted from pay for them but each was good for a litre of beer at the inns associated with the brewery. Helmuth especially loved this aspect of my apprenticeship.

Walter was now taking his final exams as an architect and father was district court judge who, as such, was one of the most important men in Ingolstadt. There were no Nazis among my classmates and my mother, as a devout Catholic, naturally detested the radical right and left as most of the older generation did. There was no anti-Semitism either. I had one Jewish friend, 'Bubi' Rosenbaum, a nice rosy-cheeked stubby chap, a violin player like me in our school orchestra.

He once took me home to introduce me to his parents, but their reaction seemed somewhat distant. I assume that rising anti-Semitism made them suspicious of everybody outside their Hebrew community.

In these years the economy came to a near standstill with one *Notverordnung* [emergency legislation] passed after another. The Nazi Party became stronger and pushed its main rival the Communist Party against the wall. There were more and more ugly scenes of street demonstrations and fighting and I wished the monarchy would return. This had reasonably strong support in Bavaria, but I knew that it could never solve the mounting problems. The left was out of the question for all of our family and friends, but nobody liked the Nazis either for their sharp practices and loud mouths. Sadly, the other right-wing or centre parties were hopelessly inefficient. Our younger generation only saw hope in a strong hand, which was not ideally that of the Nazis.

The Nazi influence grew stronger within the universities and it came to the point that all students were pressured to join some organisation that the black shirts controlled. Walter and Helmuth didn't want to get involved. Walter had a problem when one such student body insisted that he be expelled from the Technical University for dishonourable conduct. This was merely because in an argument he defended himself by hitting his opponent in the face and didn't answer the fellow's challenge to defend his honour with the sabre. His adversary was well versed in the use of the weapon which Walter had never handled. He laughed the challenge off and his university administration was still strong enough to withstand the already considerable political pressure. He had no further trouble in spite of not joining any Nazi organisation.

After the Nazis came to power in January 1933 in a legally democratic way, everything changed and they created plans to eliminate joblessness. A brewer exchange programme was initiated in which every trainee brewer could move every six months to another brewery of his choice in Germany. I selected northern Germany and transferred to work in a larger brewery at Dessau/Anhalt.

While there, during my almost daily walks to the Mulde river, or pushbike rides onto the Elbe flood plains, I could not fail to hear the sonorous sound of aircraft occasionally flying overhead and realised that the Junkers aircraft factory was in the other direction in unattractive flat countryside. One day I drove to the airfield and was bewildered by what I saw. There were some of the single-engine low-wing all-metal monoplanes parked near the road, Junkers W 33 or W 34s, I think, and further away a Ju 52/3m of which I had heard but not seen before. It made an immense impression on me as it took off over my head, representing so much power and industrial achievement that I was

filled with pride that our impov-
erished country could manufacture
such things. In the far distance I
could see a vast industrial complex
taking shape which I thought was
surely not intended for making gas
water heaters, which was supposedly Junkers' main product in
addition to aircraft manufacture.

By this time, I had become
friendly with Lotte Mahn, a girl
whom I had as a partner at our
dancing lessons. It became a long
association which ended only

*At the Schultheiss Patzenhofer brewery in Dessau
with some of my colleagues. I am on the far right.*

years afterwards when she decided she wanted to marry somebody else and I
was still not ready, not having finished my studies to take up a profession. We
parted without recrimination in 1940 and I never saw her again.

Two friends from Berlin joined me at Dessau, Lothar Krebs and Kurt Rieger.
After having worked at the brewery for six months Lothar came up with a new
idea. The son of the family he lodged with had joined an SS Sturm troop and
told Lothar many glowing accounts of the organisation, of their youthful leadership and high morale. They were looking for more men to join. At first I was
not very keen on the idea, but when Kurt joined I followed. It was a mistake.

It was June 1934 and we had beautiful summer weather and I had been
with the SS troop for two or three weeks when tension arose between us few
of the SS and the bulk of other younger brewers, who were in the Sturmabtei-
lung (SA). They had up to that time constant brawls on the weekends with
other young people in the surrounding villages where they went dancing and
drinking. They often appeared on Mondays with black eyes and boasted of
their prowess in fights. We others never took part in this and thought that this
separateness was the reason for the tension.

One day near the end of June, Lothar, Kurt and I were called away from work
to report at once to our SS headquarters, a two-storey villa in a suburb, for a
field exercise. So we went home, got our uniforms and hurried to join. It was
early morning and a lot of people were already there and others still coming
and nobody had a clue as to what was going on. We were only told not to
leave and wait and finally a roll call was ordered and the Sturmführer told us

in a tense voice that there had been an SA revolt which was nipped in the bud by Hitler himself but that nobody knew how widespread this revolt was and if it would come to an armed confrontation. Everybody was asked to collect any weapon he could lay his hands on and re-join the unit immediately. As we three had nothing to collect we stayed put. After a short time, people came back with old army pistols, rifles slung over their shoulders and long-handled hand grenades pushed into their belts. How dangerous it was, became obvious when the chap sitting next to me, at a table inside, started cleaning his Luger. I watched him emptying the chamber by pulling back the breech when a shot rang out and his face became pale. He had shot himself through his thigh, through the calf of the same leg slung under and for good measure through the foot of the chap sitting opposite him. The 'revolt' had taken its toll and we were two down already. Nothing else happened all day except for some more rumours, but no fighting anywhere. This was the so-called *Röhm Putsch* [The Night of the Long Knives].

By this time, I had become disillusioned with the SS. I didn't like the so-called 'honour' rituals, or the arrogance, or the drunken leadership and managed to wriggle out of the organisation when we were transferred to the Schultheiss brewery in Fürstenwalde/Spree, the largest in Germany, in October 1934. It was not very easy to get out of the SS once you had joined up. I had to negotiate with the Sturm leadership in Fürstenwalde which was a different crowd altogether to the Dessau one, with more sophisticated directors and comrades.

It was very hard work at the brewery, with day, afternoon and nightshifts alternating week after week. Fritz Peppke and I were in the same shift and we became good friends. We grew more and more critical of the National Socialist system and kept out of its way as much as we could. But still there was a lot in this movement which satisfied our patriotic feelings, which was much depressed by the outcome of the last war and the cruel arrogance of the victors which we considered senseless, immoral and brutal. There seemed to be no way in the twenties to ever throw off this burden.

When I wanted a driver's licence I had to be in the NSKK[3] or other establishment. The KdF[4] organisation took care of recreation, had liners for sea travel, organised and administered the building of the Volkswagen works and the future

---

3. The NSKK (*Nationalsozialistisches Kraftfahrkorps*) or National Socialist Motor Corps were a paramilitary organisation, part of the Nazi regime.

4. The KdF (*Kraft durch Freude*) or Strength through Joy.

car's marketing. You could already
make a down payment. Dozens of
organisations now existed with their
own brass hats and of course, uniforms. You had to have some sort of
uniform to be somebody. How we
could stand all that beats me now. I
was never harassed after having opted
out of the SS. I had had enough of it
in spite of the fact that it did not have
the devilish reputation it achieved later.

The spring of 1934 had seen the
decrease in the long dole queues and
the future in Germany looked a lot
better. At this time the compulsory

A group of us working the Arbeitsdienst *at
Ingolstadt in 1935. I am standing on the far
left of the photograph.*

Reichsarbeitsdienst [State Labour Service] was formed, an organisation which
pulled many young people off the streets and into camps of uniformed youngsters. Their purpose was to perform physical work with the additional aim of
bringing all classes of people together. At the same time, us so-called intellec-
tuals were directed to join to give us a taste of manual work and kill any
snobbery which we may have had. As Fritz Borchert and I wanted to study
the following year we thought we had better do our *Arbeitsdienst* now and be
done with it.

On 8 March 1935 a letter came from father in Ingolstadt that Fritz and I could
join the *Arbeitsdienst* there for the usual six months, after he had pulled some
strings again. He could still do that, not because he had party connections,
but because of his position as a respected judge. He had nothing to do with
the Nazis, but was able to hold his position despite the Nuremberg laws on
racial purity. There were ways to circumnavigate the rules.

I gave notice to Schultheiss-Patzenhofer, collected my papers on 15 March
and, after a short holiday, reported to the labour service on 2 April. Its headquarters was housed in an old Dominican monastery. In the large open space in front
of the building, we lined up with our spades, which we learned to handle like
a rifles in a military fashion. To work in the surrounding countryside, we rode
in columns on pushbikes and dug and shovelled to drain boggy ground, build
roads or irrigation trenches for which the rural communities were charged. The
latter of course complained that we worked too slowly and this made the charges

overly high. However, the aim of bringing people together under primitive conditions, hailed by sociologists, to form a one-class nation, was never achieved.

In November 1935, after six months with the *Arbeitsdienst,* I joined a small brewery in the Holledau, a hop-growing district between Ingolstadt and Munich. It belonged to a country estate, called Neuhausen, which had a big agricultural holding in hop growing, cattle breeding and a rye distillery. I had a good time there with reasonably satisfying work in the company of other young folk, who liked to go dancing and drinking, with an occasional relatively harmless fight in the villages of the neighbourhood.

By mid-March 1936 I had had enough of country life and was eager for another environment before beginning studies at the Weihenstephan Brewery College. I was then offered a job at the Waldschlosschen Brauerei in Dresden. I said goodbye to Neuhausen and its very basic lifestyle and transferred by rail to Dresden. I liked the city at first sight. The very clean widely spread town on both sides of the wide River Elbe running along the southern hills, had an air of modernity, with its quiet and fast modern tram cars and a fleet of river boats. I revelled in it all and took every free moment, as shift work allowed, to explore the city and its beautiful environment on foot or my pushbike which I had brought with me. I loved pedalling for the sheer exhilaration of the exercise, uphill and downhill and for some considerable distance. In the evenings I used to take a walk along the Elbe, just down the road from my room. Dresden was by no means parochial. It had an international flavour through its culture and industry. There were some beautiful areas including the Zwinger palace built in Rococo style, the world renowned *Grüne Gewolbe* museum, the opera and the castle.

The Zwinger palace in Dresden was built in 1709. Partly destroyed during the bombing of Dresden in 1945, it was rebuilt between 1994 and 2005.

Of course I had to go and see the 1936 Olympic Games in Berlin and went with the KdF on a dreadful rail tour to the event. What did they offer us on this cheap run? An evening exhibition of baseball of all things – between two top American teams. First it started an hour late, and then it was so boring that the crowd shouted louder and louder *"Baseball nicht unser*

Fall." ("Baseball is not for us.") and people left the stadium in droves to have a drink. The packed night train disgorged a thoroughly dispirited crowd in Dresden early next morning. That was the celebrated Berlin Games for us. "Never again!" we yelled. But the international show in Berlin was magnificent and the general atmosphere was good.

In September I enrolled at the Weihenstephan Brewery College, in Freising, and was accepted. The Hofbrauhaus brewery in the town is still quite famous. Meanwhile father Emil had reached his pension age of sixty-seven and the whole household moved to Munich. Why did we move to Munich, the capital of the state of Bavaria, then a city of about 800,000 people? Many retired upper echelon public servants congregated there, after having had their last posting somewhere in the provinces, to try to re-establish contact with old acquaint-ances and their families. There was an abundant variety of cultural offerings to be had, a university for the last years of their children's studies, the vicinity of the Alps as a holiday resort and a magnificent air of free and easy life for mind and body. There was always something going on. For me it was only a short train ride to Freising, where I began my studies.

Meanwhile Helmuth had finished his diploma of engineering in Stuttgart as a civil engineer and was now with the big construction company, Philipp Holz-mann AG in Hamburg. He then joined us in Munich for a week and we all

went out together with Helmuth's friend, Edi Hirsch, who had studied civil engineering with him and later joined the *Reichsbahn* [state railways]. He eventually became a director there. Edi was a jovial fellow who looked very Jewish (with a crooked nose), but despite this he became a party member, so he had good papers. It was all you needed, good papers to prove that you were a true blue Arian. As Göring said in the case of Erhard Milch[5]: "I'll decide who is a Jew." Some of the top Nazis were not pure Arians either. Just look at Hitler's face. Not quite a Germanic soldier's! The whole racial business was nothing but ideological rubbish, a

My brother Helmuth in 1937.

---

5. Erhard Milch oversaw the development of the Luftwaffe and its re-equipment under Göring.

mixture of hatred, envy and greed to get hold of other people's fortunes, and pompous arrogance; the latter being the most devastating.

On 7 March 1936 Hitler had decided to move our newly established German army into the Rhineland which, since the Treaty of Versailles, was supposed to be completely unmilitarised. We were jubilant as we saw this imposition as an unjust act substantiated by the myth that Germany was solely responsible for starting the First World War. But the Treaty of Versailles had created a European imbalance of power which found unarmed Germany encircled by politically hostile alliances of nations like France, England, Poland, Czechoslovakia and Yugoslavia, all heavily armed and ready to pounce.

There was a general willingness in my generation to do military service and many volunteered, but could not be accommodated by the facilities which were then at an early stage. It was easy to get into the footslogging infantry, but that was not my favourite idea. Some people were already getting drafted and, in order to avoid this, I volunteered for service in the Luftwaffe by making an application for the short term instruction course for air crew, preferably as a trainee pilot. My enthusiasm was dampened right at the beginning when I was told that pilot training was not for people of higher education in the reserve. They were needed as navigators in bomber and photographic-reconnaissance units.

On 26 June 1937 I passed my pre-examinations and, on 5 July, received orders to join the Luftwaffe at Herzogenaurach near Erlangen. About forty of us assembled, most of us about my age, many of them teachers, students or engineers. After reporting to the airfield early in the morning nobody knew what to do with us. After being told to come back during the afternoon we all went out for a drink. We did not skimp on the alcohol and we were already singing by the time we reported back at 3.00 p.m. "You are in the wrong place," we were told and were loaded onto two open trucks and shipped to Lager Lechfeld south of Augsburg where there was a bomber training school. Lechfeld was a park-like compound of two-storey barracks with meticulously kept lawns and hedges, sports facilities and a heated swimming pool, arenas and, most importantly, a long row of hangars on the wide airfield. Accommodation was in two of the long houses, four men to a room with good bunks. Meals were taken in a wide hall with long rows of tables and chairs. Everything was neat and architect designed in good taste.

After initial theoretical aviation instruction, we were given flights in sport biplanes like the Focke-Wulf Fw 44 Stieglitz and Heinkel He 72 Kadett. Our pilots were flying instructors in civvies who took a devilish delight in shaking out our breakfast when we lost our way, which easily happened in the misty air at low altitude. Our theoretical teachers were old First World War officers who were out of date in most things concerning modern flying. Navigation, weapon instruction, meteorology, Morse code, wireless direction finding, bomb aiming: it was a lot we had to learn during the first three months of the course.

In addition, we had to do army drill. One day, while doing just that on the tarmac on a fine morning, a sudden humming in the air grew into a frenzied noise which raced low over our heads and disappeared in a southerly direction. To our astonishment we could just glimpse the shape of a low-wing fighter for a split second. Next day we heard of a successful world speed record by a Messerschmitt 109 piloted by Hermann Wurster and realised what we had seen. I think the top speed was about 670 km/h, a speed we thought not possible then.[6] How could I anticipate that seven years later I would push an aircraft just for fun out of a dive at 800 km/h (497 mph) just a couple of metres above the ground and think nothing of it?

After final examinations we were sent home and the successful participants were immediately recalled for a two-month advanced course which was again staged at the Kampffliergerschule[7] Lechfeld. Now we were approaching winter and the air was colder, but we were mostly seated in more protected environments

Luftwaffe ground crew manhandling an Arado Ar 66 two-seater trainer. This aircraft type had the open cockpits typical of those which gave us 'plenty of fresh air'.

6. Wurster's record was actually 611 km/h (379.38 mph) [Ed.]
7. Bomber training school.

like Ju 52s or W 34s, although we were still flying in Ar 66s, He 46s and Do 23s which gave us plenty of fresh air. Especially in the forward gun and bomb-aiming position in the Do 23; a lofty place in which one was anchored to the floor by a strap between the legs from the parachute harness. At negative G one was lifted off the floor and floated like an angel praying that the strap would hold. "Don't forget to put on your parachute," a teacher used to tell us, "as we don't like sweeping up your remains on the ground." Very reassuring, we thought.

By the end of November, the second navigator's course was over and I was dismissed as Gefreiter and returned to Weihenstephan to take up my studies six weeks late. Fortunately, Fritz Borchert and Hans Korting had been there from the beginning and brought me up to date very quickly.

At Christmas the whole family met again in Munich, Walter from Bremen where he was in a Luftwaffe architect's bureau; Helmuth from Hamburg, where he worked

Working on our brewery studies at Weihenstephan in 1937. From left to right: me, Fritz Borchert, Hans Korting and Rolf Kurtz. It was at this time that I first joined the Luftwaffe as a reservist.

for the international building construction firm Philipp Holzmann AG, and Paul from Leipheim, where he did his two-year's military service, in a Luftwaffe technical support unit.

After the Christmas break, work in Weihenstephan began in earnest with me catching up with studies for the end of term examinations which were to be in February. I copied all of the notes of my friends, made technical drawings for them and did quite well with the biological and chemical experiments. My favourite subject was energy technology under Professor Fischer, a fine and convincing man who was dean of the institute. Suddenly, because he was not a party member and a somewhat sarcastic critic of the Nazis, he was replaced by a youngish chap, a Dr Netz who sported the party emblem on his lapel. We opposed the new dean and made it difficult for him by our passive resistance.

He may have had expertise in his field, but he seemed useless. After the war, to my astonishment, I found his rather elaborate death notice in my Munich paper as vice president of Munich University. He must have wriggled himself out of his predicament after the war quite convincingly.

My last term at Weihenstephan began in April 1938. The aim of my studies was to gain the certificate of master brewing. I studied hard till the end of June when the final theoretical examination took place as I did not want the years of hard physical work I had endured to be in vain. Should the result be satisfactory I was determined to continue studies for another year in Berlin at the VLB (Experimental and Development Brewery) which was attached to Berlin University. Fritz and Hans had the same idea, so we decided to stick together.

We young people, as well as our parents, had a pretty active social life. We met with old acquaintances in coffee houses with famous music bands, at the weekends at band concerts and especially in talking to friends at the *Feldher-rnhalle*. But we never went through the *Residenz Strasse* where there was a memorial to old Nazis who died there at the hands of government police in the Nazi demonstration march in 1923. We would have had to salute with raised hands while going past, which nobody wanted to do.

To keep our population's mind occupied and prevent them from becoming bored with constant attempts at ideological indoctrination there was always a political show staged at every occasion. The flags went out, military bands played, streets were decorated and of course massed demonstrations of support for the SA, SS, NSKK, and the *Arbeitsfront* [unions] with uniforms galore. Every organisation, no matter what its size, had to have its own uniform. This was to prove that he was an honest citizen. According to the Nazis all criminals and the politically obstinate and unreliable were in concentration camps to learn a good trade. So nobody knew and didn't care much about the 'corrective services' of the concentration camps. There was certainly no inkling of Jews being rounded up to be put into these camps.

We all did well in our final exams in June 1938 and made immediate application to Berlin University for the next two semesters for the Diploma Brewery Engineer degree. In front of me was a three-month sabbatical which I used to earn money. I applied for, and got, a job as a brewer in the Durlacher Hof Brewery in Mannheim and, after only two days at home in Munich, arrived there on 4 July in pouring rain. I found the manual work hard after two years of study and my back ached and the skin on my hands became noticeably thinner. But it was fun, meeting new friends, this time from the Rhineland, and life outside the brewery was easy going.

One of my friends, Kurt Wiedmann, had the family car for his use, and we used it every free hour to visit our circle of acquaintances which covered an increasingly larger area. People just seemed to love to have a change and the opportunity to open a good bottle and have a light-hearted talk. All this was in sharp contrast to the political reality of the time. Hitler wanted, as soon as possible, to re-occupy the places on the European map created by the Treaty of Versailles to the disadvantage of the old German Reich. After marching into the Rhineland and the Austrian *Anschluss,* Hitler felt that he had to eliminate the threat from Czechoslovakia on our eastern border. To do this, a supposed threat to the large German element within this artificially created country was used to create international alarm. The right of the German element had to be guaranteed and, to do so, Hitler threatened to use military force.

The general nervousness resulted in a telegram reaching me on 27 July 1938 ordering me to join the bomber group, I./K.G. 355 at Ansbach, immediately. I took the next train to Ansbach, where nobody seemed to want to have anything to do with us reservists. We had good accommodation and food, but were sent away on leave for the weekend and after a week were sent home again.

After a period of relative calm, I was called up again on 14 September. I had to join an obscure unit at Regensburg/Obertraubling immediately. So off I went again to meet a jolly little band of reserve airmen who were gathered together to form a *Kurierstaffel*. There was a pilot, an observer and a mechanic to each crew and we got a couple of corrugated aluminium single-engine Junkers W 34s. My pilot was Karl Ritzenberger, a nice chap with whom I hit it off straight away following our familiarisation flights to the well-known coffee and cake spots such as Ainring, in the Alps.

A week later, when Prime Minister Chamberlain came to the Obersalzberg, more pressure was put on and we were moved to a little airfield near Pocking in Lower Bavaria, near where I was born. There we waited, flew around and lived well, sometimes carrying secret documents to Berlin and back again in what I would consider a very unreliable service, as we were neither instrument rated nor did we have wireless equipment. What a great Luftwaffe!

Then came the Sudeten crisis and, on 29 September, Chamberlain, Daladier and Mussolini all agreed to Hitler's demands to take over mainly German-speaking Czechoslovakia. Everything calmed down and our troops moved into the border areas. Not a shot was fired. At the end of October, we were dismissed and I returned to Mannheim, travelling via Landsberg on the way, where I met father and mother who were staying with Oberstleutnant Kolb for a short holiday. I collected my military papers on the way and was pleased to read that I was

At the Brewery School (VLB) in Berlin from 1938 to 1939.
The three in the centre are Hans Korting, me and Fritz Borchert.

now promoted to Unteroffizier (corporal) of the reserve.

I returned to Berlin during the chilly autumn of 1938. Fritz Borchert had already found accommodation for us, the location of which was unfortunately not to my taste at all, but as he had signed on for himself there and paid, I had to be content with Pankow and its dreary *Grundungsarchitecture* without a tree to be seen. I soon got used to it though, as I became quite busy with my studies.

The Nazi Party had a strong grip at the VLB college at the Friedrich Wilhelm University and all students had to be a member of one of the Nazi organisations. Following long deliberations, we three joined the NSKK because there seemed to be no other way. Our calculations were right, as we were excused from active service almost immediately because of our upcoming examinations. We didn't even have to buy a uniform.

Early in December all the big shots in politics, arts and the theatre, and of course film, mingled with the population in the streets as part of the 'Day of People's Solidarity'. When Fritz, Hans and I went to Friedrichstrasse we were able to joke with Goebbels, who was there in the middle of a crowd with his wife Magda and two little daughters, plus Frau Ribbentrop, the wife of the minister of the exterior, and Heinz Ruhmann and Werner Kraus, two famous actors.

In February 1939 I managed to go to the Opera House to see *Die Zauberflöte* [The Magic Flute] and *La bohème* while my studies at the Seestrasse research brewery went on and we had pre-examinations. Then something dreadful happened. One morning, when we went to the S-Bahn station[8], people were milling about the streets looking at SA men smashing shop windows and

---

8. Above ground local rail network.

looting from them. No police were in sight. We were disgusted, but hurried past to see the same thing happening elsewhere. A synagogue was burning. At the college we found out that these were demonstrations against the Jews who were held responsible for the murder of a German consulate official in France. We all were disgusted with this type of mob action and could not see what harm was done by the Jews who, quite legally, traded in German produced goods. Up to then nobody denied them this activity, which was legally theirs, by strict laws for the Jews, for centuries. They were practically forced into these activities, as well as into banking, by old restrictive regulations. Now it was to be denied them. Jews were to be outcasts and forced to wear a yellow star. I met nobody who agreed with this, but the outcry was muted for fear of retribution.

The semester ended in March and I signed up with the Paulaner brewery in Munich as a laboratory assistant. The laboratory was under the direction of an old white-haired doctor of chemistry whose main task was to lead the *Weisswurst* ceremony every Thursday at the laboratory. He was the only one allowed to collect the hallowed pots and tongs, set up the cooking operations at precisely nine in the morning, and cook the product of a trusted local butcher. When the time was right he yelled out of the window in a strong Bavarian accent, *"Die Weisswurst san fertig"* ("The sausages are ready") and the directors and master brewers rushed to join in the feast with us.

It was a wonderful summer in Berlin in 1939. During the hot weeks, whenever there was a free half-day to spare from college work, we swam in the pool in the Olympic stadium in the Grunewald. We also joined the annual pilgrimage of the Berliners to Werder during cherry blossom time. Every fruit orchard had rough tables and benches under the flowering trees. Around them merry drinkers gathered to sample the local produce of last year's wines. These tasted quite agreeable and were easy on the tongue (and on the purse too), but potent in a sly way, so that most of the merrymakers only realised this too late and were found snoring wherever there was grass which was not trampled on. We missed the last train too, like so many, and had a 'singing' night out until the first train arrived at five in the morning by which time we were cold and sober.

In August the last semester came to an end some months before the final examinations for our diploma were to take place. Meanwhile, everyone looked for provisional employment. I got a job as a laboratory assistant at the central laboratory of the giant Schultheiss-Patzenhofer brewery at Karlshorst, while Fritz and Hans went somewhere else. The weather was still mostly fine and hot and, with all the lakes around Berlin, it was good to be alive.

On the other hand, the political prospects did not look so good. After all the successes of Hitler's policies, there was still a sore point on our eastern border. The Treaty of Versailles had given over parts of the old Reich to the Poles, with the Polish Corridor and the free City of Danzig forbidden to join the Reich again. Hitler pressed for a solution to this injustice. Encouraged by the support of the English and French governments, a considerable arrogance was felt on the side of the Polish government and military. Then, Hitler's masterstroke of concluding a non-aggression treaty with the Soviets, robbed the Poles of their rear guard. Things got heated and consultation carried over to demands and finally to irrational actions. Still most of the populace didn't in its wildest dreams believe that things would come to violent conflict. Hadn't Göring been a good hunting friend of Marshal Piłsudski?[9] Wasn't there a constant cultural exchange with Poland? We heard of cases of Polish spying, which cost two women of the German nobility their lives and the bad treatment of Poles of German descent was infuriating, robbing them of their native language, customs and rights. The accusations went forwards and backwards, but we thought nothing would come of it.

---

9. Marshal Józef Klemens Piłsudski (1867-1935) had been the military dictator of Poland from 1926 to his death in 1935. Hitler repeatedly tried to suggest a German-Polish alliance against the Soviet Union, but Piłsudski declined, instead seeking precious time to prepare for potential war with Germany or with the Soviet Union. Just before his death, he stated that Poland should maintain neutral relations with Germany and keep up the Polish alliance with France, and improve relations with the United Kingdom.

CHAPTER 3

POLAND AND THE PHONEY WAR

I was ordered to join the Luftwaffe on 7 September 1939, eventually joining Kampfgruppe 100 at Köthen as a Feldwebel.

Things were to look very different when I awoke on the morning of 1 September 1939 and turned on the radio as usual. I was surprised and dismayed to hear that Germany had just invaded Poland. More details were given in the morning paper which I picked up on my way via the S-Bahn to the brewing laboratory where I worked. Apparently the invasion was to clear the air once and for all and to set things right. My God! I thought, was it necessary to do that? Was there no other way? And Hitler, who was hurt in the last war, said that he would see to it that there were to be no repetition of these sufferings. Maybe it would blow over. But it went on. The Polish generals, so full of arrogance had to have their mouths shut.

Then Britain and France, who had guaranteed Poland's independence, declared war on Germany. Why we thought, it's not their business? All of a sudden we became patriotically involved and nobody questioned our right to fight for our lives, as it then appeared to us. We felt that the invasion of Poland was purely to regain some of the territory which Germany had lost after the First World

War. But the declaration of war by the Allies was something different and nobody had the moral right any more to refuse to take up arms. Let's settle the problem with Poland, we felt, and then try to come to terms with the Allies. When the Polish forces had been overcome, which actually took three weeks, we would have no enemies in the rear and we could exploit the rich forests and the agricultural land of the east. We would be able to deal from a strong position.

What we didn't anticipate was Russia later declaring war on Poland and advancing westward. Did Hitler see a danger in this movement or was it as planned? That the Soviets invaded the Baltic provinces afterwards must have made Hitler see the real Russian intentions, so we thought, not knowing that he had sold the Baltic States out to the Russians. The fact that the Soviet aggression against Poland did not inspire the Allies to declare war on them too was especially disquieting. Was there some sort of secret collusion between them? Was the old policy of encirclement still active?

Nevertheless, I thought, there would be peace again and I hadn't done anything to contribute to the glory, but this soon changed. During the morning of 7 September 1939, a telegram arrived at our laboratory, calling me up into the reserves with the 13th Ergänzungs [Reserve] Battalion based at Gauting near Augsburg. I went home straight away, packed my things, and gave my crackling old radio to my landlady who was mightily pleased. After packing, I took the night express to Munich. Father and mother were not unduly surprised to see me turn up unannounced and we had a hearty breakfast after which I left for the destination shown on the telegram. To my surprise I found that this was the wrong town so I returned to Munich. After enquiring further, I discovered that the unit was based at Gablingen, not Gauting! After arriving there I enlisted with the 4th Company, received my equipment, and settled down together with the other randomly assembled reservists with my level of training, all navigators.

A number of dreadfully boring weeks followed which seemed completely purposeless while the war in Poland came to an end with the Russians invading the eastern part of this unlucky country. Our role was to replace unit losses and to reinforce the squadrons of bomber groups which were being expanded. As we were all navigators, we had first to be teamed with pilots, wireless operators and flight mechanics to make complete crews. We were then trained to crew the major type of bombers in use at the time, such as the Heinkel He 111 and the Dornier Do 17.

The problem was that we had already had most of the theoretical lessons when we were reservists, but these were given again purely to keep us occupied.

We got our uniforms of course, and a *Soldbuch* (which accompanied you wherever you were posted). This included our personal particulars such as rank, unit, pay etc. We were also given an *Erkennungsmarke* [identification tag] with our personal number. At that time, I didn't give much thought that this was necessary to identify something unrecognisable by other means. I just shrugged off thoughts like that, as it 'only happened to other people'. Surprisingly, at the end of the war, I found that my anticipation proved correct for me.

As our final examinations were not to take place until the ten days between 16 and 26 October in Berlin, I got permission to complete my brewery studies. It was a jolly reunion at the university. I was the only one to wear a uniform at that time. We had a good time in spite of the pressure of the written and oral examinations which actually went quite well. Looking back, I think that everything was made easier for us defenders of the fatherland out of growing patriotism.

I arrived back at Gablingen airfield on 16 November 1939 and was posted to a reserve unit at Krakau [Krakow] in Poland. Like my previous unit, this was non-operational but purely a collection of reserve crews for bomber units. The weather and the general environment was cold, wet and bleak. No refinements such as we were used to in Germany. Old cavalry barracks, dirt tracks, mud and a lousy grassed airfield about five kilometres from the old town. It could only be reached on foot. In addition, there were a large number of wrecked Polish fighters and other aircraft strewn about.

One consolation was meeting a good friend, Jochen Meinholt, a very young fresh-faced blonde Friesian boy who had a great sense of humour. Together we explored the old city, and had cups of hot black coffee with brandy in one of the big local cafes; a treat which we could not find any more in Germany. Jochen and I had no personal contact with the Poles, but fraternisation went on quite openly in spite of orders forbidding it. A loaf of bread smuggled in to the town immediately opened up family connections, especially with the very willing females. This, they hoped, would please the soldiers and gain protection for their families.

The Krakau intermezzo lasted only until 3 December when Jochen and I were both posted to an active Luftwaffe unit, Kampfgruppe 100 based at Köthen/Anhalt in Germany. We were happy to pack our bags and left by train, first for Berlin, and then next day to Kothen not far from Dessau. I had lived there during 1933-34. It was very flat country, formed from the glacial deposits of the past ice ages which had covered much of northern Germany.

Kampfgruppe 100 had been established following the invention of the X-Verfahren target-locating device. Its purpose was to test the equipment under operational conditions. Formed on 26 August 1938, the unit was initially designated the 7th and 8th Kompanien of the Luftnachrichten Schule und Versuchs Regiment [Air Signals Training and Experimental Regiment]. The two companies were the first in the world to undertake this type of operation. Both were initially equipped with Ju 52s.

Following a period of experimental distance flights, the unit carried out a small number of operational sorties over Poland. The companies began to re-equip with the He 111 from 7 October 1939 and were redesignated the 1st and 2nd Staffeln [squadrons] of Kampfgruppe 100. Their first commander was Major Heinrich Pusch who was replaced by Oberstleutnant Joachim Stollbock on 22 November 1939. Initially K.Gr. 100's aircraft carried four-letter identification markings but these were replaced by the code 6N followed by the black cross national insignia and two other letters indicating the individual aircraft and the Staffel.

Jochen and I arrived at K.Gr. 100's airfield just outside Kothen and reported to the Stabs [headquarters] office. After a short interview I was told to join the 1st Staffel while Jochen went to the 2nd Staffel. We had no idea what awaited us, or the role that the unit was to undertake apart from the fact that it was a bomber group as its designation (Kampfgruppe) implied. After I found my way to the 1st Staffel office I was informed that it was equipped with Heinkel He 111s and had special tasks such as long-distance flights and night-precision bombing.

The Staffel had just lost half a crew on a night-training flight when the pilot collapsed and the machine crashed. Both the pilot and navigator were killed while the radio operator and mechanic/gunner bailed out safely. I was to replace the navigator and the pilot's replacement was scheduled to arrive soon afterwards. He joined us two days later. He was a short fellow with a wrinkled face but with enormous vitality, quick witted and full of purpose. His name was Horst Götz and he came from the Telefunken Company in Berlin where he had worked as a test pilot for electronic

After joining K.Gr. 100 I met Hortz Götz for the first time. This photograph shows us just after we met with Horst on the left.

development. He was a year older than me, and because of his career, had become acquainted with a number of people in politics, as well as in the military and industry. This was to prove extremely useful, as he was often able to pull strings if he found it expedient. His most important contact was 'Papa Cornberg', Oberst [Group Captain] Wilfried von Cornberg, the head of the personnel department of the Reichs Luftfahrt Ministerium [German Air Ministry].

Horst pulled strings immediately by organising his wireless operator at Telefunken, Gerd Albrecht, to replace the previous one who had bailed out and had lost his nerve. He was nicknamed *'Der Dicke'* [the fat one] because of his tall lean figure. The original mechanic, Erich Kraft, stayed with us for the time being. He was a short guy from Hamburg who was full of native jokes. He was the only one of our original crew who didn't survive the war. When we moved to France in September 1940 he also lost his nerve and asked for a transfer to a quieter unit which flew mainly transport operations. However, during one of these, his aircraft crashed into a low hill in Normandy in broad daylight and he and the remainder of his crew were killed. We buried them at Vannes in Brittany.

Our aircraft, on which we began training the same week, was a He 111 H-3. It was brand new, but a consistent troublemaker. Its electrics occasionally broke down in mid-flight. The reason could not be established for a long time as ground testing revealed no problems. Our squadron aircraft, nine of them, as well as the three from the Stabsstaffel [Headquarters Flight], looked different from a normal He 111 because they had three radio aerials sticking up above the back of their fuselages. These were the installations for the top secret X-Verfahren, a shortwave radio-directed target-finding device for bombing in bad weather and at night.

X-Verfahren was a system of radio beams designed to locate a target. Each beam was named after a river. The main beam, Weser, was sent out by the Wotan I ground station to cross the intended target. It operated at a much higher frequency (around 60 MHz) than the previous Knickebein device and consequently could be pointed much more accurately. This beam was crossed by a series of three very narrow single beams, named Rhine, Oder and Elbe respectively. At about 30 kilometres (19 miles) from the target, the radio operator would hear a brief signal from Rhine, and set up his equipment. This comprised a special clock with two hands. When the second Oder cross beam was received, about 10 kilometres from the target, the clock was started automatically causing the two hands to begin to sweep up from zero. When the final Elbe beam was crossed, five kilometres from the target, the clock reversed, at which point one hand would stop and the second would start

I am sitting in the navigator's seat of our He 111 with the special X-Verfahren bombing clock.

moving back towards zero. When zero was indicated by the second hand reaching this point, the bombs would be released automatically after the bomb aimer opened the bomb doors and switched on the electrical fuses. When installed in the aircraft the equipment was known as X-Geräte.

At this time our Gruppe was training on long-distance night flights to the Mediterranean and back. We were not told the reasons for these sorties. After a couple of these flights, both our Staffeln transferred to Rotenburg near Bremen on 16 December. This was a grassed airfield with good barracks some miles from the North Sea coast. Now Christmas was upon us. We were all sent on leave, which I spent in Munich. I have no recollection of who I met there, but travel restrictions then applied generally in Germany, preventing big family reunions.

After our return, training began in earnest to catch up with the high standard of the professional crews. We undertook a series of night circuits, bad weather landing procedures, landing with the Funk Bake navigational system and even with Z-Z-Verfahren, an experimental landing procedure under zero visibility. Then, on 17 January 1940, we did our first training flight with the top secret X-Verfahren in which the pilot followed his directional beam and I, as navigator, listened to cross beams on different frequencies.

Long-distance flights followed. During these an electrical fault, which had been causing us the considerable trouble previously mentioned, was finally located by an engineer from a very small airfield. This after all the big shot electricians had failed to find the problem. Then a really hard winter set in with temperatures of minus twenty degrees and high winds causing the ground mechanics and crew a hard time in trying to keep the aircraft ready for immediate action. In this period no actual combat was taking place, apart from some minor aerial skirmishes and desultory British bombings over the coastal areas. We were not allowed to retaliate. Morale was high, but it received a blow when our Kommandeur [commander] Oberst Joachim Stollbrock, and his crew were

Horst seated above the cockpit of our K.Gr. 100 He 111. Note the Viking ship emblem, which was painted on all the unit's aircraft.

lost during a training sortie over the Thames Estuary at dusk on 13 February. We discovered later that their He 111, 6N+AB, had been shot down by Spitfires. He was replaced by Hauptmann Artur von Casimir. Other crews took part in sporadic shipping raids at night along the English east coast and, later in February, the complete Gruppe transferred to Lüneburg which was to become our home base for more than a year.

It was from there, during the night of 2-3 March 1940, that I made my first operational flight. This was with another crew because Horst Götz and Gerd Albrecht were on leave in Berlin and the crew of Oberfeldwebel [Flight Sergeant] Heseler had its navigator missing. It was a strange feeling being out at night over the North Sea near to the hostile British coast with only the faint lights of ships visible in the otherwise complete darkness. We released our bombs on dark shapes of ships which blacked out immediately. Some machine-gun fire came from below but we could not see the results of our attack and turned back into the rose-coloured morning light to the east. The attack was carried out at low level after which we climbed to 2,000 metres (6,500 ft) to preserve fuel. After an hour we saw the rock of Heligoland in the far distance. This was a most welcome sight. We turned around the rock then to run in over the coast at a predetermined corridor through our coastal defences. When we landed, we found one crew had made a belly landing. Jochen, who had been out during the same night with his Staffel commander Oberleutnant Gerd Korthals, proudly showed me some holes in the wings of their aircraft from the ship's machine guns. I could show nothing. A report by me of this flight was used by a *Propaganda Kompanie* reporter, Major Adler, in his little book *Wir greifen England an*. This dreadful piece of prose still exists amongst my books after surprisingly surviving the war at home.

At this time, it was a leisurely war with both sides testing the other's strength. We still thought the possibility of a compromise was feasible. But then Churchill was appointed as the new British prime minister and we felt this, together with the 'Roosevelt Brain Trust' effectively ruled out any compromise. It made the defeat of Germany and its government which they hated, a distant possibility. We, on the other side, had the feeling that the moral actions of the Allies in no way out-shone those of Nazi Germany. They broke treaties in the same cold-blooded way and their actions were just as questionable. We felt that the war had begun long before the official outbreak. The USA broke their neutrality status constantly and had begun re-arming in a big way by building up its shadow industry. It colluded with Britain in reporting German ship movements and denying us certain materials but assisting Britain and France with arms. We felt that the USA was practically at war with Germany, but our government felt arrogantly secure behind their trumped-up military strength, which they demonstrated at every opportunity. Of course, at this time we were superior in war technology and determination. This was good for the short term, but how strained our resources already were at this time showed up in the events which were to happen shortly afterwards.

The Luftwaffe still conducted its affairs with ease. There was no immediate threat it could not handle. Some crews of merit were even sent on 'recreation' to ski lodges in the Alps and I was one of the lucky ones. On 13 March I was posted to Radstadt in Austria for a fortnight's skiing. I had a great time with much better food. All Germany had been on rations since the beginning of the war. I had several relaxing skiing tours from a hut high up in the mountains but snow blindness put me out of action for a couple of days. Our caretaker, a lanky weather-beaten Austrian, shortened the days by letting me help to draw secretly on the rum supply for the 'convalescents', for which it was issued. He gave me an occasional little nip in a tiny glass, while he put the big glass balloon to his mouth and gulped deeply. I doubt if anybody else ever knew or saw anything of this rum. After this act of Christian charity, he felt better and started to sing until, at ten o'clock, the *Jause* was served. This was a bowl of fresh thick sour milk with spicy dark bread. At the end, I returned to my unit again, brown as a berry.

Lüneburg was a fully equipped station with fine barracks and modern instal-lations and amenities. As with most of our airfields at that time, it had no concrete runway. Only the aprons in front of the long row of hangars were hardcore. Our training went on. By the end of March, a higher state of readiness was ordered. On 6 April, our crew received a new aircraft, coded 6N+IH, which would serve us for the next year until the end of our assignment on the Western Front. The X-Verfahren equipment had temporarily been removed from our Heinkels.

CHAPTER 4

THE BATTLE FOR NORWAY

Two days later, on 8 April, we transferred to a rather primitive airfield further north at Nordholz. From there we trained briefly with fighter escorts and they simulated fighter attacks which might take place during our bombing runs. For bomb aiming at higher altitude we used the old mechanical bomb sight, the Görz 219, which wasn't very accurate.

During the evening we were called to a top-secret briefing which revealed that there was intelligence that British naval forces were approaching Norway, with the intention of landing troops there. The German government could not stand by and allow this, so early the next morning our troops were to move in. We were not to leave the airfield or talk to anyone. Readiness would begin immediately. Anticipated take-off, after further briefing, was at 0500 hours. We were stunned. It was a terrible blow for Horst, who had good friends in Norway. As a youngster he was cared for, as a hungry boy in Berlin, by a fishing family at Andenes on the Lofoten islands in the far north. He could speak Norwegian fluently, and was very upset about the prospect of attacking the country. But what could he do but obey orders? We all had a very disturbed night.

Next morning, we were woken early. It was still dark with clear skies. The sky showed only strips of cirrus; it would be fine flying weather. After the briefing, which informed us that our target area would be inside the Oslo Fjord, we had a good breakfast. We were served strong Brazilian coffee, hot sweet milk porridge which I liked most, and an egg, all privileges for an aircrew in action. In addition to this we each received a packet of biscuits with a round disc of chocolate and an apple for sustenance during our sortie. Then we wrapped ourselves up in our flying gear, parachute harness and leather helmet with microphones and oxygen mask. We declined the vacuum flask of hot coffee for the cockpit, for reasons of 'difficulty with disposal'. It was cold at our usual operational height of 4,000 metres – around minus twenty-five degrees. We felt pretty helpless with all this gear within the confined space of the cockpit, and with fingers stiff from the cold in spite of our woollen and leather gloves.

As navigator I sat on a small seat on the right-hand side of the extensively glazed cockpit of the Heinkel. This could be hinged backwards when not needed. In front of me was a sliding floor panel beneath which I, doubling as bomb aimer, lay. When slid shut, I could lie on top of this if I had to use the flexible MG 15 machine gun in the front of the Plexiglas nose cone. On my right-hand side, against the wall, was my parachute which I could attach to my harness if needed. Adjacent to this was a sheet metal container in which I could stow an assortment of maps for navigation. Above that was the artificial lung (a regulated oxygen dispenser) into which I tapped my oxygen mask and the Patin radio direction-finder compass.

To my left sat the pilot Horst. He was much more comfortably placed on an adjustable seat which contained his parachute.

The cockpit of the He 111. The pilot's seat is situated on the left with the navigator's to the right. In this photograph the bombing clock is on the right and the forward-firing machine gun is in the extreme nose.

Despite this he was equally restricted in movement by all the paraphernalia. Behind us a bulkhead separated us from the bomb-storage compartment. This consisted of eight vertical housings which accommodated either eight 250-kg bombs or alternatively thirty-two 50-kg bombs or incendiary containers. I could control the electrical fuses with a switch in the cockpit, if I wanted them to have delayed action or not. A narrow corridor between the bomb-storage compartments led from the cockpit to the rear compartment in which the wireless operator was housed high up under a Plexiglas cupola, with his machine gun facing to the rear. He was able to swing sideways to operate his transmitters, receivers and switchboard, while our mechanic/gunner, Erich

Kraft, lay on his belly (in flight only) in the 'bath tub' beneath the fuselage. He had a rearward-firing MG 15 gun. Entry and exit was through a lockable trapdoor on which he was lying. Not a safe place to be in a belly landing! A man could be squashed and killed standing on the trapdoor, which was against regulations. This happened once in an emergency.

At 0608 hours we took off in formation to the north in a clear sky. For no apparent reason we had to circle over the North Sea until 0900 hours before entering the Oslo Fjord. There we were to attack the coastal town of Horten in case there was continuing resistance from Norwegian forces. As no white flares were visible, as a sign of surrender, we unloaded our bombs onto the fortifications. There was a big oil patch on the water there. We found out later that this was the grave of the German cruiser *Blücher* which had been torpedoed by the Norwegian fortified land batteries. After a magazine exploded the ship had sunk with major loss of life. The wreck remains on the bottom of the fjord to this day.

Apart from this there appeared to be no activity below except for the smoking remnants of a ship on the shore. Meanwhile, after aimlessly milling around, we joined up with the Heinkel of our Staffel Kapitän, Hauptmann Hermann Schmidt. All of a sudden a slight puff of smoke appeared on our port side followed by more puffs. We could see parts of Schmidt's wing hanging from a sizeable hole and we indicated that we would escort them to our home airfield of Lüneburg. On the way, at the southern entrance to the fjord, we passed over the semi-submerged wreck of a German torpedo boat. I learned some forty years later that it was the *Albatros*, which had run aground during the night. Our landing at Lüneburg went without a hitch at 1325 hours. After partaking of refreshments at the airfield, we flew back to our temporary base at Nordholz.

Next morning, we were given the task of reconnoitering the North Sea between the Orkney Islands and Norway. We were looking for the Royal Navy and hoping to discover any of its movements which could threaten our own operations along the Norwegian coast right up to the Arctic. Everything seemed to have gone well with landing our troops except at Narvik. There was a problem there because our destroyer flotilla had run into superior British naval forces. The outcome was unclear. We discovered a smallish ship off the Orkneys and attacked it because it failed to show any recognition signal. We sprayed it with machine-gun fire but without visible effect.

It might be interesting here to give a brief history of the Narvik campaign. When Germany invaded Norway on 9 April, some 2,000 troops from the German 3rd Mountain Division under General Eduard Dietl were landed by

Hauptmann Hermann Schmidt's He 111, coded 6N+NH, following its crash-landing after being shot-up by RAF Hurricanes on 10 April 1940.

ten destroyers at the strategically important port of Narvik. Next day five British destroyers attacked the German naval force. Two destroyers were sunk and three more damaged for the loss of two British ships. Three days later an attack by nine more Royal Navy destroyers, this time led by the battleship HMS *Warspite,* resulted in the loss of all eight remaining German destroyers. Eventually British, French and Polish troops, supported by the Norwegians, launched an attack on Dietl's forces and managed to recapture the town on 28 May 1940. However, before this, on 10 May, the Germans had invaded France and the Low Countries and Allied forces had been ordered to withdraw from Norway on 25 May. Norwegian forces were only informed of this decision on 1 June and shortly afterwards the country fell.

After our time was up in the sector which we were patrolling, we returned alone, flying just beneath the clouds at 2,000 metres for fear of fighter attack. Suddenly, an SOS came over the radio from Hauptmann Schmidt's aircraft, 6N+NH, saying that it had been hit. He seemed to cop all the flak wherever he went, but he managed to return home despite having one engine shot out and two of the crew, Oberfeldwebel Richard Röder and Unteroffizier Alfred Traupe, wounded. Although the rescue boats had been alerted, they were not needed as Schmidt managed to crash-land safely.

In the days that followed, we shuttled backwards and forwards to various bases including Schleswig, Aalborg in Denmark and Trondheim/Værnes in Norway. No definitive plan seemed to exist. We felt that there was no proper planning behind the whole operation. We got further proof of this later.

We transferred to Schleswig/Land on 12 April during a very cold morning. The grass runway was covered in thick frost. We had just turned to starboard after taxiing in when, to our left, another Heinkel passed us, still going at considerable speed. 'He'll never make it', we thought and watched as it raced towards the border embankment where it sheared its undercarriage off and finally came to rest on its belly. The pilot turned out to be Oberleutnant 'Bubi' Russell, (so-called because of his young looks). This kind of thing was not taken lightly at that time and I think 'Bubi' lost his wings. It was one-and-a-half years later that I was to sit opposite his desk as *Offizier zur Besonderen Verwendung* (assigned to special duties like an adjutant) at the Ergänzungs Staffel (reserve squadron) at Hannover/Langenhagen where he was then the boss. He survived the war suffering the indignity of the reduced rations allocated to those who stayed at home.

Next day we were told to return to Lüneburg, then to Tutow in Pomerania for compass adjustment, and finally back again to Schleswig. On 15 April we were ordered to transfer to Christiansand in Norway, but on arrival we were told to get the hell out of there as the airfield was extremely overcrowded. So we returned to Schleswig. Scarcely back on the ground, the order came to fly immediately to Oslo/Fornebu. We finally arrived there, exhausted, with night approaching, only to find that there were no barracks, no room to bed down, no transport. All that was there were the wrecks of the transport machines which had crashed during the first day's action. These only made things look more uncomfortable. It was a cold sleepless night on the concrete floor of a corridor in an airport building. By dawn we were up again, jumping around in an attempt to get warm. There was no warm food for the second day running, but hot coffee did arrive. The morning dragged on until a briefing took place in the control

Our group of He 111s at Trondheim where we always had beautiful weather. The sun was so hot that the air over the airfield shimmered. We craved for the coolness of higher altitudes.

tower. We were to reconnoitre along the coast of Norway and the fjord into Narvik, as there was no clear picture of what was happening to our forces there.

Our leaders seemed to have no idea as to the ship movements of the enemy. There were no weather reports and no navigational aids anywhere along the coast. Even more infuriating was the absence of any maps, to any scale, north of Bergen, just above us in Oslo. We had pointed this out days ago. We had packs of maps in the metal cases which had been issued to us as navigators, but these did not cover anything north of Bergen! This shows how badly the whole operation was prepared. It seemed no forethought had been given to the undertaking, everything being done on the spur of the moment, possibly with a fortnight's preparation. The only thing to be found for the area north of Bergen to the very top of Norway was a weather map stuck to the wall of the control tower. So we found some sheets of tracing paper and each navigator copied the coastline of Norway onto it. That was all, good luck, see you afterwards at the little frozen lake east of Trondheim! We were to fly in loose formation and only use the radios in an emergency.

We took off at 1142 hours flying in unison, tanks full to the brim, with some bombs in case of a good target. Widely spread out, just holding visible contact, we cruised north out at sea skirting the numerous islands. At least it was warm and cosy in the sunlit cabin except for a cold draft from an air leak by my right leg. We had lost contact with the others when we crossed the Arctic Circle and approached a longish island at 2,500 metres. This was just outside the rocky coast with its many fjords and glaciers. Approaching closer we saw ships entering the channel between the island and the coast from the north. After a second glance we realised, to our utter surprise, that there was a whole line of ships. This consisted of several destroyers, possibly a battleship, and a cruiser. These began to open up on us with orange flashes coming from their decks.

After a split second, lots of smoke puffs were surrounding us and we had no choice but to immediately dive down to sea level and turn to port. This brought us behind the island for cover. We innocents had waited one second too long for evasive action and we seemed to have little chance. Even the big guns of the battleship had fired and placed the waterspouts so accurately in front of us that we nearly hit them when down near the water. We immediately reported the battleship as HMS *Warspite* and the movement of the naval force, but got no acknowledgment. It must have cost Mr Churchill a lot of money we thought, all this ammunition they had wasted. We didn't receive one hit or even a splinter which was quite important to us at the time. We continued on northwards, but we later found out that the whole British battle group had also turned to the north as a result of our encounter and being detected.

At the entrance to the Vest Fjord we discovered nine ships lying idle, among them three destroyers and three bigger merchantmen. Inside Narvik harbour itself we saw nothing but destruction. All our destroyers had apparently been sunk or scuttled on the rocky beaches. Only a single merchantman in the harbour looked like being on even keel and seemed to be under steam. At Harstad, north of Narvik, we found a cruiser and a destroyer, clearly enemy ships, but no troops seemed to be disembarking. We attacked these with our 50-kg bombs but apparently without result.

As we returned to base, we thought about the precarious situation of the few sailors and soldiers of General Dietl's mountain division who had survived and landed before the destruction occurred. Without doubt a decisive push by the British, French, Poles and Norwegians would have immediately overcome them. But we saw no signs indicating such a move. The hills were covered in snow and the landscape made a bleak and desolate impression. An attempt to supply the remaining troops with light artillery had already taken place. Fifteen Ju 52s laden with the disassembled guns were dispatched on 13 April, a one-way mission to land and discharge their cargo on the frozen Hartvikvann Lake north of Narvik. Of these, two returned to base due to mechanical trouble, three were shot down by destroyers while circling low to come in to land, while the remaining ten landed and were left on the ice due to lack of fuel. They were later to sink through the ice after the summer thaw set in. Four of them were recovered in 1986 from a depth of 75 metres (246 feet) out of the icy clear water in remarkably good condition. They are now prized relics. One

is now in Delmenhorst in northern Germany.

After completing this sortie, we returned and landed at our new make-shift base at Jonsvatnet, east of Trondheim, the last aircraft of the Gruppe to do so. As soon as we got on the

The He 111, coded 6N+IH, in which Horst and I flew most of our missions.

ground we began rolling 200-litre (44-gallon) drums of aviation fuel over the ice to pump the contents into our almost empty fuel tanks. It was hard work. Afterwards we were driven to Trondheim to eat a fantastic smorgasbord dinner at a hotel and have a night's rest. Sadly, though, this was interrupted at about midnight by air raid sirens as the Tommies tried to bomb our aircraft on the lake, but without success.

Next morning, we completed the refuelling from drums which we had put on sledges. Petrol was in short supply as many of our naval tankers had been sunk on the way up the coast. Then we were ordered back to Lüneburg, had two days' leave in Berlin, and then transferred back to Aalborg in Denmark for the next sortie over Narvik. We used every excuse possible to touch down on a Danish airfield for the rich food which was available there throughout the war. Denmark had special protected status and was not picked clean by the ever-hungry Germans.

On 21 April we took off again for Narvik with orders to bomb anything hostile and to land again on frozen Jonsvatnet near Trondheim. Again we were flying far out from the coast, in the wonderful world of water, mountains and ice, with our automatic pilot doing much of the flying. The rearward crew were not speaking on the intercom, so it was quiet and cosy warm apart from the monotonous singing of the reliable Junkers engines and the manually adjustable variable-pitch propellers. I saw Horst closing his eyes against the glare, or so I thought, but then I realised that he had dozed off. Doesn't matter I thought, the crate flies by itself and in an emergency I can take over by swinging the control column over to my side. All of a sudden we both woke up. The pitch of the engine noise was a little higher, and the variometer (rate of climb and descent indicator) was showing that we were in a shallow dive.

Startled, we realised that we were a little bit too far out to sea. Looking to starboard over the mountains we could see little specks in the sky going southwards. Another unit returning, we reassured ourselves. We asked Albrecht for his opinion over the intercom and he too replied in a very sleepy voice that he hadn't been keeping a look out. On we went towards Harstad where we found 5/10ths cumulus cloud cover when we reached the target area. Almost immediately the Allied cruisers and destroyers began firing ferociously at us. There were also some merchantmen off the coast which had just discharged their troops and equipment. Still alone we made three bombing runs on the ships below from 3,500 metres, passing through the black cloud of exploding shells. Fortunately, we escaped unhurt but we could not see if we had caused any damage because of the cloud. After making a note of the position of the enemy fleet we came back on course.

Meanwhile the weather along the coast had deteriorated badly. Low clouds drifted in from the sea concealing the mountain tops. Then we flew through snow drifts and the aircraft began to ice up so we were lower than we would have liked. As we had better charts by then we found the entrance to the Trondheim Fjord with no problem and sneaked in under the black clouds. Running short of fuel, we realised that we would have to land on the lake there but, at the end of the fjord, we had to climb over a range of forested hills before touching down. Horst took the risk and in spite of the low clouds approached the area. Suddenly we spotted the white area just in front and under us.

The undercarriage and flaps were already out. We slid in and touched down, taking a deep breath of relief. Our taxiing run created a very rough rumbling sound and we passed a Ju 88 lying upside down. Thick snow fell. Finally, we came to a halt tilting slightly to the right. When we emerged from the cockpit we found we were standing in 20 cm (8 inches) of fresh snow which was concealing the deep ruts from aircraft which had previously used the landing strip. Our starboard wheel was in one of them. For half an hour we worked hard to push the aircraft, with the engines revving hard, out of the ruts and onto a reasonably firm patch of ice. There was nobody about but the crew of the unlucky Ju 88 two kilometres away. No help, no organisation.

We made our way on foot over the frozen lake to the old maintenance area. Here we found that the undercarriage of our group commander, Hauptmann von Casimir, had broken through the ice, leaving his aircraft on its belly. Damn it, how come we were not informed? Perhaps there was a recall over the radio but, like the rest of us, had 'der Dicke' been asleep? Of course he said he never heard anything, but wouldn't admit it if he had. We found our commander on the shore of the lake. Initially he was not at all pleased to see us, but mellowed when we explained how things had happened and how we too ended up here. He liked active and aggressive crews and we seemed to fall into this category in his eyes.

Again we stayed at the hotel in Trondheim, enjoying the smorgasbord and the wide variety of food. Next morning, we were driven out to the lake. No more snow had fallen during the night and the air was frosty and crisp. There were hundreds of fuel drums on the lake and on the shore, but they were all empty. There was nobody about from whom we could ask questions. Eventually we found a hand pump and a hose in a half-empty drum lying on a sledge. Gradually we discovered more drums containing petrol until we had enough to get us to nearby Oslo. Just enough to enable us to lift off the soft ice covered with thick snow.

The four of us then trampled all over the surface of the lake to try and locate a safe stretch without concealed ruts. This took us ages but eventually we mapped out a strip from which we could take off. After warming up the engines, Horst applied full power. No need to hold the brakes for a short run. At first she didn't move but then, at last, she began to crawl. As our speed increased, she began to wobble about. Then there was a loud crunching sound or two as we bounced over ruts in the ice which we had failed to detect. Fortunately, they also gave us a slight jolt which lifted us into the air. With fingers crossed, we skimmed the ice and flying at a crazy angle managed to make it over the fir trees ringing the shore – just.

After landing at Oslo/Fornebu, twenty minutes or so later, we found that we had left the tail wheel behind on the ice; no doubt torn off by a rut. This meant a three-day stay at Oslo while our Heinkel was repaired. There were already a number of He 111s from other units there. I had a pleasant surprise when I recognised a pilot getting out of his aircraft after he had parked it nearby. He was an old rowing mate from Ingolstadt, Ottl Allwang, who was now with K.G. 4 and who I had not seen since 1933. We had a brief talk but we never saw each other again. I heard a year later that he had been shot down and killed in the Battle of Britain.

Next day the patch-up job had been completed, but we still could not leave as a splinter from an enemy bomb had burst one of our main-wheel tyres and we had to wait until a spare was flown in the next day. This was the only damage caused in this night attack on the airfield.

This suited us well as it gave us a chance for a short holiday in the city where we peeled shrimps on the harbour quay and chatted with the Norwegians. At this time at least, they were mostly happy to talk to us, but we could sense considerable reserve in their manner. Horst talked freely and tried to explain and apologise. The Norwegians were treated fairly and with respect, which we think they appreciated. They were not harassed by anybody except when they were involved in clandestine military activities. This was the same for the Danes.

On 24 April we were able to return to Lüneburg where all our mechanical complaints were rectified. Two days later we joined the remainder of our Staffel at Aalborg in Denmark. Just after arriving we took off again to combat the British landings at Andalsnes. The British were trying to cut Norway in two between Trondheim and Oslo. They had already been beaten back from the south and their supplies had been cut off by attacking Luftwaffe aircraft and German U-boats.

As we approached the target area I saw for the first time in my flying career an enemy fighter bearing down on us. It was an uncomfortable feeling being exposed to bullets while sitting in the 'glasshouse' canopy with no protection. At this time, we only had a single machine gun firing forward and no armour plating whatsoever. The enemy turned out to be an old-fashioned biplane, a Gloster Gladiator.[10] It didn't fire a shot and took off when our gun opened up.

After we had plastered the ships of the landing fleet in the bay at Andalsnes we separated from the rest of the squadron. We still had some 50-kg (110-lb) bombs in our bomb bays so we dived into the valley where the road and railway ran eastwards into the mountains. We attacked a viaduct but nearly hit a hospital behind. We only realised this as we skimmed over its roof, flying very low close to the valley floor. Then we headed back westwards again towards the sea. The road was now on our right, cut into the hill down in the valley. We kept a sharp look out for retreating enemy troops, when all of a sudden there was a rattle in the cockpit and bits of chart were flying about like confetti.

Erich Kraft yelled over the intercom: "Horst! The port engine is burning!"

The rattle stopped as fast as it began. I crawled back through the corridor to look for myself and saw a dirty white discharge pouring thickly from the port engine. But Horst had already reacted and cut it and feathered the propeller pitch to zero so that the blades didn't turn anymore as the temperature rose. I assured him that it was not flames that were coming from the engine. We then veered gently away from the road from where the machine-gun fire had come, and settled down on the far side of the valley as it widened out.

The fire had come from British troops who were retreating on the road from Lillehammer and going towards Andalsnes. The road was overgrown with trees and had concealed their movements. The confetti came from my chart holder, which was hit by a bullet. The rotating projectile had turned madly inside the tight container. Another bullet had hit my parachute beside my thigh and rolled itself up inside the silk like a corkscrew. I had it for a long time as a talisman in my wallet until I lost it, and the wallet, in 1943.

Horst never batted an eyelid and carefully climbed up the slopes of the southern mountains to get us over the 2,000-metre-high glacier. We finally made it by a cat's whisker through a gap in the mountains. Now at a safe height we flew steadily on south towards Aalborg, our home base. We landed there in a clear night sky at 2225 hours. The squadron had already given us up.

Because the engine and other damage had to be repaired, we flew back to Lüneburg in a Ju 52 to obtain a replacement aircraft. We found a Heinkel which

---

10. This was probably an aircraft from the RAF's 263 Squadron as the Gladiators flown by the Norwegians had been destroyed by this time.

had just been repaired and transferred to Trondheim/Værnes which was situated towards the end of the fjord. The airfield was occasionally bombarded by fire from the British navy and also suffered some bombing attacks. This forced us to operate, in between attacks, from Stavanger, which was equally exposed but not so crowded. One night while we were there, a British cruiser's guns hit the airfield, liberating thousands of chickens from the adjoining farms. This meant that we didn't have to rely on our frugal Luftwaffe rations for a while. It was a hot early spring and we even had cases of sunstroke during briefings in the open. Our main task was to act as tactical support for our paratroops at Narvik who were fighting a desperate battle to keep alive against overwhelming odds. We attacked ships and enemy troops from high and low level between Harstad and the Gratangen.

At the beginning of May 1940 I was promoted from Unteroffizier to Feldwebel and all our crew were awarded the EK II (Iron Cross Second Class). I left the medal with my parents in Munich when I visited them on leave. The conditions in the north were never easy for operations. The weather was always unreliable and could change rapidly, especially bad when we undertook long-distance flights. In addition, our petrol was often contaminated with water as it was pumped from our supplying submarines at Trondheim. This caused the engines to cut occasionally and splutter until the fuel injection cleared itself. At Trondheim/Værnes we often got bogged down in the mud when taxiing. When this happened British and Norwegian prisoners helped by pushing together with soldiers from German infantry pulling on long ropes.

On 20 May we attacked Polish troops on top of the mountain ridge to the south of Narvik with machine guns and 50-kg bombs. We flew at low level just above the rocky ground. When we returned to Værnes, Jochen Meinholt enthusiastically rushed up and told me what had happened after we had turned for home. Flying as navigator/bomb aimer with Gerd Korthals, he had dropped a widely spaced stick of bombs along the ridge running north towards the shore of the fjord when the very last of the twenty-four bombs overshot the steep hill and hit something just offshore. This blew up with a tremendous explosion. He had hit the Polish destroyer *Grom* which sank immediately. The bomb had hit live torpedoes lying on deck.[11]

At this time the German offensive in the west began and all of a sudden increased activity by the Allies in the north was apparent. They still hung on

---

11. Erich's date is probably wrong as most sources say that the destruction of the *Grom* took place on 4 May. A total of fifty-nine sailors were killed and thirty wounded amongst the 154 survivors. [Ed.]

The destruction of the town of Bodø as seen in 1942.

to Bodø, south of Narvik, and naval attacks on the latter intensified. Our aircraft had in the meantime been equipped with the much improved Lotfe 7C bombsight. This was an optical gyro-stabilised automatic device with far superior accuracy and our success rate improved dramatically. Enemy ships never had it easy while they were within the range of the Luftwaffe and without fighter protection.

Now there was a last serious attempt by Allied forces in northern Norway to capture the ore port of Narvik. The German land forces were pushing north to relieve their beleaguered troops but had been held up at the coastal town of Bodø. The Luftwaffe was called on to break the resistance of the British troops there and we attacked town and harbour with disastrous results for the township, which was completely razed. When we were in the second wave of the attack we saw with growing horror that the town was doomed and attacked the wharf with our high-explosive bombs and then threw the incendiary bombs into a swamp to the south.

Later, in 1957 while heading a building company in Australia, I built houses at the Mary Kathleen Uranium mine in Queensland. One hot evening I happened to sit beside a young man in the pub. We fell into conversation and he told me that he had emigrated from the town of Bodø in Norway. He was a young boy when the attack took place and told of the German forewarning whereupon the populace made for the hills from where they saw the terrible destruction. We talked quite openly and I gained the feeling that he held no personal ill feeling against me as a former Luftwaffe man.

On 28 May, Allied forces took Narvik while we bombed the British ships which were supporting the operation. One of our aircraft hit the flak cruiser HMS *Cairo* in the bow section with two bombs. As we followed it in, Horst held our Heinkel steady despite the shells coming from the ships below and bursting around us. It always surprised me how much space there was around a solitary aircraft for the fireballs and splinters from over 100 guns. Horst took no evasive action as he could have just as easily steered into the path of one of the shells. I discovered in 1985 from British naval sources after I sent them my aerial picture with dates and location that our bombs had disposed of the cruiser's main antennas. As the *Cairo* was the lead vessel for the attack, Admiral Cunningham had to shift his command to another vessel.

Next day we bombed the newly established airfield at Skaanland near Harstad. This was reported to be the base of British Hurricane fighters. This attack was to cost us our Gruppen Kommandeur, Hauptmann von Casimir. He was flying as an observer in Oberleutnant Wolfgang Metzke's 6N+AB. After the war I discovered what had happened. Their aircraft had reached its target when it was attacked

We found some British helmets at Trondheim which I couldn't resist trying on.

by two Hurricanes from No. 46 Squadron RAF. In the action that followed the Heinkel was badly damaged but Metzke managed to make a forced landing south of Narvik in the Efjorden. One of the crew was killed and two more wounded, but both von Casimir and Metzke escaped unhurt, only to be taken prisoners by Norwegian troops. They were handed over to the British who immediately shipped them to Glasgow for interrogation. Von Casimir's place was later taken by Hauptmann Kurd Aschenbrenner.

This was the last action in Norway with which we were involved. Shortly afterwards we were recalled to Germany. During our time in the north, German forces had overrun the French and British armies in France and Belgium and had taken up positions on the Channel coast. The Luftwaffe was now preparing to attack the British Isles. Just as German troops in Norway were to be interred by the Swedes, several of the Allies were now doing the same if they could not be evacuated. It was the end of the war in Norway.

We flew back to Lüneburg, our home base, where we were all given five days leave. I made my way from there by rail to Munich to see my parents. The mood was generally good as there was no apparent danger to anybody at home. Our rations were still adequate. My father and mother were in rude health. As for my brothers, Walter was now on the island of Sylt, Helmuth was in Hamburg, while Paul was serving with a Luftwaffe ground-support unit on the Western Front. He was not too happy with his job of driving an arrogant unit commander.

CHAPTER 5

NIGHT-BOMBING MISSIONS

After returning from leave on 6 June 1940, our Heinkels had been refitted with their X-Verfahren target-location equipment. The next few days were spent very quietly, in training with the device and indulging in sporting activities. Then, on 20 June, the whole of Kamfgruppe 100 (which still only comprised two Staffeln plus three machines from the headquarters flight) moved from Lüneburg to the small tactical airfield of Gabbert in Eastern Pomerania. This was a remote field surrounded by miles of forests and a string of glacial lakes from the Ice Age bedded deep into a flat landscape. It was like paradise. The weather became rather hot and we were happy to escape the heat by swimming early in the morning and then flying at altitude where it was cool.

The transmitter for the main beam of the X-Verfahren which we were using was 150 kilometres (90 miles) away and was cross directed at a bombing target nearby. As we grew in confidence with the device, we managed to get our practice concrete bombs within an average of 150 metres (500 ft) from the target. We alternated in practising bombing dummy ship targets from low level and attacking installations with our machine guns. Around this time our ground crew applied a temporary soot black finish to the underside of our Heinkels. This, it was hoped, would make them less visible from the ground at night.

Kurd Aschenbrenner had just been appointed as our new group commander but, unlike von Casimir, he was not universally popular. We found him a rather dour man, but he did possess considerable experience in signals work. Around this time a third Staffel was added to the group by a nucleus drawn from the other two squadrons. Its commander was Oberleutnant Eberhard Schnürpel.

While flying over the scorched landscape, we sometimes had occasion to report forest fires in the distance. One sultry day, with thick thunderstorm clouds towering above the airfield, we descended from high altitude to see a patch of oil in the small lake at the end of our landing strip. It was, we were told afterwards, the spot where one of our He 111s had overshot while landing. This was due to a recent heavy rain shower which had caused the aircraft to aquaplane. It had raced through the pine trees, down an embankment and into the water where it promptly

A He 111 (6N+FH) en route from Lüneburg in northern Germany to Vannes in Brittany on 11 August 1940.

sank. The pilot was a recent arrival to the squadron. He was a young lieutenant, and as his crew told us later, he was so distressed that he hunched down in his seat and determined to go down with his aircraft. This was until his navigator forced open the hatch and kicked him out of the flooded cabin. Both men surfaced without further mishap, but the pilot had to bear the scorn of the remainder of the squadron for this incident for a long time afterwards.

By 8 August we were ready to fly back to Lüneburg but, instead, we were ordered to go westwards to Brittany to be thrown into the Battle of Britain. It was thought that our night-bombing capability would be a great advantage. It looked at this time as though Germany might be able to force the British to capitulate, especially after France had been defeated in such a spectacular fashion. Instead, this was to prove the beginning of a war of attrition in which both sides suffered heavily.

On 11 August we flew westward to Vannes under low cloud. Vannes was a beautiful 16th century town on the south coast of Brittany with brightly coloured half-timbered houses. Its airfield at Meucon, about eight kilometres to the north, was quite wide and positioned on a high plateau. As we flew towards our new home we passed over areas where recent ground battles had taken place. We saw the destruction of the towns, rivers and harbours. We also reflected uneasily about the landscape of Normandy with its fields surrounded by stone walls, which would make safe emergency landings almost impossible.

After landing at the airfield our aircraft were rolled into the adjoining paddocks and camouflaged. We were then driven to town in buses to find our quarters at the Hotel Moderne. This was managed by an elderly, fat and resolute lady, a formidable disciplinarian who stood no nonsense. In the end we all grew to like her as she was always good for a joke. How we tucked into the rich French cuisine including an enormous langouste which we couldn't finish. On top of this the French wine was flowing freely!

Our operations against Britain began with bombing attacks in and around Birmingham on the night of 13-14 August. We were allocated as target the Spitfire 'shadow' factory at Castle Bromwich. It was a moonlit night which we preferred because it helped us control the accuracy of the beams which were laid over targets of strategic importance like aircraft factories, harbour installations and other clear military objectives. No towns or civilian targets were to be bombed at this time.

An excellent contemporary account of this first operation was given by one of my compatriots in K.Gr. 100, Feldwebel Hilmar Schmidt.

'At 1900 hours the pre-flight briefing was held. Our target was the Dunlop Works, east of Birmingham. We were given all the necessary papers and instructions. As always, ours was the last aircraft of the second Kette (Flight) to take off. Our prescribed route was Taunton-Swindon-Birmingham-Carmarthen-Brest and back home. The fact that we did not exactly adhere to the second part of this plan was due to no fault of ours, but was brought about by adverse circumstances.

'The complete Stabs-Kette took off ahead of us, followed by the three Ketten from the first Staffel and finally our own second Staffel, a total of twenty-one aircraft. A half-hourly spacing had been ordered between each Kette, and each aircraft within its Kette went on a different route to the target.

'All the flying crews had their pre-flight meal together in the hotel and Paul Wiersbitzki (my pilot) and I went to have a little rest afterwards. Then a coach took us to the airfield. As the engines were run up I stood listening to the drone of the motors. What a spectacle on a moonlit night like this, before the dark silhouette of the trees one can't help being impressed by such a scene. Then the motors were running at full throttle, demonstrating their power, their exhaust pipes glowing red in the darkness. Then, as before in May, we were putting on our life jackets, flying suits and parachutes. Now fully prepared, we were aware of that feeling of cool confidence a man gains after fighting both the weather and the enemy and knowing that he can win by trusting his machine and having faith in himself and his fellow crew members.

'We fastened our seat belts and I again flashed a signal to Bernd (our No 1 maintenance mechanic) and we were taxiing out to the take-off position which was marked by lamps. It is rather strange, but it has become a long-standing habit that I make a goodbye sign to the mechanic, thereby acknowledging on behalf of the crew his friendly wishes for a good trip. Our flight is only made possible by his untiring work on the aircraft. I really feel that something is amiss if he is absent, as was the case when we were operating from Stavanger.

'The flight itself was routine at first, but I heard absolutely nothing of the first X-Verfahren beam over the Channel. Nevertheless, the English coastline could be identified with no trouble and we could see dimmed lights. Of course this was of little concern to us for we had no work to do here. About half an hour before we were due to reach the target I began to experience a lack of oxygen. On checking I found the pressure indicator was falling to zero when I inhaled. Luckily, with our bomb load we could get no higher than 6,000 metres so I just sat and moved as little as possible in order to cope with the lack of air.

'Occasionally I switched on my lamp to glance over the map, but down there on the ground a ghostly brightness had sprung up; like the fingers of a corpse a great number of powerful searchlights were groping for us, trying to seize us but only touching us and slipping off our soot-black coat of paint. Then there were lights and red flashes on the ground along the direction of our flight. Was this to indicate our track to night fighters? We were on the alert and Kurt Braun thought he saw a fighter on one occasion.

'Bomb release was due soon so I carried out all the necessary settings, went through the procedure and the bombs fell as programmed. However, "big fires and explosions" were not observed.

'The homeward flight was to result in a lot of trouble for us. Even allowing for the slight eeriness normally experienced when night flying, one could almost feel the uneasiness that pervaded the atmosphere on this night. The flak was not bothering us much as yet; it certainly was not as furious as our German flak which, it is popularly believed, induces the English airmen to partake of alcoholic drinks. Dying is supposed to be easier that way. Actually, I think that they, too, are daring chaps. These night raids are quite a problem and no one should be blamed for not

A He 111 showing the temporary black under surface applied for night operations. This often resulted in a rather battered appearance.

always hitting military targets in darkness. That is no reason to deny a man the attribute of personal courage! We, too, are only too glad to get rid of our bombs. We must not worry about who is being killed by them. And nor do we worry. The first time, at Harstad in Norway, I still had such worries, but never afterwards. On second thoughts, yes, over Bodø I also had such feelings. That attack, against an open city, had not been to my taste. But we are flying against England now.

'During the turn our aircraft appeared to slip away rather badly. The auto-pilot had ceased to work and the master compass failed. We could have been anywhere in the darkness of that night, wandering around and looking at the direct reading compass now and then. If only that damned water below us had not been there! But here was land again. We saw it with gratitude.

'Then we heard Caesar Heinrich (CH the phonetic alphabet call sign of 6N+CH) transmitting an urgent PAN signal and requesting a QDM.[12] However, it made an emergency landing on the beach.

'Suddenly we were over Brest, establishing our position by means of the light beacon there. Bearings obtained from radio beacons could not be relied upon because of the beginning of morning twilight, but we still had plenty of fuel. QDMs were most inaccurate, too, and we missed the airfield several times, but at last we got down, dog-tired, apathetic, dead beat. We had had enough. The Kaufmann crew, a new one to our Staffel, had been unlucky. Feldwebel Kaufmann, who had

---

12. PAN was an international signal indicating urgency but not a Mayday full distress situation. A QDM, again in international wireless telegraphy, is the magnetic heading to steer to reach the ground station.

been sharing our room, had lost control of his aircraft and gave orders to bail out. His wireless operator had just gone overboard when the machine recovered. This happened near the target and after landing it was found that one of the antenna masts had gone, too.

'Leutnant [Pilot Officer] Seebauer of the other newly-arrived crew had somehow managed to fire off a signal pistol inside the aircraft. He then scrambled back towards the rear compartment. In consequence Feldwebel [Sergeant] Knier (who had been unfortunate enough to lose his chance of becoming a reserve officer after doing some illicit stunt flying at Warsaw) and Seebauer had burns and blisters on their hands.

'Our Kommandeur, who had not been with us on our flight, was waiting in his armchair. After delivering our report we went to the hotel and had a good sleep. Our aircraft is unserviceable for the time being.'

During the following weeks, in August and September, targets varied frequently all over the British Isles until London was subjected to constant attack from October. On 24 September, our mechanic, Erich Kraft suffered health problems and he was transferred to a transport crew in our Gruppe. He was later killed in a crash on 23 March 1941. He was replaced in our crew by Gefreiter Spitznagel. Night flying was now routine. The only thing to worry about was the take-off with heavy bomb and fuel loads and the return, with bad weather conditions closing in. On more than one occasion we saw the burning debris of an aircraft over which we roared after take-off. The crews we buried in the local cemetery.

On one occasion I noticed an old French woman in the middle distance sneering from behind a tombstone in apparent delight that another couple of Germans had been killed. I remember this sending a shiver down my spine. I still lived with the opinion that death was sacrosanct, a feeling I never lost through all the cruelty of war. Maybe I never grasped what war was all about, the destruction of your enemy by whatever means possible. The British seemed to perfect it without any apparent scruple. But I shouldn't forget what our own people did to prisoners, Jews and political adversaries. It was only after the war that we found out about these atrocities, which were concealed from us until then. At that time, I still had a feeling of compassion when confronted with a young British bomber crew. They were standing in their flying gear in front of our airfield headquarters, after being brought in from a nearby airfield on which they had mistakenly landed their Wellington bomber.

It was not until the end of October that the first order came to bomb a city. The target was supposed to be the Birmingham gasworks but this was in the centre of the city. We were told that we were to do this in retaliation for British aircraft having indiscriminately bombed civilian areas in Hamburg. I had seen this for myself when I had stayed with my brother Helmuth on weekend leave from Lüneburg.

We did not take part when the much publicised attack on Coventry took place during the night of 14-15 November. We had taken off during this night in a borrowed aircraft which was so full of faults that when all our radio equipment failed, Horst as pilot, decided to throw in the towel and return. In addition, bad weather was forecast for our time of anticipated return from the target. Of course Coventry was a clear military target with essential war industry dispersed throughout the city. Each of our bomber wings was given a special target within the area, but this meant that the whole city was involved. I felt that the important thing was that a lot of industrial targets, producing war machinery, were put out of action for weeks.

Our losses were bearable at this time. They usually came from navigational errors or technical failures. In most cases it was the novice crews which suffered most while the old hares survived through the experience they had gained and the value they had for their own lives. Sometimes a seemingly cowardly expert is worth a lot more in the end than a reckless hothead. He might be called a hero after he was dead, but his worth was only to be held as a memorial to inspire the living. In the end it is the one with a little daring but with a lot of prudence who can look back satisfactorily on his achievement.

Up until the time we were transferred from this theatre in May 1941 we laughed off the enemy defences. Night fighters were reported, and we were on the lookout for them, but we only had the barest glimpse of the shadow of one on a couple of occasions. The flak didn't worry us as it was mostly badly directed. We also desynchronised our engines which confused the acoustic listening

devices on the ground. We always flew above the height of the barrage balloons.

On 24 September 1940 I was awarded the EK I (Iron Cross First Class) together with the rest of our crew and promoted to Oberfeldwebel eight days later. On 25 October I went on leave and

The main Luftkriegschule training building at Dresden in 1941.

visited Hamburg to see my brother Helmuth and then on to Munich to see my parents. I returned on 10 November and flew my next operation two days later. More raids followed until, on 27 November, I was ordered to transfer to the Luftkriegschule (Air War Academy) at Dresden/Klotsche to undergo training as a commissioned officer.

My departure meant that our crew was split up, though only temporarily. Horst and our radio operator Gerd Albrecht flew on with other crew members for eight sorties. Horst then managed a temporary move for himself and Albrecht to Telefunken, the company from which he had been transferred. Here they undertook a number of research flights.

The Air War Academy facility at Dresden had been designed and built in 1935 by Ernst Sagebiel who was also responsible for the RLM [Reichs Luftfahrt Ministerium or German Aviation Ministry] headquarters in Berlin and Tempelhof Airport, then the world's largest building. Our complex was hidden in the woods. There were all sorts of people of my own rank there. They were to be introduced to the task of leading autonomous units and all had some war experience behind them. Administrative skills, deportment, leadership training, sports, tactics for all three services were taught by the young and brash, as well as old and somewhat outdated teachers. They kept us busy non-stop for three months. Some candidates fell by the wayside but about half were successful.

At Christmas 1940 we were given a week's leave. I managed to get home to Munich by rail despite the deep snow. All my brothers turned up. Walter came from the island of Sylt and Helmuth from the Channel coast where he was engaged in fortification building. On one occasion he had picked up Adolf Galland the fighter ace, after he was shot up and had escaped by parachute.[13] Paul came from the Alsace. It was a merry encounter and father, mother and Marie the housemaid were happy to see us all unharmed and in good spirits.

Father and mother still had their social life with all their old friends and acquaintances. Father did a lot of reading of books he borrowed from the numerous local libraries. Nobody thought there was a threat to Munich or a bad end to the war and everything seemed to be going well. They were short but beautiful days full of fun and prospects. Only our parents seemed to be cautious and in anguish, which was understandable.

---

13. The only reference to Galland being shot down was on 21 June 1941. He had destroyed a Spitfire east of Boulogne, but was then shot down by the Polish ace Boleslaw Drobinski of No. 303 Squadron, RAF. He bailed out but was wounded. [Ed.]

A Heinkel He 111 of the 2nd Staffel of K.Gr. 100 carrying the identification code 6N+EK mounted on a compass-calibration platform.

On the way back to Dresden the express train got stuck in deep snow in the *Mittelgebirge* (Central Mountains) and we were immobile for two days at Hof until a powerful snow plough cleared the tracks. Back in Dresden the harsh winter continued until almost the end of our course. It was the last time I saw the stunning Zwinger, a stately building and park area with museums in the centre of the beautiful city of Dresden. I had loved my previous stay there in 1935 but I would never see it again. Nor would I return to Ingolstadt to which I was attracted by my girlfriend, Lotte, and her family. But the war had forced us to drift apart, as happened with many of my friends' liaisons. She told me bluntly that she wanted to marry somebody else. Although this was painful at first, I soon began to feel free.

The course at the Luftkriegschule ended on 25 February 1941 and I returned to Kampfgruppe 100 at Vannes by train. My return was not without trepidation as I would not be able to re-join Horst and my old crew there and would have to fly with strangers. I quickly settled down again, but it was not the same as before. I now had to billet and eat with the officers. This arrangement cut communication with the non-commissioned personnel which I didn't like. People came, and went missing, without me taking much notice. I was surprised to learn that by the end of my tour of duty in May 1941 our Gruppe had lost its full complement three times over since April 1940. I couldn't understand this, but it was apparently a fact.

It was fortunate that the proposed British commando attack on our bus (see opposite page) did not take place when we had a flat tyre on the way to the airfield in 1941.

Early in 1941 a plan was introduced to give the crews some respite by letting them have a week's leave at a villa to the south of Vannes. This was situated on the shore of the Morbihan, a bay on the south coast of Brittany. It was managed by a French lady on behalf of the Luftwaffe and we had some relaxing days strolling along the shore, exploring the rocky surf and going out fishing with the local fishermen. They left in their sailing boats early in the morning with the outgoing tide. We serviced the hooks of all four lines with bait. The rods were on outriggers. When we hit a shoal we pulled in masses of mackerel. It was great fun. We came back at noon with the incoming tide which was flowing strongly. While we considered the British enemies the Bretons appeared to really hate them for some reason. I thought the reason was probably two-fold. Firstly, the Bretons are of Celtic origin like the Irish. Secondly they were very much upset by the British naval action at the Algerian port of Mers-el-Kébir on 3 July 1940. This was the bombardment of the French navy which had refused to join the Allies. It had resulted in the deaths of 1,297 French sailors, the sinking of a battleship and the damaging of five other ships. The slogan *'N'oubliez pas Oran!'* ('Remember Oran!') appeared on placards and large posters all over France.

It was round about the middle of March 1941 that we escaped another disaster of which I was not aware until long after the war. The British War Office produced a plan to eliminate the 'infamous' Kampfgruppe 100 after their electronic countermeasures had been found not to be quite as effective as expected. We experienced crews could still differentiate our beams from the maze of other signals. So with this plan, the British hoped to eliminate the dangerous German practice of 'bombing on the beam'. Despite the objection of the chief of Air Staff, Sir Charles Portal, who said it would be unethical, it was decided to blow us up. This would happen while we were making our normal transfer by a bus from Vannes to Meucon preceding one of our night missions. They knew about this from the French underground.

I only found out about this plan in 1976 when Horst Götz told me about it. During a NATO refresher course in Salisbury in England in 1968, he had met, in the officer's mess, a French officer who told him, in the course of an extended conversation, that he was a paratrooper in 1941. He was to take part in the commando mission to blow up the Kampfgruppe 100 bus. He said that his group had hidden in the bushes beside the road to Meucon for several days but no bus came through. What they didn't know was that each crew was now travelling in separate cars. As it was senseless to blow up a car with a single occupant they decided it was not worth taking the risk. So, after a few days, they buried the explosives and mingled with the civilian population. I remember well the time we began travelling with crews in separate cars as I flew then with Leutnant Albrecht Zetzsche whom I considered as bad a driver as he was a pilot. That change happened at this exact time. It was not the last event in which the hand of Churchill (who had forced the plan through) made itself felt in my personal affairs. We'll see this later.

I was one of the first in our Staffel to receive the Frontflugspange in silver. Pictured from left are Sigi Simon, Wischnewski, me and Schulte.

There were of course quite a lot of critical moments in which we narrowly escaped destruction. Bullets flying around us, aimed or un-aimed. Being caught by searchlights and passed on to the next intersecting beams of blinding light, of exploding shells all around us in concentrated flak over Plymouth or rocked by radar-controlled shells fired from previously unknown batteries south-west of London.

On 27 March, having flown sixty-one missions, I was one of the first in the squadron to receive the Bomber Frontflugspange (operational flight clasp) in silver. As mentioned, I flew with a number of different crews up until April 1941. At last, and to my great joy, both Horst Götz and Gerd Albrecht returned from Telefunken on 21 April. The old crew was now back together with Willi Sprickerhoff as engineer.

After March, losses from British night defences began to rise. Targets became more difficult to hit in a concentrated attack. Ideally, all the bombs from our Gruppe should have hit the same spot on account of the automatic release with the X-Verfahren. If this had happened, it would have caused utter devastation in this area and would have guided other bomber units to the target. A way of checking the efficacy of our X-Verfahren attacks was then devised. One aircraft would take off first, stay over the target until the last of the incendiary bombs from our group was recorded, and then report, after landing, the time and accuracy of their impact. This task usually fell to us from mid-March until the end of May because we were the most experienced crew. We flew twenty-three of these missions in all. Nevertheless, we survived while younger crews sometimes managed only three missions before disappearing from the roll call.

Occasionally these losses were caused by technical mishaps. One pitch-black night, for example, we were taxiing in driving rain from our dispersal along the winding steel mesh grid to the take-off point. The soft ground at the dispersals in which our aircraft were parked would make the heavily laden machines sink in while taxiing and taking off, so an overlay of metal grids was laid on top of the grass. This followed a winding track through the typically Breton border hedges. We were guided along by a series of pitiful paraffin lamps.

After we took up position at the start of the runway, still faintly illuminated by the lamps, we got the green light and roared off down the track into pitch darkness with the instruments our only guide. Having got the heavy tail up and reaching the required airspeed, Horst lifted the overloaded bird off. Carefully watching him and the instruments, I noticed that our rate of climb was struggling. The speed was not increasing and Horst was working with all his strength to keep the nose down. He yelled for assistance and I, sitting to his right and slightly lower, put my left boot against the control column giving Horst the opportunity to get his right hand on to the trimming wheel between us. With an effort, he broke it free from some obstruction and turned it forwards, just in time before the aircraft ploughed into the ground in a stall. Following that, the aircraft behaved quite normally and we completed our mission. Next morning our ground crew chief, who had followed up Horst's complaint from his maintenance list, told us that we had reason to celebrate our good fortune. He found that we had dented the tail cone, under which was positioned the rear trimming-wheel sprocket. This resulted in it becoming jammed, probably from us rolling over the lamps while taxiing.

Another aircraft which crashed and was totally lost that same week was not so lucky. It happened in front of our eyes, in a ball of fire and smoke. Horst Götz told me after the war that he met a member of the family of one of the ill-fated crew members who told him the full story of the crash.

During the afternoon of 26 May 1941, while still at Vannes, our Gruppe was put on alert for immediate action. We had already been informed of the breakthrough of the German battle cruiser *Bismarck* and the cruiser *Prince Eugen* from Norway into the North Atlantic. There had been major action between our two ships and a Royal Navy battle group two days earlier. During this the British flagship, HMS *Hood,* was sunk and the battle cruiser, HMS *Prince of Wales*, badly damaged. The *Bismarck* was not seriously damaged in this fight but had been hit in the forward fuel cells. Becoming short of fuel, it changed course to make for Brest in France, sending the *Prince Eugen* off on its own. It reached Brest safely a couple of months later.

The night passed and early in the morning the *Bismarck's* position was calculated to be within range for us to give assistance. It was still pitch dark when we were alerted again and briefed about the situation. The whole of the British Home Fleet was now hunting the damaged battle cruiser and we were given the estimated area where to meet her. *U-77,* one of our submarines, was near to her and giving direction signals to guide us.

I still have the oil-smeared notebook into which I entered the most important points from the briefing. We were only allowed to write down the most important items for navigation because of security reasons in case we were shot down and the notes discovered.

They read:

> Enemy naval forces — One aircraft carrier, three battle cruisers, more cruisers and destroyers (in reality there were far more).

Target in plan square 3812 (on our grid map this was about 900 km west of Brest).

U-77 on location sends half-hourly signals of five-minute duration at 443 KHz from 0615-1620 then 0645-0650.

Break off search after four hours and thirty minutes.

Height of attack 4,000 metres.

Bomb load six SC 250 (cylindrical high explosive bombs of 250 kg). Set fuses to 'with delay'. Bomb distancing to 40 metres.

Estimated QFF (barometric pressure in target area 1,012 Kilobars).

Take-off time 0545 hours.

It was still pitch dark when we took off in formations of three Heinkels each but soon lost contact with our other two and were all on our own on our intended course. I checked this constantly with bearings I got from our transmitter near home. Dawn came around 0730. The sky was cloudless but the sea below seemed a bit rough from a strong wind coming in from the west. At 0810 we passed over two little light-coloured ships down there running southeast, probably fishing vessels. The half-hourly signals from *U*-77 came through loud and clear and at the regular times we anticipated.

By 0915 we should have been close to the anticipated position of the *Bismarck* but we were now out of range of the submarine's signals. Meanwhile, altocumulus cloud cover at around 800 metres above sea level had increased to about 7/10ths. Because we were too high to see anything we decided to go beneath the cloud cover only to find that visibility down there was just as bad. The range of visibility in the prevailing mist was now no more than four kilometres: a situation made worse by the sun's rays breaking through the gaps in the clouds. We then searched in all directions, trying to find any ships which were supposed to be congregating in this area or the *Bismarck* herself. But there was nothing but rolling waves with white caps as far as the eye could see.

Then, at 1002, the signals returned but they came from a direction much further north of our target area. As they were also outside the anticipated time schedule and the 'handwriting' of the signaller was very different from before, I distrusted them. They have forced the sub under water and someone from the enemy fleet is sending false signals to pull us away from the scene, I reasoned. Consequently, we decided to follow our original general direction in our zigzag search pattern until the time came to break off the hunt and return to base. More than half our 3,400-litre (750-Imp. gallon) fuel load was gone. With a sinking heart and in a seemingly hopeless situation, we turned for home at 1022. After half an hour we climbed through the clouds again to our most economical cruising height of 4,000 metres (13,000 feet). There was dead silence in the air. No signals, no aircraft to aircraft communication, nothing. After an uneventful return flight, we touched down again at Meucon airfield at 1322.

When we entered the command hut for debriefing we heard the sad news that the *Bismarck* had been sunk at around the same time that we had been forced to break off our search. This had taken place 100 km (60 miles) further to the west than we had anticipated. We didn't know at the time of our sortie that the *Bismarck* had suffered damage during her first battle and had lost part of her fuel reserve. In addition, she had later lost control of her rudder from a torpedo launched by a Swordfish biplane from the aircraft carrier HMS *Ark Royal*. These factors had considerably reduced her speed and prevented the possibility of her reversing her course at some point. There had been no hope of rendezvousing with her after the signals from *U-77* ceased. On the bus to the hotel from the airfield no-one spoke a word. It had been a terrible blow to us all.

Next day, 28 May, we took off again in an attempt to bomb the British fleet, but by then the capital ships were out of range. Nevertheless, we continued to fly up the Irish west coast when we received a signal which gave the co-ordinates of some British destroyers which were running into a wide bay. We immediately made for the area and found four destroyers which greeted us with intense flak and began zigzagging around like mad things. We attacked from 3,000 metres and in the melee two destroyers were badly hit. A Tribal class destroyer, HMS *Mashona*, was sunk and another, HMS *Maori*, sank later.[14]

One of our comrades signalled that he was hit and asked for assistance. On approaching him we found that a flak shell had pierced his port wing. It had gone right through the inner fuel tank but failed to explode. Fearing that he would be out of fuel on the long way home we decided to accompany him. The southern sky had become more and more covered in cloud so when we came into the designated corridor west of Brest, to cross the coast onto land, we felt quite safe. Then the aircraft which we were escorting signalled that it had no significant fuel loss thanks to the inside tank coating which closed up any reasonably small-sized holes. But to close a 75-mm (3-inch) hole was quite an achievement.

---

14. In fact, HMS *Maori* was not sunk in this action. She was eventually lost on 12 February 1942 in Valetta harbour.[Ed.]

All our Heinkels were fitted with self-sealing tanks. These were constructed of aluminium. Inside them was positioned a second rubber tank. This second tank had a 25-mm (1-inch) thick coating of 'Kautschuk', a very flexible material similar to that used on the soles of the boots worn by German athletes. It was a light-coloured yellowish fluffy rubber. The material automatically sealed the holes in the tanks when a shot passed through.

As we neared our base near Brest someone shouted, "Fighters behind!" We immediately pulled up into the clouds, losing contact with the other machine. After landing at Vannes we were told that it had been shot-up by Messerschmitt fighters on patrol in this sensitive area. They opened fire before asking questions but thankfully our comrades landed safely at Brest though with two badly wounded crew. They had taken cover in the clouds a split second too late.

After this mission we flew only one more sortie, to Liverpool, and that was the end of our assignment with the front-line unit. I was to be put out to grass, so to speak. Horst, who did not like the prospect of flying with another navigator, immediately went to his protector in the RLM and managed a transfer to the Luftnachrichtenschule [Air Signals School] at Strausberg near Berlin. He was safe there for the time being. Before leaving the squadron I was awarded the Frontflugspange in gold, having accomplished the requisite 110 missions (actually nearer to 130).

CHAPTER 6

TRAINING AND REPLACEMENT

On 1 June 1941 I was transferred to the Ergänzungsstaffel [training and replacement squadron] of Kampfgruppe 100 at Hannover/Langenhagen. This unit had been formed on 24 August 1940 as an Ergänzungskette and expanded to squadron strength on 24 January 1941. It had the dual role of training replacement crews and readying new aircraft for the operational parts of K.Gr. 100.

Although still a non-commissioned officer, I was appointed Officer z.B.V. [officer on special duty] and adjutant to the Staffelkapitän [squadron leader], Oberleutnant Enno 'Bubi' Russell. From now on I sat quietly at my desk opposite 'Bubi' (who you may remember I mentioned earlier) doing my daily paperwork. My duties included scrutinising and filing secret and top secret (g.Kdos) telex messages from the High Command. I also gave practical lessons to fledgling crews who had just come from basic crew bomber training schools. They had scarcely flown together, and certainly not under difficult conditions.

For night-flying exercises I transferred with some of our aircraft and crews to areas in eastern France which were not affected by the steadily increasing British night bombing of the German-held territory. We code-named the areas which were subject to enemy bomber streams MYO areas. Obviously we had to train in areas which had no MYO warnings whatsoever. So we moved first to Chartres in France and later to Silesia so as to leave the skies free for Luftwaffe night-fighter operations. I found these training flights nearly as dangerous as actual missions! Despite this I only lost one of my pupil crew's aircraft. This somersaulted after coming in to land in very poor weather and overshot the runway in Silesia. The wireless operator was killed. We always had two or three, sometimes four, aircraft in a group, but they were always under my charge.

After three weeks at Langenhagen, on 20 June 1941, I was presented with the Ehrenpokal der Luftwaffe, a silver goblet. This was instituted in February

1940 and awarded on the authority of Reichsmarschall Hermann Göring to Luftwaffe personnel *'für besondere leistung im Luftkrieg'* (for special achievement in the air war). It was accompanied by a certificate signed by Göring and was engraved with my name. I didn't actually like it and took it home on my first leave to Munich where it survived the war. I still have it and it is said that on account of its originality and certification, which is in my files, it is now worth quite a lot of money. Don't forget the last words, whoever gets it eventually, but keep the pot and paper together!

Myself after being promoted to Leutnant.

On 1 July 1941 I was at last promoted to Leutnant. I then had to buy a new uniform. For this, I was indebted to my brother Helmuth who, with his civilian status, regularly travelled to Paris. He had many connections with the burgeoning black market in which one could get almost anything. He obtained for me the fine blue-grey cloth for my parade uniform and a coveted long leather coat which is still hanging in my wardrobe. The whole outfit looked quite smart with all the metal of merit attached to it and I felt I was really something. This rapidly wore off somewhat during the early winter when the frostbitten and rebellious infantry came back from the Russian front and made me feel like an *Etappenschwein* (literally a 'stage pig' – a show-off).

Meanwhile, while I was on leave in Munich in June, Hitler had invaded Russia, an event which turned my stomach. I could see the difficulties which we already had in the west which were being cleverly glossed over by Goebbels' propaganda machine. It was Hitler's ruthlessness and Goebbels' media power which engineered Germany's downfall with equal weight. The power of the press can shift anything. Ink is stronger than blood; never forget this.

Throughout my time at Langenhagen I stayed in contact with Horst, my former pilot. I got to know his wife, Ilse, and his two daughters well during my occasional visits to his house in the Lichterfelde Ost area of Berlin. There were always relatives visiting like his wife Ilse's sister, Ursula, with her husband, the lean and blonde Fritz Schilgen. Fritz had become famous for carrying the Olympic Torch up the stairs in the stadium to light the Olympic Flame on 1 August 1936 in Berlin. It was always a light-hearted and joyful crowd full of exuberance and likely to celebrate till far into the night. Except for Horst, that is. The man of the house himself regularly dropped off to sleep on

Horst pictured with his newly acquired Retinette camera. This was taken during our time off at his home.

the lounge couch at about 10 p.m. in the middle of a conversation. This remarkable feat probably helped him to live a long life. He was still capable of doing it when I met him in 1993 at Nieby on the coast of the Baltic Sea. He just fell asleep as usual in the middle of a conversation!

During the winter I was commandeered to attend a course in astro-navigation at Strausberg east of Berlin. I never had occasion to put it into practice, but since then I have always had an interest in the stars.

While in this area I occasionally visited Uncle Karl who lived in Zehlendorf nearer to his son, my cousin Karl 'Karlchen'. He had a house in Siedlung which was beautifully furnished in modern style. He lived there with his wife Lore, whom I had met in 1935 and his two sons, Peter and Michael. I could not avoid the boys' affection as, at this time, I was 'loaded' with goodies, such as chocolates and biscuits. This cache came partly from my saved flying rations and as the result of mercy packets sent by my scarcely remembered mates from Berlin University days. They insisted on sending these to my Feldpost number for which I regularly gave thanks. The other person to get her share of this treasure was my cousin Hans' daughter at Wertingen. Hans had recently been called up and was based at Neubiberg. I was not so bothered about the sweets but I kept a sharp eye on the spirits. I could occasionally lay my hands on these when I was at Chartres or other parts of France.

One spring day a bunch of film stars appeared at Langenhagen when one of our Gruppen returned from Russia to collect their new equipment. They had previously met at Sechtchinskaja where the stars and starlets had entertained

Fita Benkhoff on the cover of Film Woche *promoting the 1939 film* Spassvögel [Joker].

them. It was a great evening with joyous recollections on both sides. We drank and danced until early morning and I swung quite a leg with some of the famous. These included Fita Benkhoff and Herta Vorell and I talked a lot with famous male actors whose names I have now forgotten. Fita Benkhoff appeared in more than 100 films from 1933 to 1967.

Meanwhile Horst and Gerd Albrecht had become restless in their civilian role. One diversion was when they were given the task of flying some Telefunken technicians to Minsk to investigate what the Russians were achieving in the electronics field. He told me of their surprise at what they found and how advanced the programmes were on which the Russians were working. He also informed me, as had my brother Paul, who had come back from the north-eastern front to take up studies, of the executions of Jews by Lithuanian militia. Horst had also heard of Jews being executed by the SS in the occupied territories, Ukraine in particular. He described how their technical team had tried to save the Jewish engineers from this fate and to bring them back to Germany to work at Telefunken. They were partly successful he was pleased to report.

This account left an uneasy feeling with us. We thought that this SS action (being part of the aftermath of recent fighting in this area, in which partisans had been involved) would cause extensive problems to us behind the whole front line. On top of its brutality we felt that it would lead to a hostile reaction of the Russians 'liberated' from Bolshevism. We cursed our government politicians who abandoned the rule of law in this occupied country with their '*Goldfasanen*' (an expression we used for the gold-braided Nazi officers based behind the front line). The army also strongly opposed party politics and had no part in this awfulness.

Despite this, we never heard any rumours of camps for the mass eradication of Jews or even of maltreatment of prisoners of war who came in from the east in their millions. It was not until the end of the war that these horrors were revealed to the German populace in general.

As I mentioned before, the early and harsh Russian winter of 1941 put an end to German advances in the east. Russian counter attacks by an enemy well equipped for winter warfare surprised our troops who were not equipped with the proper clothing to cope with the bitter cold. In addition, their ground transport and armoured vehicles often became stuck in the deep mud and could not move. The morale of the largely frostbitten infantry, who were brought home after their ordeal to be replaced, was very low. They refused to salute any officer, as in their eyes they were all *'Etappenschwein'* who avoided the hardships of the front. It came to the point that one day, while journeying into Hannover, I saw some of these pitiful figures approaching and had to look the other way to avoid embarrassment. Afterwards I felt ashamed because instead of sympathetically communicating with them about their past hardships, I had ignored them.

By this time, both Horst and I found our inaction increasingly depressing and he finally found a way out of this situation by again approaching his protector, 'Papa' Cornberg, to give him a more satisfactory task. As a result of this he found himself, in January 1942, transferred to a support unit based in Wiesbaden flying He 111s for the Kontroll Kommission Afrika of the Armistice Commission. This was based in Casablanca, the capital of Morocco. He was told that he should stay there for a while until something more appropriate was found for him.

CHAPTER 7

DIVERSION TO CASABLANCA

On 15 December 1941, Kampfgruppe 100 was redesignated the first Gruppe of Kampfgeschwader (bomber wing) 100 with a second group being formed from the third Gruppe of K.G. 26. At the same time our Ergänzungsstaffel became 13th Squadron of K.G. 100. In early May 1942 we were transferred from Hannover/Langenhagen to Schwerin/Görtes.

During the relocation flight to Schwerin I had the opportunity to fly over the town of Lübeck, which had been attacked by the RAF during the previous night. I saw the awful destruction of the whole of the old centre of the medieval Hanseatic Town. The vast armament industry complexes just to the east of the town were untouched by any bombs. It looked like a terror attack with only one aim. The sight was depressing as it seemed that nothing could have been done to prevent it happening. Hitler himself was so infuriated by the bombing that he ordered the Baedeker raids, retaliatory strikes on British historical towns. The German publisher, Karl Baedeker, had founded a series of world-wide travel guides in 1827 including, of course, one for Great Britain, hence the name chosen by Hitler. The problem was that the Luftwaffe was now fully engaged in Russia, and the bombers that remained in the west could only inflict pinprick retaliatory strikes.

I had scarcely settled down in Schwerin when the RLM ordered me to transfer to the Wastico based in Casablanca. Wastico was the name given to the Waffenstillstands Kommission [Armistice Commission] of which the Casablanca division was called Kontroll Kommission Afrika. After the invasion of France, its Arab colonies, including Morocco, were placed under the control of the puppet Vichy French government. At this time there were approximately 55,000 French troops in the country. The job of Kontroll Kommission Afrika

The He 111 H flown by Horst with me as navigator while serving with the Kontroll Kommission Afrika. Our aircraft, W.Nr. 2457 was repainted pale blue and given the civil code D-ARAJ.

was to monitor the neutrality of Morocco and produce aerial maps of possible strategic installations.

My transfer to Casablanca sparked an immediate protest from my Geschwader Kommodore [wing commander], Oberst Heinz-Ludwig von Holleben, but to no avail. I had to report to Generalleutnant Heinz-Helmuth Wühlish in Casablanca as his new Bildoffizier [photographic officer] by 1 June 1942. I was puzzled about my new task, as I had only theoretical knowledge of reconnaissance work. I was assured by Horst that this appointment was only a temporary one to bring our crew together again for more important tasks.

Eventually, Horst, Gerd Albrecht and I rendezvoused at Wiesbaden and flew from there to Casablanca in a He 111 via Tunisia. While at the latter we had to disarm our aircraft to comply with an agreement with the Vichy government. In addition, our machine was painted in civil markings. French Morocco, of which Casablanca was the capital, was a French protectorate, not a colony like Tunisia or Algeria and so it was declared neutral. There was still an American embassy there doing just the same clandestine spying as we did but we had no social contact with them whatsoever. For us they were already clearly enemies without any war being declared between us and them. (I found out later that the famous film, *Casablanca,* was set in this environment.)

Gerd Albrecht, me and Horst felt rather conspicuous in our white tropical uniforms.

For some time, it had been anticipated that a joint American/British intervention would take place in the area. By this time, we had already finished the aerial mapping of all the airfields and marine installations along the coast. Our military intelligence had its presence all over Morocco and up to Tangier across the straights from Gibraltar, monitoring British and American naval movements. As I was billeted in a nice modern hotel on the beach south of Casablanca I had the task of working out a defence system with the light armament which was neatly stashed away. There was an agreement with the Sultan of Morocco, the titular head of state, not to wear our uniforms in public so we walked and travelled in civvies – except at official functions. For these we wore white tropical uniforms in which we felt rather ridiculous!

Surrounded by lush walled gardens, the splendid Maison Blanche was the headquarters of General von Wühlish and his administration. I also had my office there. The building was of modern tropical design and belonged to a Casablanca newspaper proprietor who had been temporarily displaced. Previously it had been known as Villa Maas after its owner.

My tasks were simple. The general knew of my temporary status. We ate and drank well, except that I didn't like the cooking in olive oil very much. There was constant black market dealing, our middlemen being, oddly enough, old Austrian communists who had fled their country in 1932. They had been swept along with the tide of European immigrants to these shores where they were now stuck. Once, when we had one of them in our car, doing a deal, he hid his face when a French policeman came in sight.

Occasionally I travelled out of town on my own in Major Mahnke's little car which he let me borrow when he was in Marrakech or some other odd place. We often went swimming together in the beautiful surf next to our hotel in the afternoons when the daily clouds (regularly at two o'clock) came in and suppressed the humidity. Horst and Gerd were flying backwards and forwards to Germany most of the time on courier business. They ferried all the goodies which they had purchased on the black market, such as coffee beans, clothes, olive oil and chocolates. I collected some of these too of course for when my anticipated transfer back was ordered. This actually came only five weeks after we had arrived and just in time to prevent boredom setting in.

Horst told me that von Cornberg now had a choice of two tasks for him and his crew. One was with a Heinkel He 177 test unit, the new four-engine bomber. The other was with the VfH [Versuchsstelle für Hohenflüge or experimental unit for high-altitude flight] of the Luftwaffe High Command based at Oranienburg near Berlin. The choice was easy. The He 177 had a terrible reputation due to its new arrangement of coupling two engines together to drive one propeller. This regularly led to fires and crashes. The second choice involved Horst being stationed near his family in Berlin and offered us a wide variety of activities. As there was no contest, Horst decided on the second option. The only mystery was how we, as an experienced bomber crew, fitted in with the primary task of the new unit which was reconnaissance.

We left Casablanca on 5 July 1942 in a He 111 overloaded with things that everyone in the Wastico wanted brought back to Germany. On the way over the Atlas Mountains one engine overheated and we made an emergency landing at the French military airfield of Fez in Morocco. From there we rang for a replacement aircraft. While waiting and unloading with the help of Foreign Legion soldiers, I met a naval captain in our hotel at Fez. He, Korvetten Kapitän von Kessler, invited me to come to his house at Meknes up in the hills for the afternoon. I accepted as I had nothing else to do and it proved a very pleasant experience. The naval captain was actually with our intelligence section. He was monitoring what was going on there and passing the information back to Berlin. He let me have a tiny glimpse into what military intelligence was up to down there.

In the afternoon we travelled by car to the not-too-distant old Roman settlement of Volubilis and wandered through the well preserved ruins. There is very little rain in these mountains, no frost and so it had suffered little natural deterioration. The only problem was the local Arabs from the holy town of Muley Idris on the flank of the hill above, who availed themselves of its building materials. Muley Idris is the burial place of a grandson of Mohammed. There is a whole district – a holy district in a part of this township – which is forbidden to non-believers. We could not enter and could only look down from the top of the town into the valley in which a beautiful mosque was gleaming in the sunlight. We were very sorry we couldn't go there, but we were classed as infidels.

Looking very serious in my tropical uniform.

The layout of the Roman settlement with its underground waste disposal canals and mosaic-decorated baths suggested that the climate must have been very different then with higher rainfall and probably lush vegetation over the hills. There were wells in the Arab town on the slope with constantly running fountains for the people and their mules. These were their main means of transport. They were all tall fellows riding tiny animals, constantly urging them on with their heels which nearly dragged on the ground.

In the evening I was back in Fez. Next day the replacement aircraft arrived from Casablanca and loading was carried out in the cool of the night. We wandered through the old Moorish fortified town and its narrow covered streets and the bustling life under the shade of the coverings. It was a fascinating sight as we seemed to be the only foreigners there. There was no danger to us as we Germans were generally regarded as friends on account of the still favourable (to us) war at El Alamein in the northern desert. They also regarded us as Allies against the Jews towards whom they had hostile feelings. There was a sharp separation in the Arab townships between the two races of which the Jews were about ten per cent as far as we could estimate. The upper classes were pure Islamic Arab and highly regarded. Of course in Casablanca there was a more cosmopolitan atmosphere due to its industries.

The next morning, we were ready to continue the flight home through Algiers where we re-armed the aircraft. Then on to Oran from where we crossed over the Mediterranean to Wiesbaden. As we were not expected at Oranienburg before 15 July 1942 we gave ourselves eight days' leave. I turned up at my parents' house heavily laden with my share of the Casablanca booty. This consisted of an enormous smoked leg of ham (which tasted rather fishy, but nobody minded) a bag of green coffee beans (the roasting of which created obvious envy amongst the neighbours as the fragrance drifted through their windows) and many other things which were no longer available in Germany.

CHAPTER 8

THE HIGH-ALTITUDE KOMMANDO

On 15 July 1942, the four of us, Horst Götz, Gerd Albrecht, Willi Sprickerhoff our engineer, and I arrived at Berlin/Oranienburg to join our new unit, the Versuchsstelle für Höhenflug. We knew very little about it except that it was a high command research squadron. That it was, for Horst, conveniently located near Berlin and was a military establishment with a strong civilian leaning, promised much. There was also the prospect of occasional front-line service which was important to us.

We soon found out that there were, in fact, three squadrons attached to the unit. They each undertook different tasks, all top secret. The overall commander was Oberst Theo Rowehl, a First World War naval flyer. We found out later that the top boss of military intelligence, Admiral Wilhelm Canaris was an old acquaintance of his. It was then that links between the two became obvious.

The Rowehl organisation had its own communication network developed by the Radione company of Wien [Vienna] which worked on UHF frequencies. This was linked to the Stern [star] network used by the General der Aufklärer. Our messages were transmitted by *Fernschreiber* [telex] which had its own coding system and was not intercepted as far as I know. Even our operational aircraft were equipped with the Radione system but, in the case of the Ju 86 R, only a receiver was installed; no transmitter. I could see Canaris' hand in this who trusted nobody. Neither did Horst or I!

Our crew was added to the first squadron of the VfH which fine-tuned high-altitude and high-performance reconnaissance aircraft and tested them under operational conditions. This part of the work had previously been performed clandestinely by Rowehl's *Hansa Luftbild* in peacetime. At that time, it was based

The Junkers Ju 86 R was a high-altitude development of the obsolescent Ju 86 medium bomber. The forward fuselage was completely redesigned, housing a pressurised cabin which could maintain pressure to an equivalent altitude of 3,000 metres (10,000 feet).

at Berlin/Tempelhof but later relocated to Berlin/Oranienburg and placed under military administration. Although we were a military unit, the buildings at the airfield were still owned by the Heinkel company. This remained unchanged until the end of the war. Our three-storey administration building housed a complex of offices, officer accommodation, and mess facilities. It was called the Katharinen Hof. At the southern part of the establishment were greenhouses for growing vegetables and hutches for the rabbits which provided meat for the table and pelts for the soldiers in Russia. In addition, there were several pig styes which supplied somewhat better rations, but I can't remember ever having had roast pork. It was always broad beans with boiled pork or vegetables with boiled pork, cooked together in a casserole and stretched as far as possible.

The first squadron, under Hauptmann Koehler, had two subsidiary Kommandos [squadron detachments] for front-line service at that time. One was based at Mykolajiw (Nikolajev) in southern Ukraine and the other at Orly near Paris. The latter, a permanent establishment, was led by Oberst Paul Achilles who, like Rowehl, had been a pilot in the First World War. We were amazed when he used to run down the hill in the depths of winter to swim in the cold and dirty Seine. Not only did his Kommando undertake operations but it was also there for the benefit of the General Staff. There were two Ritterkreuz or 'Doedl' holders (as we called them) in our squadron, who in our superior opinion had not done much to get it (about twenty low danger operations against the 130 or so which we had completed by this time). The officers who we came to join were not from a military background. Many of them had private interests in case peace broke out and observed us with some trepidation. They didn't quite know what to expect from us bomber men, but we soon gained their approval as we shall see later.

The second squadron, led by Hauptmann 'Ted' Rosarius, comprised a group of pilots who were flying refurbished enemy fighters which had crashed or belly-landed in German-occupied territory. Occasionally they had made mistakes in navigation and had completed normal wheels-down landings thinking they were in England when they were actually in France. The same happened with German aircraft. They landed over there in England thinking they were already in France. This happened a couple of times and the British used them for the same purposes.[15]

After being released by the test station at Rechlin, the enemy aircraft were flown to our fighter squadrons to acquaint them with their prospective opponents. This, it was hoped, would help them improve their tactics against them. Rosarius' squadron had some Spitfires and Hurricanes and a few American aircraft such as the P-38 Lightning and two P-51 Mustangs. Our squadron had difficulties with the Mustangs I remember. The Mustang had a very bad habit of stalling and going out of control in tight combat near the ground. This was because of its laminar wing profile which was very good for high-speed dives but very bad for low-speed sharp turns. We lost both Mustangs in this way while having imaginary dogfights with Messerschmitt 109s at low altitude.

At this time the third squadron of the VfH, under Hauptmann Edmund Gartenfeld, dropped spies and saboteurs behind the Russian lines. It used captured American B-17 Flying Fortresses and B-24 Liberators. In addition to these tasks it performed top-secret operations such as keeping political lines open to the near east including transporting the Imam and Pandit Neru into Iraq and Afghanistan. Shortly after we arrived the squadron became the First Gruppe of K.G. 200, the top-secret wing about which so many stories were later to be published, many of them fantastic nonsense.

There was not much time to sit back and contemplate our position because we were immediately sent on supply missions to Nikolajev on the Black Sea. For these sorties we had a three-engine Ju 52 transport.

---

15. The British equivalent to the 2./VfH was the RAF's No. 1426 Flight.

We were there for three days and, after returning, it was off to Kursk in the Ukraine with a Do 215 reconnaissance aircraft, then obsolete in the west. Oberst Rowehl had organised this trip to meet his Hungarian friend, Oberst Keks, Inspector General of the Hungarian reconnaissance forces. We had to land at three airfields near Kursk until we found the right one. It was well camouflaged in the corner of a paddock in the woods. Shortly after we arrived, Rowehl joined us. He was flown over in a He 111 piloted by 'Ted' Rosarius who was his personal pilot as well as leader of the second squadron. Rowehl was to meet Oberst Keks there. The Hungarian officers were very affable and we were treated to a sumptuous lunch on rough wooden tables under the trees. We left the Dornier with them, for which they were enormously grateful, and took off with Rowehl in the He 111. On the way home we put down at Shitomir for the night because Rowehl had to attend a conference at Hitler's Werewolf headquarters at nearby Winniza (Winnyzja).

Next morning, we had breakfast in the mess and we all noticed the imposing figure of the tall young Ukrainian woman serving coffee. When we were seated back in the Heinkel, I asked Rowehl with a grin, if he had noticed the mountainous bosom back at the mess, knowing that he had a keen eye for such things. "Impossible to miss it," he replied "I think if somebody tries to crush a louse on it, the louse would be propelled to this far tree," pointing to the edge of the field with a sweeping gesture. It was 24 July 1942. By noon we were back at Oranienburg.

At this time the British had introduced a new innovation, using twin-engine Mosquito bombers made of plywood to break through our *Würzburg* and *Mammut* radar screens undetected. Because of their construction, they had very low radar reflectivity. Heavy casualties in our cities and a bad effect on morale were anticipated due to the normal air raid defences being deployed. Hitler ordered Göring to do something in retaliation to support morale at home. Rowehl came to Göring's rescue by suggesting, during the conference at Winniza, that four Junkers Ju 86 Rs, destined for high-altitude reconnaissance over North Africa from Crete, were to be immediately re-equipped to carry bombs.

Consequently, a unit (later known as Höhenkommando Beauvais) was established from crews and technicians from our squadron to attack southern England from 12,000 metres (40,000 feet) in broad daylight. This would be out of reach of British and American fighters (the latter country was already operating P-38 Lightnings). To investigate whether the electrical fuses of our bombs would go off during their fall from excessive static build-up, Horst and I took the first Ju 86 R delivered to Rechlin for a test run.

To gain the utmost in altitude performance, weight had to be reduced to the minimum. For this reason, all defensive weaponry and armour plating was removed and there was only room for one 250-kg (550-lb) bomb. The comfortable pressurised cockpit only held a crew of two and radio equipment was limited to a Radione receiver, but no transmitter. As previously mentioned, the Motorola Radione high-frequency transmitter was used by the VfH for internal communication between headquarters and the different Kommandos. Its frequencies allowed for bridging of vast distances with low energy. The aircraft had pretty reliable diesel engines, at least so we thought at this time. The wings were of enormous span and tended to flex considerably. Because they were liable to fold under very little stress, we were told to go easy when manoeuvring.

We had heard that one of the earlier high-altitude variants, the Ju 86 P, had made an emergency landing in 1940 while carrying out clandestine reconnaissance work over Russian territory near Brest Litovsk. It was destroyed by its crew. At this time there were reports of a considerable concentration of Russian forces on our eastern front. This was especially disturbing because, under the non-aggression treaty between the German and Russian governments, which was then still in force, this should not have been the case. There was also the threatened occupation of the Baltic States and the invasion of Finland by the Bolshevists. Leutnant Albert Schnetz, the pilot of the Ju 86 P, told me later of his capture and interrogation by the Russians. He and his navigator, Leutnant Walter, were able to free themselves from prison during the rapid German advance after the invasion of June 1941.

This early intelligence could have been a strong reason for Hitler to begin his preventative action in the east as the war in the west was getting harder with the prospect of direct American intervention. How could he trust a man like Stalin who was an opportunist with the same ruthless nature as himself? It is a mystery to me why Stalin's alleged trust in Hitler, after the first warnings of a German attack by the British and others, remained. As I see now from letters I received in May and June 1941 from my brother Paul and others from East Prussia, there were colossal German troop movements taking place. Shouldn't Russian intelligence have picked this up? By then Stalin had shot most of his senior officers including a lot of top-ranking intelligence people and so he probably mistrusted all their reports.

After that diversion I will continue with describing our operations with the U-2-like spy-plane, now reassigned to the bombing role. By early August the first of our converted Ju 86 Rs arrived at Oranienburg. Horst and I had already been briefed about our new task by Oberst Rowehl, which was "to transfer to

Beauvais in France with (at first) two of the aircraft equipped for the task". From there we were to attack sizeable British targets, as opportunity arose, in daylight and at maximum height.

Our second crew would be made up of a Rechlin test pilot, Dipl.-Ing. [diploma engineer] Werner Altrogge with our old wireless operator, Gerd Albrecht, as his navigator. Engineers from the Junkers factory at Des-

Our Kommando relaxing after tea at Beauvais during the summer of 1942. From left to right: Ing. Heinz (a Junkers engineer), Oberst Theodor Rowehl, Feldwebel Gerd Albrecht, me, Feldwebel Horst Götz and Dipl.-Ing. Werner Altrogge.

sau would assist on site and ground crew for bombing up and refuelling with diesel fuel and GM 1 would be provided. GM 1 (*Geheimmittel 1*) was a solution of nitrous oxide held at a temperature of about minus 120 degrees. This was carried in a 300-litre (66-Imp.gal) aluminium thermos container and injected into the engine manifolds at a height of over 10,600 metres (35,000 feet) to increase engine performance. This system had been developed by our fighter aircraft establishment.

As the highest in rank I was to lead the Kommando. To establish if the whole system would work, Horst and I took the first aircraft to Rechlin for an altitude and bombing trial. It was a beautiful summer Saturday. We discussed all relevant preparations including bombing up with a 'half-sharp' 250-kg bomb which made enough smoke to be visible from extreme height on impact. As target we were allocated an area within the adjoining Rechlin test grounds. We did a short test flight to be sure all was right for a later high-altitude take-off as we were informed that Rechlin closed down for the weekend at 1200 hours and nobody would be there to service us. Was that an expression of the urgent intention of Germany to dominate the world at that time, as is still propounded by some historians?

The clouds broke up by 1600 hours and so we began our slow climb to the prescribed altitude of 13,000 metres (42,500 feet) locating our target point through the broken cirrus clouds which were at half this altitude. For the bombing run I used the old mechanical Görz bombsight which was the only one available at the time for this height, but it was still good enough for the task. The new Lotfe 7E was scheduled to arrive in a few days.

After I released the bomb we descended slowly within our speed and throttle limitations (not too high a speed and throttle not below a certain injection pressure as the engines would cut out). As the target area grew bigger under the cloud base we saw the smoke of our bomb still there in the right location. But there was something else, which turned out to our surprise to be a tractor still running and puffing smoke from its exhaust and a horse or a cow lying flat out.

We landed at the airfield and rolled to hangar E7. I climbed out to notify someone, but there was nobody there. With the engines still ticking over I tried to climb back up through the manhole entrance hatch. Because this was two metres above the ground, Horst attempted to help me by reaching down. He didn't have enough strength to lift me, so I tried to help him by jerking my legs, but I hit the calf of the left leg with the sharp edge of my right shoe, causing me to let out a cry of excruciating pain. Now I was left on the ground while Horst ran the two kilometres over to the tower to notify them of our problems. After ten minutes an ambulance arrived and my calf was bandaged in the airfield hospital. As this was being done, the orderly told me of an accident out on the range in which a farmer and two French POW farm helpers were hurt and were being brought in.

"For heaven's sake," I told the bloke, "don't tell them that I am lying next door and that I am the person responsible for their injuries. I don't want my nose flattened!" Fortunately, they were not too badly hurt. The farmer had got a

A crew memeber gaining entry to the pressurised cockpit of the Ju 86 R showing the distance between the hatch and the ground.

splinter in the ribs and some heavy bruising. One Frenchman copped it in the behind, but luckily he had his wallet in exactly the right place. The other one had just fallen over and bloodied his nose. Nobody had warned them of our bombing run and so they were there, gathering hay as usual. They didn't know how lucky they were. I had at first insisted on using a fully sharp bomb to make sure we could locate the impact point by the crater. But an engineer convinced me that a half-sharp smoke bomb would do the trick.

Everything had worked satisfactorily. The fuse performed properly. The ride in the pressurised cockpit was agreeable with us being able to sit there in our normal uniforms, without oxygen masks. Even the noise level was quite low. Soon afterwards the new Lotfe 7E gyroscopic bombsight arrived and was installed on 18 August 1942.

Following this we transferred to Beauvais, north of Paris, only to be told to get off the field immediately as it was chock-a-block full of fighters. This was because British and Canadian troops had landed at Dieppe. This was an exploratory undertaking which went horribly wrong. Of the nearly 5,000-strong Canadian contingent, 3,367 were killed, wounded or taken prisoner. The 1,000 British commandos lost 247 men. The German army had 591 casualties and the operation was over in one day.

Our dismissal from Beauvais forced us to move to Orly south of Paris, where our other Kommando was based. Here we waited for the situation to develop. Things were soon cleared up, so I returned to Beauvais on 20 August. This time I flew with Werner Altrogge in one of our four Ju 86 Rs, this one coded T5+QM. After returning we began to prepare for our missions. We were now under the direct tactical command of Luftflotte 3 in Paris and received our orders from there.

Then Reichsmarschall Hermann Göring put his oar in. He sent a telex in which he communicated his wish that 'predominantly railway targets' had to be attacked. If he had only known how far off he was with assuming that such targets could be hit with a high degree of accuracy from 14,000 metres…! We contemptuously put the telex aside and ignored it.

Our first sortie was against the military training area at Aldershot. Horst and I took off at 1414 hours on 24 August in T9+PM and landed at 1722. Next day we bombed Luton (the British reported our target as Stanstead) but we had to land at Rouen. Our Junkers spent more than an hour over Britain, our intention being to sound as many sirens as possible and cause maximum disruption. The British authorities refused to play this game however; single intruders were treated as reconnaissance aircraft without bombs. The sirens remained silent. Some Spitfires were, however, scrambled in an attempt to intercept. We watched as interested spectators while these zig-zagged thousands of feet below with their exhausts smoking in an attempt to gain altitude. There was much chatter on their radios which gave our listening post, at Meldekopf Birk near Cherbourg, the opportunity to locate British units and plot the frequency ranges which they were using. We got a two-page report from them after every flight, telling us what fun they had at the listening station after months of boring silence in the ether.

That evening the German propaganda ministry jubilantly announced that our Hohenkampfkommando had carried out the first of its daylight revenge attacks on Britain and that all aircraft had returned safely. They failed to mention that our unit only had enough crews to operate two aircraft.

We gave little thought to civilian casualties until our third mission which took place on 28 August. Our bomb landed on Broadmead in Bristol city centre, smack in the middle of three buses full of people. I couldn't see this from our altitude and between gaps in the clouds below. I thought that the bomb would hit the southern

The aftermath of our bomb hitting Bristol showing one of the wrecked buses.

part of the city. I had switched the electric fuse to 'non delay' to ensure that the explosion would make as much noise as possible on hitting the ground or the top of a roof. That night, listening to BBC radio, we heard the bad news that forty-six people had died in Bristol as a result of our attack and many more were wounded. How could this have happened we wondered?[16] I later read this report from Ken Wakefield who witnessed the bombing:

16. Long after the war I found that British war cabinet minutes recorded that there was to be no more alerts when we flew over England as our results were negligible and did not warrant such costly action. I also learned that Churchill took an intense interest in the measures taken to get us down and requested a daily report.

'At 9.15 a.m. on 28 August 1942 a high-flying aircraft approached Bristol from the south, flying in absolutely cloudless conditions. It was leaving a short contrail as it approached directly overhead. I identified it with the naked eye, but with no doubt on my part, as a He 177, provisional silhouettes of which had appeared in *The Aeroplane Spotter* some time previously. No air raid warning was given but a single bomb was dropped, duly followed by sirens and a few bursts of wildly inaccurate anti-aircraft gunfire. The aircraft continued on its course over the centre of the city and carried out a gentle turn to port to leave on a south-westerly heading.

'The single bomb dropped, reported to have been a 500-lb effort, caused the worst single bomb incident suffered by Bristol throughout the war. The bomb fell on the Broadmead area in the centre of the city, hitting a car. As a result of the subsequent explosion one of three nearby buses was seriously damaged by the blast, while petrol from the car's fuel tank was sprayed in a more or less atomized state over the other two which immediately burst into flames. The death toll was horrific with forty-six being killed, many burnt to death in the blazing buses, with a further forty-five injured. In terms of loss of life this was the single most serious incident to occur in Bristol during the Second World War. The crater was the size associated with an average high-explosive bomb and was probably a standard 250 kg.

'Newspaper reports of the period insisted that this was a fighter-bomber attack, but I remained convinced it was a He 177. However, since the end of the war, I had occasion to doubt my spotting accuracy when details of the He 177 became available which seemed to indicate that it did not go into operational service until much later. Also a heavy bomber dropping one bomb of approximately 500 lbs? I did consider that it could have been a Ju 86 P, but I was still inwardly convinced that it was a He 177. At this time, I was a very keen ATC (Air Training Corps) cadet and a member of the National Association of Spotters Clubs.'

Next day we bombed Swindon, still flying T5+PM. Chelmsford followed on 30 August, this time in T5+RM. Our remaining sorties were flown in T5+PM, against Ramsgate on 4 September, on Luton next day and Gloucester on the 6th.

Meanwhile, the RAF had established a 'Special Service Flight' at Northolt, north-west of London, to modify a Spitfire to attain the altitudes at which we were flying. To their credit they managed to achieve their aim on 12 September

Junkers Ju 86 R-2 coded T5+PM. Our aircraft was painted pale blue-grey overall with black identification markings.

when Horst and I were on our way to Cardiff. Our other crew were to follow shortly afterwards. Just beyond Southampton I was scanning the sky when I saw, looking back through the plastic bubble on the cockpit side through which I was able to see aft, a fine condensation trail just below our height. At first I thought it was Altrogge and told Horst that they were behind us. Then I realised that this aircraft was catching up fast and was already higher than us. Just then it passed us high on our starboard side and I saw to my horror that it was a Spitfire. Horst later remembered:

> 'Suddenly Erich, sitting on my right, said that there was a fighter closing in from his side. I thought there was nothing remarkable about that – almost every time we had been over England in the Ju 86, fighters had tried to intercept us. Then he said that the fighter was climbing very fast and was nearly at our altitude. The next thing, it was above us. I thought Erich's eyes must have been playing tricks on him, so I leaned over to his side of the cabin to see for myself. To my horror I saw the Spitfire, a little above us and still climbing.'

Horst immediately opened up the air vent to reduce inside air pressure while I jettisoned the bomb to lighten the aircraft. Now about 25 kilometres (15 miles) north-west of Southampton, Horst turned back trying to out-climb the Spitfire, but to no avail. It was a most uncomfortable feeling knowing that somebody with 20-mm cannon blazing could pounce on us any second. We were completely unprotected by any armour plating and had nowhere to hide. Our only defence was our tight turning circle which we used to full effect. As soon as the fighter took up position for an attack I told Horst, who could only see forward. When I saw the first gun lighting up the leading edge of the Spitfire's wings I yelled to Horst who pulled the Junkers round in a tight right-hand turn.

Almost immediately we were shot through the port wing although we were still climbing. We performed the same manoeuvre during the second attack, but seeing little hope with this tactic, we began to make for home, repeating our turns to starboard. The chap behind didn't manage to get another shot into our aircraft as we confirmed afterwards. There was no cloud for hundreds of miles, but we had penetrated a misty layer on the way up at 11,500 metres (38,000 feet). This didn't seem to be much protection at first while looking straight up or down, but gave a little help when looking through at an angle.

We continued to pull tight turns at the moment of each attack and, during the fourth one, the Spitfire passed over our heads. I took a photo with the Robot 35-mm automatic advance camera which I had with me on this day, but it only showed contrails in the distance. Horst then cut the throttles back and put the nose of the Junkers down, aiming for the slim protection of the layer of mist below. Then we saw with growing horror thick grey smoke coming from our dying engines which had both flamed out. That's it, we thought, waiting for the *coup de grâce*. We were now breathing heavily with the aid of our oxygen masks which we had donned the moment Horst had opened the air valve. This was to avoid becoming unconscious if a bullet penetrated the pressurised cockpit. Now we feared that at any moment our backs or skulls would be ripped open by exploding cannon shells but, to our amazement, the Spitfire had disappeared.

Horst let the aircraft dive as fast as our speed would allow without the long wings flexing too much. He hoped that we could then re-start the Jumo diesel engines at 4,000 metres (13,000 feet). We were now above the Isle of Wight and below the mist we had the vast expanse of the Channel in front of us and to our relief no conventional fighters were in sight. To our intense joy the engines came to life again in the warmer air at low level. We headed for the protection of the sea by just skimming the waves with the French coast in the distance. The next danger was the German guns opening fire on us while crossing the coastline in this strange aircraft, but miraculously no shot was fired. Hugging the terrain, we headed for Caen where we finally landed.

Many years later I learnt that the pilot of the Spitfire was Prince Emanuel Vladimirovich Galitzine who had been spirited out of Russia as an infant after the Revolution of 1917. He was the great-grandson of Emperor Paul I (a son of

Catherine the Great). Before the Revolution, his father had served as aide-de-camp to Grand Duke Nikolai, head of all the Russian armies until 1916. He then grew up and worked in England until 1940 when he was accepted to serve with the Finnish air force which was fighting against the Communists. However, before he could take up that duty, he heard that his mother had been killed in the London Blitz and he accepted a commission in the Royal Air Force Volunteer Reserve. In November 1941 he was transferred to No.611 Squadron equipped with Spitfires based at Redhill in Surrey. During the summer of 1942 he was detached from this squadron to experiment with a Spitfire which had been adapted for high-altitude flying. This is his description of the interception of our Ju 86:

Prince Emanuel Vladimirovich (1918-2003). Following the interception of our Ju 86 R, Galitzine transferred to the RAF's 124 Squadron equipped with Spitfire VIIs designed for high-altitude work. After the war he became a successful business- man in the aircraft industry.

'At the end of August 1942 I was flying Spitfires with No.611 Squadron at Redhill when, following a medical examination, I was pronounced fit for very high-altitude operations and sent to join the Special Service Flight which was then forming at Northolt. On arrival there, I learnt the purpose of the new unit. During the previous couple of weeks, the Germans had been sending in single Junkers bombers at altitudes above 40,000 ft to attack targets in southern England. Conventional fighter units had found these high-flying raiders impossible to catch. With medically selected and specially trained pilots flying modified Spitfires, we hoped to do better. There were six of us in the Special Service Flight which was under the command of Flt Lt Jimmy Nelson, an American ex-Eagle Squadron pilot.

'Training for the new role began immediately. First of all, we were put on a special diet which included plenty of sweets, chocolate, eggs and bacon, fresh orange juice and other things which at that time were either strictly rationed or else unobtainable. There is now some doubt regarding the effectiveness of this diet in improving our performance at high altitude but it certainly did a lot for our morale and increased our standing with the girls.

'As part of our training we were sent to Farnborough where we underwent tests in the decompression chamber and had a short course of lectures from the doctors there. To conserve our strength and delay the onset of oxygen shortage at high altitude, we were enjoined to make all our movements slowly and deliberately. Everything had to be done in an icy calm manner.

'At the end of the first week in September the Flight received the first of our Spitfire IXs which had been modified for very high-altitude operations. The aircraft, serial BF273, had been lightened in almost every way possible. A lighter wooden propeller had been substituted for the normal metal one, all of the armour had been removed as had the four machine guns, leaving an armament of only two 20-mm Hispano cannons. The aircraft was finished in a special lightweight finish, which gave it a colour rather like Cambridge blue and all equipment not strictly necessary for high-altitude fighting was removed. It had the normal wingtips. A pressure cabin would have been very nice but the HF VII, essentially a Mk IX with a pressure cabin, was not yet ready for operations.

'On 10 September I made my first flight in the modified Spitfire IX and found it absolutely delightful to handle. During the war I flew eleven versions of the Spitfire and this was far and away the best. The 450-lb reduction in weight was immediately noticeable once airborne and with the Merlin 61 she had plenty of power and was very lively. I made a second flight that day to test the cannons, during which I took her up to 43,000 feet. I stayed above 40,000 feet for some time and found it quite exhilarating, it was a beautiful day and I could see along the coast of England from Dover to Plymouth and almost the whole of the northern coast of France as far as Belgium and Holland. During this flight I wore an electrically heated flying suit which kept me warm and comfortable.

'On 12 September I made my second high-altitude flight and this time it was in earnest. That morning, it had been my turn to wait at readiness and at 0927 I was scrambled to meet an aircraft being watched on radar climbing to height over France; it looked suspiciously like another one of the high-flying raiders.

'Climbing away at full throttle, the Spitfire went up like a lift but there was a long way to go – 40,000 feet is about 7.5 miles up. I climbed in a wide spiral over Northolt to 15,000 feet then the ground controller informed me that the incoming aircraft was over mid-Channel and heading towards the Portsmouth area. I was ordered onto a south-westerly heading to cut him off. After several course corrections I finally caught sight of the enemy aircraft as it was flying up the Solent. I was at about 40,000 feet and he was slightly higher and out to starboard. I continued my climb and headed after him, closing in until I could make out the outline of a Junkers 86. By then, I was about half a mile from him and we were both at 42,000 feet to the north of Southampton.

'The German crew had obviously seen me, because I saw the bomb jettison, the aircraft nose go up to gain altitude and turn for home. My Spitfire had plenty of performance in hand, however. I jettisoned my 30-gallon slipper tank and had little difficulty in following him in the climb and getting about 200 feet above the bomber. At this stage I kept reminding myself "Take it easy, conserve your strength, keep icy calm". The grey-blue Junkers seemed enormous and it trailed a long, curling condensation trail. It reminded me of a film I had once seen of an aerial view of an ocean liner ploughing through a calm sea and leaving a wake.

'I positioned myself for an attack and dived to about 200 yards astern of him, where I opened up with a three-second burst. At the end of the burst my

File Ju 86⁰ W/Cr Bartow. and Room 216/7

REPORT FROM FIGHTER COMMAND
INTELLIGENCE AT 0915 HOURS - 13.9.42.

Interception of Ju 86 P.

F.C.I. reports that a special Spitfire 9 left Northolt at 0927 hours on 12.9.42. to intercept raid 59.

On reaching 38,000 ft. over Bath pilot observed black trails above him. Climbed, and when at 41,000 ft. was still below E/Ac. Spitfire then jettisoned petrol tank and climbed to 42,500 ft. He was then at the same level as E/Ac which he identified as 86 P-1. Spitfire climbed to 43,000 ft. and was then same level as E/Ac who jettisoned a bomb. Spitfire closed to 300 yds. and gave 3 sec. burst, cannon. One strike observed in starboard wing. One cannon jammed. Spitfire got into slipstream and lost contact but then climbed to 44,000 ft. and got above E/Ac. Spitfire dived to 43,000 ft., closing to 400 yds. but E/Ac did steep turn for such an altitude and Spitfire was unable to follow. Contact regained over I.O.W. and Spitfire climbed 1,000 ft. above E/Ac, who was now a bit lower. Closed to 150 yds. and gave 2 secs. burst with one cannon but no strikes claimed. One jammed cannon and also frosted windscreen interfered with aim. After contact E/Ac carried out other steep turns and was finally lost.

The first page of the RAF Fighter Command intelligence report on the interception of Götz and Sommer's Ju 86. Note that the report wrongly identifies the aircraft as the earlier Ju 86 P high-altitude variant.

port cannon jammed and the Spitfire slewed round to starboard, then, as I passed through his slipstream, my canopy misted over. It took about a minute to clear completely, during which time I climbed back into position for the next attack. When I next saw the Junkers he was heading southwards, trying to escape out to sea. I knew I had to get right in close behind him if I was to stand any chance of scoring hits, because it would be difficult to hold the Spitfire straight when the starboard cannon fired and she went into a yaw. Again, I dived to attack but when I was about a hundred yards away the bomber made a surprisingly tight turn to starboard. I opened fire but the Spitfire went into a yaw and fell out of the sky; I broke off the attack, turned outside him and climbed back to 44,000 feet.

'I carried out two further attacks on the Junkers. On each of them my Spitfire yawed and fell out of the sky whenever I opened fire with my remaining cannon, and my canopy misted over whenever I passed through his slipstream. By the end of the fourth attack the action had lasted about 45 minutes. My engine had been running at full throttle for an hour and a quarter and my fuel was beginning to run low. So when the bomber descended into a patch of mist I did not attempt to follow. Instead I broke away and turned north-east for home. How I cursed that jammed cannon, had it not failed, I would certainly have shot down the Ju 86. As I neared the coast it became clear that I did not have sufficient fuel to reach Northolt, so I landed at Tangmere to refuel.'

After Galitzine lost us he presumed that we had carried on at altitude and headed straight for Cherbourg. This was later also assumed by the British radar plotters. After Galitzine returned to Northolt his feat was enthusiastically celebrated. Churchill was of course informed immediately and went personally to the airfield. He must have had a bad conscience since the effect of our attack on Bristol, and wanted to shake the pilot's hand. But Emmanuel was by then well and truly filled up by his mates and no longer in any state to be presented. Someone found the convincing excuse that he was already on another assignment.

Some thirty-three years later, the author Alfred Price managed to bring Horst and Emanuel together in London. They then reminisced about the battle over a bottle of whisky and discovered that they were distantly related. Horst was a descendant of a Polish princely house (Druki-Lubeki). Their meeting was covered by the newspapers. At four o'clock in the morning (London time) they called me on the telephone in Adelaide, singing merrily!

The hole in the port wing of our Ju 86 R from Galitzine's cannon shell. My brother, Helmuth, is on the left at the bottom of the photograph.

At Caen airfield we examined the damage caused by the cannon shell and considered it not serious enough to prevent us from returning to Beauvais. Meanwhile a crowd had gathered and a staff officer among them made the remark, after hearing we were attacked at 43,000 feet, "that is not possible". Horst retorted contemptuously, "Herr Major, do you think we made this hole ourselves?"

When we came to a halt at Beauvais airfield I saw to my pleasant surprise my brother Helmuth in the reception committee of technicians. We embraced heartily, the more so as we had been so lucky that day. When we inspected the damage inside the port wing (not the starboard as Galitzine had reported) we found a head-sized hole in the vertical member of the main spar which must have weakened it considerably. But luckily it had held during our dive and tight turns both of which had exceeded the specified safety limits.

Helmuth had come from Guernsey and was on his way to Paris where Philip Holzmann, his firm, had its French headquarters. He stayed with us at our villa for a couple of days. The next day I was told to report to the headquarters of K.G. 6 (Kampfgeschwader 6). Its commander, Oberst Walter Storp, showed me a telex stating that our Kommando would be enlarged to squadron strength and be known as the 14th Staffel. K.G. 6 was a mixture of dive-bombing remnants of decimated wings from all over France. Oberst Storp had earlier become a successful dive-bomber pilot who was now at a loose end. He was hoping that our Kommando would become very successful so that he could go shopping to Luftflotte 3 and so regain his status. When I told him of what had happened the day before and that the British now had fighters that could reach our operational height, he immediately saw the end of his dream. After a lengthy discussion he told me to get on with what I had been doing and he would not interfere.

When I returned to our villa in Beauvais, Horst and Helmuth were lying in their deckchairs on the back lawn in an exhausted state with a cognac in their hands. They told me the sad story that they had cleaned out the fishpond under the fountain and washed all the algae down the gurgler. When they reappraised their achievement the goldfish were missing. They had gone down with the turbid water. Grounds for an extended wake! Our ever ready 'Funker' (radio operator), Gerd Albrecht, was already weaving a not too straight a line across the lawn towards us, clutching more bottles.

This was the end of our unarmed sorties. Horst and Albrecht returned to Oranienburg while Altrogge and I made another attempt, without a bomb and with minimum fuel, to gain another 2,500 feet. This was to establish what the ceiling of the Spitfire would be. We again avoided London, which was ruled out of bounds to us throughout the operations of our Kommando. This was not the only time as you will see later. We penetrated east of London on 2 October 1942, heading towards Tunbridge Wells and returned without being intercepted. This was despite a number of fighters trying to climb to our altitude. 'Our' Spitfire, a special Mark IX, was not among them but the intelligence report we received at night from Meldekopf Birk, showed that the British lost two Spitfires during the action. One was shot down by their own flak and the other as the pilot bailed out at high altitude. He was unable to pull his aircraft out of a flat spin after he had stalled it while trying to get a lucky shot at us from his maximum ceiling of about 900 metres (3,000 feet) below.

The remaining Ju 86 Rs were then flown back to Orly and put into the Zeppelin hangars there. Altrogge returned to Rechlin. He was killed on 16 April 1944 when testing the second prototype Dornier Do 335 V2. Just after being diverted to the Luftwaffe airfield at Leipheim the aircraft's rear engine caught fire. Altrogge immediately shut it down and activated the fire extinguisher, but to no avail. Realising the situation was hopeless, he decided to use the newly installed ejector seat. He unlocked the canopy in order to jettison it, but rather than being flung away from the aircraft the forward edge of the canopy crashed down on his head, fracturing his skull. His loss of consciousness caused the aircraft to crash and he was killed.

This left me alone at Beauvais unclear as to what was to happen next. I remained there for four months, awaiting news of an improved high-altitude reconnaissance aircraft which was supposedly under development. Several designs were being considered, the Dornier Do 217 P, the Henschel Hs 130 E and the Ju 86 R-3. All three were to employ the HZ-Anlage system in which a Daimler-Benz DB 605 T engine was mounted *inside* the fuselage driving a two-stage supercharger for the two 'normal' engines. Both the Do 217 P and the Hs 130 E were powered by two 1,750-hp DB 603s, but the Ju 86 R-3 was to utilise two 1,500-hp Jumo 208 Diesel engines. Only the Do 217 P and the Hs 130 E were produced in prototype form. One other design, the Ju 186 powered by four Jumo 208 engines was also proposed. Nothing actually came of any of these aircraft and I was left to my own devices – going hunting in the countryside, visiting museums in Paris and helping other crews on night reconnaissance test flights with flares. I didn't fly any operations during this time.

One day, I think it was in January 1943, Sepp Binder, an Austrian Oberingenieur from the 2./VfH (our enemy aircraft squadron under Rosarius), arrived at Orly to retrieve a twin-engine RAF Hudson. This had crash-landed on the water's edge beneath the cliffs of southern Brest, and he was to establish whether it could still be salvaged and refurbished. Before the war Binder had been a motorcycle rider with the Velocette racing team in Birmingham. I accompanied him on the night train and it was interesting to listen to his reminiscences. He had a former assignment (on account of his familiarity with the English language and localities) of interrogating captured British air crews collected together at the Oberursel POW camp. While there, he had extracted the identity of a mystery bomber (which was completely destroyed after crashing) as the 'Mosquito'. At that time almost nothing was known about this aircraft. These subtle interrogations were the lever with which air intelligence could penetrate the silence of tight-lipped English personnel. Force was never used in these camps. We arrived at Brest the day after the highest ever recorded wind speed of just over 300 km/h (186 mph) over Europe and they had considerable damage at the airfield. I returned to Orly alone, after inspecting the Hudson's crash site under the cliffs, while Sepp stayed on.

While at Orly I remember quite an amusing incident which took place there. One of the pilots from Ted Rosarius' squadron desperately tried to start the engine of their captured Typhoon outside the Zeppelin hangar, in order to fly it to Oranienburg. After a time, the damned thing was surrounded by an enormous number of spent cartridge cases. The huge 24-cylinder engine was started by cartridges, but unfortunately we didn't have the correct type. Eventually, after a lot of swearing, he managed to get her started.

Over Christmas and New Year, I was given leave and spent it in Munich, but I have no record of which of my brothers were there too. Paul certainly was, as he was on study leave at the time from the technical college, studying for an automotive engineer's degree. Walter was then at the naval *Bauamt* (construction department) at Wilhelmshaven and bored stiff.

A year previously, Hitler had declared war on the USA in support of the Japanese. In their first major action in the west, in November 1942, United States forces landed troops in French Morocco to push to the north and the east. This was to link up with British forces advancing west along the

The captured Hawker Typhoon of 2.Versuchsverband (Zirkus Rosarius) coded T9+GK. The aircraft had bright-yellow tail surfaces for recognition purposes.

Mediterranean coast from Egypt. Casablanca was occupied during the month and, in January, a meeting of President Roosevelt and Churchill was arranged at this location to discuss with their staff the continuation of the war. Stalin was invited, but declined to attend.

It is interesting to read in Jan Calvin's book *Chief of Intelligence* (published in 1951) about Admiral Canaris that German intelligence had knowledge of this meeting about a week in advance. He writes that they were baffled by the location in Casablanca and the White House, where the meeting was to take place. By chance I was paying a visit to Oranienburg from Orly at this time and was in discussion with Horst and Oberst Rowehl on the tarmac when Rowehl told Horst and me of this telex interception. Obviously we were able to tell him about the Maison Blanche in Casablanca which had been our head-quarters. We immediately suggested intercepting this meeting. Oberst Rowehl went to Berlin that night.

What Jan Calvin then writes about a Ju 86 reconnaissance aircraft spotting a bomber carrying Churchill is of course nonsense, as our Ju 86s were then not operating in France. They had transferred to Crete and were flying with the reconnaissance squadrons there. But I am pretty sure that Oberst Rowehl discussed our proposal with Admiral Canaris that night. This was to attack the White House in Casablanca with a Ju 88 carrying a big bomb. We would take off from southern France, crash-land the aircraft in northern Morocco and then go home on foot through Spain. We got the thumbs down. It is anyone's guess what was behind the refusal. Rowehl told Calvin later that he was told of an order to assassinate Churchill (given by Hitler to Canaris). Canaris was against any such undertaking for ethical or other reasons. A direct bomb attack surely was not blatant assassination, like Churchill's plans to blow up our K.Gr. 100 bus from Vannes to Meucon in March 1941. Our plan would just have evened the score.

I have to mention here an encounter I had after our Ju 86 R operations had ceased. Horst and Albrecht had left for Oranienburg after my last flight with Altrogge on 2 October 1942. As it became very boring to sit by ourselves in the evening in our country house we sometimes drove to Beauvais/Tille airfield after tea. This was to have a chat in the officer's mess and partake of a glass of wine. During one of these nights, at about 11 o'clock, I was sitting with a small group including the airfield commander, a Hauptmann, when a group of people entered, wrapped up in long coats. The nights were already cool. The group consisted of an SS Sturmbannführer, a man in civilian clothing and a woman in her late fifties of somewhat striking appearance. The airfield commander seemed to know them as he greeted them cordially. He hurriedly introduced them to us so that no name stuck in my mind and ordered some refreshments for them from the orderly. We settled down with them at our table in the corner of the deserted room and a lively conversation ensued. We all spoke French as the lady seemed not to be fluent in German.

The reason for their being on the road so late did not come up in the discussion. After a time, the officers and the civilian became deep in conversation, now speaking German. I then began to talk to the French lady who was sitting on my left and I pondered how a lady of such distinguished bearing and looks came to be in the company of two Germans. Remember, that at this time, the French resistance movement was already making it dangerous to collaborate with our occupying forces. We talked for a considerable time, but I never found out how she came to be in such company. I mentioned my fear of what could befall her if she was not under the protection she apparently enjoyed at that time. Her handbag was between us on the bench. With a wry smile she opened it slightly and with her elegant hand poked about inside. Without removing it, I could see that she had a small pistol. Horrified, I pointed out that such a pea shooter would surely not be enough to make rough and well-equipped partisans throw up their hands and surrender. She just responded to my joke by looking in the direction of her companions and lifting her shoulders. My God, I thought, is she game! After an hour our guests got up and disappeared into the night again towards Paris.

Coco Chanel.

That was forty-nine years ago and I never gave it another thought until May 1992 when I read an article about Coco Chanel. During the Second World War she had a romantic liaison with a German diplomat, Hans Günther von Dincklage. This made me sit up and brought the above-mentioned encounter back to my mind, as the lady would have been the age of Coco then. A couple of weeks later I saw quite by chance, a biography of her on the shelf of the local booksellers. I opened the copy and the face of 1943 stared at me. It was without a doubt the lady with whom I had talked.

The biography recorded that she worked for General Walter Schellenberg, chief of SS intelligence. At the end of the war, he was sentenced to six years' imprisonment for war crimes at Nuremberg. He was released in 1951 owing to incurable liver disease and took refuge in Italy. Chanel paid for Schellenberg's medical care and living expenses, financially supported his wife and family and paid for his funeral upon his death in 1952. She had a dislike of the Jews, reportedly inculcated by her convent years and sharpened by her association with society's elite. She thought that Jews were a threat to Europe. During the German occupation she resided at the Hotel Ritz, which was also noteworthy for being the preferred place of residence for the upper echelon of German military staff.

In September 1944, Chanel was called in to be interrogated by the Free French Purge Committee, the *épuration*. She survived, handling her defence with aplomb. "I am not a politician," she said, "and never ask my acquaintances for their identification papers." This related to the German diplomat, who was from a noble family. By the way, the SS officer was also a man of culture, of no military self-importance, at least as long as we spoke French.

CHAPTER 9

RADAR
KOMMANDO GÖTZ

Two Ju 88 D-1s of Kommando Götz pictured at Sarabus. Note that both aircraft have black under-surfaces and the national insignia blacked out for night operations.

Horst had returned to Oranienburg in November 1942. He was then given a new assignment to join Kommando Koch based at Grosseto in Italy. This Kommando, under the leadership of Major Adolf Koch, was a special maritime radar-reconnaissance and electronic-jamming unit equipped with eleven He 111 H-6s and a Ju 88 A-4. It was attached to the II./Luftnachrichten Versuchs Regiment. Because of Götz's considerable experience in flying reconnaissance missions and his knowledge of radar with the Telefunken company, it was thought he would prove invaluable to the unit. Perhaps because of this he was promoted directly from Feldwebel to Oberleutnant and therefore climbed to a higher rank than myself.

Meanwhile, following the Stalingrad catastrophe, Russian pressure from the Caucasus towards the Crimea was growing in intensity. Soviet forces had already landed at Taman and in spite of relentless attacks against them they could not be dislodged. Their plan was to cross the straits and take Kerch which would gain them a foothold in the Crimea. In order to interrupt their supply route across the

Black Sea, Rowehl again came up with an idea. This was to establish an airborne radar Kommando to carry out night attacks against the Russian transport ships. It would be equipped with Ju 88s carrying Lichtenstein S forward-looking radar, with which Horst was also familiar as it was another Telefunken product.

Early in February 1943 I was recalled from Orly to join Horst again as navigator. The new unit, designated Kommando Götz, was to be equipped with four Ju 88s and a He 111. Unfortunately, the quality of the other crews was hampered by a lack of general experience. The He 111 pilot was not even trained in night flying and Horst had his doubts about him. There was no time to complain because, on 17 February 1943, we were on our way to Sarabus, just north of Simferopol, the Crimean capital. What a contrast the terrain and the facilities that awaited us in the area! We were billeted in primitive farm houses in the village. Everything was deep in mud after the spring thaw. No bitumen anywhere, only hard rolled taxiways and concrete aprons in front of the rickety old Soviet hangars. Sarabus had previously been a Russian air force base. Everything was very archaic by Western European standards.

We found that the population was quite standoffish but, to a small degree, sympathetic. This was to cost the whole population expulsion by Stalin later. They were looking for independence at this time, which the German government had promised them. Again the Nazi party machine made a mess of that too as they did in the whole of the east, making fierce enemies out of potential friends which it needed so badly.

For administration and supplies we were dependant on another unit, 4.(F)/122 – the Fourth (long-range squadron of Reconnaissance Group 122). This squadron was led by Hauptmann Kaspar Georg von Wedelstädt, who proved to be a jolly and nonchalant fellow. We began our time by conducting a series of short training sessions for the new crews. At the same time Horst and I flew practice missions to establish the tactics to best exploit the radar system. We scanned the German supply lines to Sebastopol, across the Black Sea, for Russian submarines. On one occasion we got strong signals, but could not see anything down below in spite of us dropping flares in the vicinity. After checking in daylight we found that floating ice had tricked us.

Our sorties began in earnest with flights all along the eastern Crimean coast. Our aircraft at this time was a Ju 88 A-4 coded T5+UB. We flew our searches in continuous circles at a distance of about 10 kilometres (6 miles) out to sea. This was so that we could distinguish target-radar traces emanating from Soviet ships from our own coming from the mainland. The problem with this was that it considerably shortened our endurance. A solution to this was the installation of side-scanning radar. We asked immediately for this but had, for the time being, to manage with the front-scanning aerials.

We had flown about ten nocturnal sorties on our own before we had our first casualty. Our He 111 crew was undertaking some night-training circuits when their aircraft fell out of the sky during a snow storm. The accident was probably due to pilot error. It was the young pilot Horst had warned me about before. Horst told me that he thought he was a bit arrogant and had ignored many of the lessons and detailed warnings which he had passed on from his considerable experience in nocturnal flying. Götz was always meticulous with his preparations, leaving no room for error, something this chap seemed to find irritating. The only thing I could criticise Horst for was that he didn't kick him out of the unit, but then he would have killed himself somewhere else.

On the night of 14 March 1943 we found a target approximately five kilometres out from the port of Adler on the Caucasian coast. We lit it up with our parachute flares and circled it. Approaching from the darkest part of the sky, we throttled back for a low-level bombing attack. Before we could drop our bombs, the tanker, which was silhouetted in the glare of the flares on the water, suddenly exploded in flames. It was not from our bombs, but a torpedo from an E-boat on patrol from Feodosia on the Crimea. It just happened to be at the right spot at the right time. Horst and I flew over to the E-boat squadron on the following day to discuss co-ordination in the future, but this achievement was not to be repeated. Either the target was too far away for them, or the sea was too rough for a run in on the target or some other thing.

In March 1943 our Ju 88 D hit a bomb crater with the starboard wheel digging into the hole. This photograph was taken shortly after the accident.

One night, I think it was 19 March, but Horst's logbooks say two days earlier, we suffered a Russian light-bomber attack on our airfield. This was just as we taxied out in pitch darkness. Some bombs fell in the vicinity. We rolled on in the faint yellow light to the take-off point far away, when the right-hand undercarriage fell into what we afterwards discovered was a bomb crater. Up went the

tail of the Ju 88, causing it to fall back
heavily with the starboard propeller
throwing stones and mud at the cabin.
After firing a red flare, the take-off
crew came and towed us out of the
crater with a tractor. The aircraft had
broken its back and needed a new
engine. After temporary patching,
Horst flew it back to Schönefeld near
Berlin, reporting that 'it flew like a
porpoise'.

He eventually returned with a brand
new Ju 88 which was equipped with
side-scanning radar in addition to the
forward-looking equipment. The only
problem was that it had reduced
range. With the former we had a radar

*In order for Horst to fly the damaged Ju 88
back to Germany, a temporary metal patch
was attached to the rear fuselage.*

range of 220 kilometres (135 miles) which was good for navigation as we
could pick out all the high peaks around our corner of the Black Sea and
draw bearings from them.

The new radar was developed by the marine scientist Professor Scherzer and
was looked after by a marine engineer, Herr Borngesser, who accompanied us
on a couple of missions. It worked very nicely, but still we wanted to extend
our operational range to enable us to attack ships in Poti harbour, the Russian
submarine base. To attain this, we were supplied with 750-litre (165-Imp.gallon)
auxiliary fuel tanks made of plywood. The only problem was that we found,
after filling them, that they all leaked due to being stored too long in dry conditions. We finally found one good one and another which only leaked slightly
and so we decided to give it a try on 12 April. We started the engines without
chocks under the main wheels, so that we could roll forward immediately in
case one of the tanks caught fire from the flames coming from the exhaust.

Just then our flak began firing on a Russian night prowler.[17] We took off in
pitch darkness from the blacked-out field right over our flak battery which

17. At this time the Russians were flying obsolescent biplanes at night to carry out harassing
attacks on our airfields. The Luftwaffe imitated this tactic with their Störkampfstaffeln which
were equipped with such types as the Ar 66 and Go 145.

was firing at the end of the
runway. Seconds later red
flames were mirrored in the
cabin glass. The leaking
starboard auxiliary fuel tank
had caught fire. Horst
pressed the release button
and both tanks fell away
streaming flames. Thank-
fully our Ju 88 seemed to
have suffered no damage
and we continued on to fly
a mission of shorter range
than originally planned. As
we never used our radio
except for emergencies, we
returned to a surprising
welcome. Everybody saw

The marine scientist, Professor Scherzer (left) and Horst share a joke over the Ju 88 which hit a bomb crater while taxiing. Note the Narvik shield on the left arm of Horst's uniform jacket.

the spectacle of our take-off and thought that we had been shot down by our own flak. The search for the wreckage was still going on.

Some days later, another of our Ju 88s had just been loaded with bombs and was ready for us on the concrete apron, when a night intruder threw a stick of bombs right across it. The aircraft blew up with a tremendous bang, also setting fire to a nearby Ju 52 transport. Horst and I were just leaving our quarters on a motorbike and side car when the blast shook us although it was six kilometres away. At the same time a fire broke out in the roof of our mess building. We established later that this was caused by a broken electric cable, but it was soon put out without serious damage.

The scene at the site of our aircraft looked quite different. There was a huge crater where the aircraft had stood and its engines were lying about 400 metres (1,300 feet) to the right and left. It had received a direct hit. This was very lucky for us as we used to ignore the Russian 'sewing machines' as we called the light bombers and went on with our business in spite of the sirens. So the Luftwaffe had lost four aircraft on this field during the time of our presence at Sarabus. I recently read in *The Official History of the Soviet Air Force in World War II* that the Russians claimed that 260 German aircraft were destroyed on the ground at Sarabus and Saki (on the western coast of the Crimea) during our time there. This was confirmed by their aerial reconnaissance. I wonder what they saw?

As the battle for the Taman Peninsula heated up, without the Russians being pushed out, we flew concentrated night attacks against their support shipping, occasionally sinking a vessel. We lost one crew while bombing a tanker off Suchum. On 18 April we flew two sorties. In one of these we nearly blew ourselves up during a low-level attack. This was due to the wrong fuse having been installed in our bombs which detonated on impact a short time after release. Fortunately, our wings held and only the bomb bay covers were bent out of shape.

We made an interesting observation one day when interference was seen on the radar screen which mainly affected the distance indicator tube. As it was noticeable only on the Lichtenstein S systems frequency and not on Professor Scherzer's, we suspected the possibility of the Russians having a radar-jamming installation near the port of Adler. Supporting this suspicion was the fact that on crossing this coastline north of the port at our usual operating altitude of 4,000 metres, we were fired on repeatedly by pretty accurate heavy flak, operating without searchlights. Our reports were treated with scepticism, but we thought that our people underrated the capability of Russian technology.

On 26 April 1943 we suffered a bad crash-landing during a night of tricky weather, marked by layers of icing-up clouds. On the same night another good crew, led by Leutnant Horst Dumke, crashed in the same way, but again nobody was injured.

During early May, the Kommando was handed over to the control of our host squadron 4.(F)/122. We had trained some of their crews too as well leading to Oranienburg ordering our crew back for other tasks. We finally left Sarabus on 14 May. During the campaign Horst and I had both received the Deutsche Kreuz in gold. I think that the main effect of our activities was the cutting or diminishing of Russian supplies to the embattled troops on the Taman Peninsula. But after seven months of fighting the battle was finally lost later in the year.

At Oranienburg we found that a number of changes had taken place. Just after we had left, in February 1943, the Versuchsstelle für Hohenflüge had been redesignated Versuchsverband Ob.d.L [experimental unit of the commander-in-chief of the Luftwaffe]. Our aircraft code was then gradually changed from 'T5' to 'T9'. In addition, and more importantly, our previous commander, Oberst Rowehl, had resigned his post. We thought this was due to a rebellion of some of his officers who had gained considerable approval and support (even from Hitler), because of their expertise and reputation in the technical field. Prominent among them was Hauptmann Siegfried Knemeyer who was famous for his mathematical and technical skills. He was suddenly catapulted from a mere underling of Rowehl's to the position of chief of development (Chef GL/CE) of

The Allied bombing raids in 1943 forced us to move the family valuables to Uncle Josef's house in Landsberg for safekeeping. From left to right: Walter's wife Inge, Helmuth's wife Hedwig, Paul and my father.

aircraft and weaponry and gained complete command of the Oranienburg establishment.

Upon our arrival at Oranienburg we were given a fortnight's leave, which I spent with my parents in Munich. I found them healthy but obviously somewhat depressed as the war situation was becoming grimmer by the day. My brother Walter had been called up as had brother Helmuth. He had already served with a pioneer unit in France. Before Helmuth went into action and while still in France, he arrived at Munich for a brief period of leave. He brought his bride, Hedwig 'Hed' Geier from Duisburg, with him and we all went sailing together on the Ammersee. Paul was still studying at the *Technicum* in Munich, but with the threat of being called up again constantly hanging over him. My cousins, Hans in Neubiberg and Karl in Berlin, were in relatively secure positions far away from danger except, of course, from the ever-increasing bombing raids being carried out by the RAF and the USAAF. The latter was already flying daylight raids on Germany.

Mother still had her fortnightly meetings with old friends at a *Kaffeekränzchen* (afternoon coffee party) while father continued his regular evening walks. I usually accompanied him in these and read profusely. They still had contact with nearby Aunt Toni and her brothers Kurt and Geo Romer. Uncle Heinrich Jolas had been bombed out in September 1942 and, following an operation, was often absent from his temporary apartment in Munich. I can't remember having ever met him after 1941.

After our meeting, brother Helmuth was transferred to the Eastern Front and was wounded in October 1943 in a Russian attack when he was shot through the leg. He had managed, after dark, to crawl back to his own front line which was rapidly retreating.

Back at Oranienburg a new chapter in my life was about to open.

CHAPTER 10

THE BEGINNING OF MY CAREER AS A PILOT

When I arrived in Oranienburg, Knemeyer, now a Major, and soon to be promoted to Oberstleutnant, asked me into his office. Although he now had a position in the Luftwaffe Führungsstab as Chef GL/CE,[18] he still had an office there. For the first time I was introduced to the development of new types of aircraft and engines. Knemeyer showed me the plans and specifications for a new generation reconnaissance and bomber aircraft, the Arado Ar 234. The first prototype of this was in the mock-up stage at the Arado works at Brandenburg. It would be the world's first jet-pro-

Siegfried Knemeyer holds open the canopy of the Horten Ho IIIc with Ted Rosarius in the cockpit, Oranienburg 1944.

pelled bombing and reconnaissance aircraft. It was a shoulder-wing, all-metal aircraft with the pilot as the lone crew member housed in a 'glasshouse' cockpit (as the Americans called it). It would be powered by two Jumo 004 turbojet engines of 960 kilograms (2,100 pounds) thrust each.

The fuselage was nearly complete but there was a delay in the supply of the jet engines from the Junkers aircraft engine factory. The new type had to share

---

18. Chief of aircraft aviation development with the Luftwaffe High Command.

these first engines with the Me 262 fighter which was already test flying. Knemeyer asked me to study the plans and to give him an opinion from the view of an experienced bomber man who had no hang-ups as regards the controversy between dive and horizontal bombing tactics. He needed someone with fresh eyes to do an assessment. There was too much fighting already in the hierarchy about the basic role of such a new development. Knemeyer himself was a reconnaissance man.

I reported back to him next day asking him if I could examine the real thing, so he arranged for an Arado Ar 66 biplane and a pilot to fly me over there. At Brandenburg I was led into the assembly area and saw the prototype airframe supported on stilts. I was then introduced to the company's chief designer, Dipl.-Ing. Wilhelm van Nes, and other engineers and civilians, all of whom were involved with this bird. It only had wooden mock-ups for the real engines. The shape of the shoulder-winged airframe was sleek and it had a beautiful finish. After a lot of explanation by the gentlemen I settled down in the pilot's seat to get the feel of it. This enabled me to check my pre-formed ideas of what I would do with such an aircraft.

After climbing out of the cockpit, I had two main criticisms to put to the gentlemen. First: why was a dive-bombing attack suggested in the plans? Everyone shrugged their shoulders. Second: why mount a mirror inside the cabin for rearward vision of the one-man cabin? It was obvious that the glazing would ice over at high altitude. My answer to the second question was to fit a periscope, similar to that developed for our armoured vehicles.

In answer to the first question, I suggested that the aircraft should use all its remarkable potential by targeting its bombs from high altitude and high speed, unmolested by enemy fighters. Dive bombing would be necessarily inaccurate because of the high gliding speed without the braking effect of idling

The wooden mock-up of the fuselage nose of the Ar 234 showing the extensively glazed nose designed for the aircraft which I saw at Brandenburg.

propellers. It would also lead the pilot into the flak danger zone and air turbulence at lower altitudes. High-altitude attacks, on the other hand, could be
planned well in advance with the Lotfe bomb aimer controlling the aircraft by
using the three-axis auto-pilot. This had already been catered for in the design.
The Lotfe was already steering other aircraft in the horizontal plane as supplied.
It should be able to do this on all three axes.

Yes, they said, and got quite excited about the idea. I left them to be flown
back to Oranienburg where I reported to Knemeyer on what I had seen and
discussed. He then made the suggestion that I should take over the role of Ar
234 *Typenbegleiter*, a person responsible for overseeing the development and
parts supply route for both the airframe and engines of a particular type. I
pointed out to him that I didn't feel comfortable in this position and that I
would rather follow up the actual tactical performance and for that I would
need a pilot's licence.

He agreed to this suggestion after I told him that I had already done solo
flying without a Luftwaffe licence. In 1940, after taking up my post as officer
zbV in the reserve squadron of KG 100 at Lüneburg, I had befriended Leutnant
Brussig, a former Lufthansa transport pilot who had an instructor's licence. I
was very eager to pilot an aircraft myself, as I had taken over temporary control
of our He 111 from Horst on many occasions. As there was a Klemm Kl 25
lying idle in a hangar, Brussig offered to train me on it to solo standard, without
official permission. So, on Saturday afternoons, when the airfield was practically
deserted, we did our circuits and I flew solo just before our squadron transferred to Hannover-Langenhagen. That was the end of my erstwhile pilot's
career as no suitable aircraft was available at that airfield. Later, in 1943, Horst
had the use of an Arado Ar 66 biplane at Sarabus, which was of Class B (a
class higher). The two-seat biplane was used by Horst for flights to the navy
in Feodosia and other communication duties. Once he sent me in it solo
(without licence) across country to pick up spare parts from Dnjepropetrovsk
and all went well. That was all the piloting experience I had to date apart from
watching and learning from Horst.

I told Knemeyer that I could be trained up to the highest class licence
within six months as long as he supported me. After thinking it over, he gave
his consent. Telling Horst what the arrangement was I reported within a week
to the Flugzeugführer Schule [pilot training school] FFS A/B 23 at Kaufbeuren.
Here I trained as any other beginner on the Bücker 181, the Focke-Wulf Fw
44 Stieglitz and other light aircraft. Within eight weeks I was flying solo and
performing aerobatics. My final report from the school recommended me for

further training as a fighter pilot, but I declined and went on to the Flugzeu-gführer Schule at Burg near Magdeburg to do further training. Mainly carried out in flying circuits, I learned to handle heavier and twin-engine aircraft together with practising instrument and night flying. After eight weeks at Burg I passed in practice and theory and was transferred to the blind flying school at Copenhagen in Denmark. Here we gorged ourselves in this land of plenty, until our stomachs complained and we were forced to revert to a more austere diet similar to that which we had become used to over the years.

As Christmas 1943 was coming up I managed to arrange an instrument training flight in rather bad winter weather to Neubiberg near Munich. I was able to see my parents and my brother Paul again. He arrived from Ingolstadt where he worked with the Deutsche Werke. It was to be the last Christmas during the war where most of us were together. Unfortunately, Walter, who had now been called up with an infantry unit, and Helmuth, who was convalescing in hospital from his wounds on the Eastern Front, could not join us.

As Walter and Inge planned to get married in January 1944 we made plans for all of us to be there at Hildesheim, where our relation, Herr Rothermund, was professor at the local art school. During my last weeks in Copenhagen I used to shop in my free time and found some nice presents for everybody. On 13 January, with all exams behind me and my licence endorsed with the EFF Schein (extended pilot licence with which I was allowed to fly all types of aircraft), I returned to Oranienburg. I was then sent on leave for three days to Hildesheim and on to Munich for a fortnight.

It was a great reunion in Hildesheim and I used my newly acquired 8-mm film camera to the full. The pictures I took are still in existence with video copies in Bobby's, Inge's and our hands. They are the only pictorial record of this historic wedding as all other cameras failed abysmally. Everybody got their presents from me apart from Hedwig. I had purchased a nice pair of shoes for her but they were stolen during my three-day stay at Oranienburg. I had left them in the locker in my room which was kept for me even when I was not there. Foolishly, perhaps, I had left it unlocked despite knowing that Russian women workers did all the cleaning. A search in their quarters in a nearby camp brought nothing to light. They were too well organised and I was only embarrassed by the exercise.

At Hildesheim the whole Sommer family was present, except for Mama who did not feel well at the time. The Rothermund relations put on a great show. After the wedding we all dispersed again. Walter and Inge went to Innsbrück for a skiing holiday on the Patschenkofel, while I went skiing

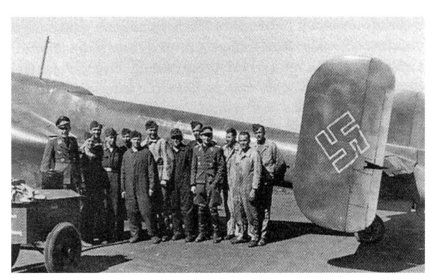

The Arado Ar 240 C-0 coded T9+GL was flown by Horst Götz. Occasionally I joined him as his 'sweating passenger'. The group of aircrew and mechanics includes Gerd Albrecht (first left) and Horst (fourth from the right).

opposite on the Hafelekar on the other side of the Inn valley. One night a Ju 88 crashed into the mountainside not far from my hotel. It was returning from a night mission to Malta. None of the crew survived. The crash was due to navigational error, as so often was the case.

I returned to Oranienburg in February and was immediately employed in transferring aircraft and personnel of all kinds until in mid-March a special task turned up. In the meantime, Horst had an Arado Ar 240 in Orly with which he tried with little success to penetrate the English air defences to get aerial pictures of the island. In total he made about forty flights in attempts to photograph England and Italy.

By then German long-range reconnaissance in the west was practically impossible. Even making a daylight show in the Mediterranean theatre was a risky business with existing squadron aircraft. That is until the Ju 88 T-series came on stream. This was a development of our earlier Ju 88 D powered by BMW 801 radial engines with GM 1. It carried a crew of three and could reach a maximum speed of 660 km/h (410 mph) at 9,000 metres (29,500 feet) after its drop tanks had been discarded. This allowed us to penetrate fighter defences. I picked one up for testing and flew it to Toulouse/Francazal in France. It had

The end of the Arado 240 C-0 (possibly the V9).
Coded T9+GL, the aircraft made a belly-landing
when piloted by Oblt Wolf Loah. Loah was later
badly burnt when the Ar 240 was destroyed.

unusual dark-blue upper surfaces over sprayed with a white 'scribble' pattern.[19]

At Toulouse I joined up with a Ju 86 R from our squadron piloted by Oberleutnant Otto Selig with Hauptmann Albert Vogel as navigator. Our job was to complete a new aerial survey of the whole of the Pyrenees as the old French and Spanish maps didn't meet properly at the border. They were not accurate enough should the Pyrenees become a defence frontier. At the same time, I was to join Horst with his Ar 240 C, coded T9+GL, to do a check on Corsica for possible naval activities of the Allies in preparation for an invasion of southern France or northern Italy. They had already taken pictures of Sicily and landed at Anzio south of Naples. As Spitfires and Mustangs were stationed on Corsica, reconnaissance by our normally equipped squadrons was too costly. Their radar-controlled high-altitude fighters saw to that.

For both these tasks I had to pick up my film cassettes at Saint Martin de Croix near Arles. This was where the 1./(F)33 reconnaissance squadron was based. Horst remembered:

'The staff at Saint Martin welcomed us with open arms and we were treated like kings because now the interpreters and staff officers finally had work again and justification for their existence. At night we flew over well-lit Switzerland and back to Orly. We were not supposed to fly over neutral territory but I am sure that nobody noticed us. After the strain of these missions we frequented the Lido in Paris. I ran into an old acquaintance of mine, a civilian translator from our unit, able to escape the invasion. After an exchange of experiences, we came upon an incident of German-Allied cooperation hardly to be found again

19. I am indebted to my good friend Thomas H Hitchcock for identifying this dark-blue colour as RLM 83 *Dunkelblau*. [Ed.]

during the war. This unbelievable incident started in Casablanca and ended for me in the Crimea.

'We had English acquaintances who were in an internment camp near Marseille. Their name was Wright. His wife wrote me a letter to ask whether I could buy some lady's stockings that were not available in the internment camp. I bought two pairs of the desired size, added some chocolate and gave the package to the translator whose French wife lived near Marseille. She managed to smuggle the package into the internment camp. Needless to say there were no written messages included for security reasons. After a while a message came to me to Casablanca via Berlin with a thank you from the Wrights and a request if I could repeat the favour. Again we got a package together and handed it to the translator. Shortly before the Americans landed in North Africa I was transferred to Berlin. The package remained in Ain Diab as reported by the apologetic translator.

'A miracle then happened. The package had arrived despite everything. I received the message in Sarabus in the Crimea via Berlin. A "thank you" from the internment camp for package number two. The Americans had found it and since it had the address it was probably sent with the help of the French resistance through the German lines to the internment camp.'

After refuelling at Saint Martin, I would climb away in my Ju 88 to the west of Corsica up to 10,500 metres (35,000 feet), turn east towards the island and increase speed by diving down to 10,000 metres and applying GM 1. This gave me an actual airspeed of about 570 km/h (354 mph). That was enough to break through any fighter screen. Then I would turn north-east and land at Vicenza in northern Italy, to deliver the film. I would then refuel again and fly back to Saint Martin to pick up new loaded cassettes and finally back to Toulouse.

Then I took on another section of the northern part of the Pyrenees until the whole aerial survey was completed. On the penultimate flight I had an uncomfortable encounter with four fighters while just completing my run west of Pamplona in Spain (we didn't care about penetrating neutral Spanish territory). Turning south-east towards home I saw these four spots at my altitude and to the north. Long-range Mustangs had been reported before in this area, so I decided to make a run for it before establishing whether or not the aircraft were friendly.

My Ju 88 T-1, coded T9+AH, at Toulouse/Francazal with its unusual camouflage scheme. It was eventually destroyed in a bombing attack on Baranovichi.

We dived at high speed towards Pau, but they gradually gained on us. I made for the relative safety of the mountains to our right and as I dived into the first steep valley they opened fire which our radio operator returned with his machine gun. I saw bullets exploding in front of me while flying tight along a rock face. I let down into a narrow mountain valley between high fir trees and wriggled my way along when all of a sudden the valley opened out. I was then confronted with an immensely high chain of mountains with apparently no way out. To do a loop would have brought us right in front of the pursuing fighters. I decided to try my luck and climbed up the towering rock wall to our left on full emergency power to try to skim over the peak at 2,000 metres. We just managed to lift her over at almost stalling speed and with a relief fell down the other side into a wide valley. We saw the fighters searching to the left in the lower hills to the east so we hugged the ground and sneaked further south and out into the open.

After putting down at Toulouse we were told that an alarm was on, as Mosquitos were active to the west. One had been engaged and shot down by a fighter-training school patrol. I rang the school at Biarritz and after a short conversation with the elated commander of the school I had to give him the sad news that his 'Mosquito' was unfortunately a Ju 88 T and it was well and alive and could be inspected at Toulouse/Francazal. Next day embarrassed members of the school came to see me. They immediately recognised their 'prey' which had an unmistakable and unusual camouflage scheme. They left without leaving a bottle of cognac for reconciliation, but then they were poor school people!

At the end of my next flight the starboard engine gave out, probably as the result of over-revving during my hasty descent the day before. I was then forced to make an uneventful single-engine landing. The aircraft still flew beautifully on one engine. A new engine was fitted and, as our task was by then completed, I flew back to Oranienburg. I only managed to get as far as Orly as the port engine then gave way. The situation was then a bit trickier as Paris had low cloud cover and all the balloons in the southern industrial area were up near Orly west of the high bank of the River Seine. But all went well again and after two days of enjoying the famous Orly cooking of its Mitropa chef I was on the final leg, still with a badly misfiring port engine. I finally arrived safely back at Oranienburg on 3 May 1944.

One of my first tasks there was to fly Oberstleutnant Knemeyer and his Führungsstab [command staff] entourage to Rostock/Marienehe, the Heinkel aircraft factory and headquarters. They were scheduled to have a conference with Professor Heinkel and his engineers. I wasn't involved in the discussions but stayed overnight at the Heinkel guest house so that I could ferry the conference delegates back to Berlin next morning. I was piloting a Siebel Si 204 D which was comfortably converted as a commuter aircraft.

Around this time, the Ascania aircraft instrument factory had developed a new automatic gyro-control system for single-engine fighter aircraft. This was to assist night flying and navigation for the Wilde Sau [Wild Boar] fighter units. These units were using single-engine aircraft for attacking enemy bombers at night and were proving relatively successful, but had a high attrition rate under adverse weather conditions. Knemeyer had a Fw 190 fighter aircraft equipped with this system standing by at Oranienburg and wanted the opinion of a novice pilot as to its efficiency.

After a day's theoretical tuition, I took off in the Focke-Wulf but found to my horror that the airspeed indicator was inoperative from the start. This meant that all the previous teaching which I had received about its stalling and landing approach speeds didn't help me at all. In an attempt to work out my own figures, I made a series of simulated landings on a bank of clouds, listening intently to the air noises as I approached stalling speed. After I got the feel of it I did a lot of loops and rolls with and without the automatic control switched on. I checked the instrument flying turn speed which was applied with the heels of the rudder pedals and landed without much trouble. Knemeyer was impressed when I told him of what happened and my experience.

I subsequently flew this aircraft several times, but the Wilde Sau pilots never got the benefit of the system. Shortly afterwards, the Ascania factory at Berlin/Tegel, not far south of our Oranienburg airfield, was destroyed in a bombing raid and with it all further development of the gadget.

On 8 May 1944 I carried out a workshop flight with a four-engine French aircraft, a prototype of the Bloch 161 airliner. This had been confiscated from

The French-built Bloch 161 four-engine airliner in German markings.

Marshal Philippe Pétain's VIP flight and was now used by our establishment. There were a lot of technical complaints about the aircraft and after three days I took it up again to test fly. Firstly, the trim mechanism was connected in reverse which nearly caused a fatal accident during take-off. Then the undercarriage would not lock in either the up or down position. I had the aircraft's chief mechanic, Feldwebel Holz, and another senior mechanic, Feldwebel Wilhelm, with me in the cockpit but none of us could do anything about it. The green lights of the down position just didn't light up, but only gave an occasional flicker.

The cockpit controls were typically French. To apply full power, the four-throttle levers were pulled back instead of being pushed forward. To check elevator trim, an indicating pointer slid along a scale to my right and above me on the cockpit ceiling. To change the trim of the aircraft I had to swing a crank hanging under the scale, clockwise for tail-heavy trim, anticlockwise for nose-heavy trim. When I reduced engine power after take-off, the aircraft tended to nose down so you had to trim towards the tail to get neutral force on the control column. But this time, in spite of the pointer indicating tail heavy, the aircraft continued to nose downwards and I had to pull with both hands and all the force I could muster to prevent us racing into the ground. "For God's sake," I yelled to the board mechanic, "swing the handle the other way!" Fortunately, he reacted immediately and correctly and saved our lives. We recovered only metres above the trees below. That was not all. The system to retract or lock down the undercarriage was partly operated by air pressure, partly by gravitational forces. To retract the undercarriage, air pressure from a reservoir was employed. If the pressure from the pump was insufficient, the wheels didn't come up fully. The pressure was too low. To lock the wheels down and lock the undercarriage braces, the wheels first fell by their own weight, but the lock-down brace had to be pushed into its final position again by air pressure. With low air pressure the whole system could fail, which it did.

After flying off most of the fuel I had to try my luck and landed her like a raw egg. At first she rolled smoothly down the runway but about halfway along the right-hand undercarriage gave way followed by the left. We slewed around on our belly and came to a halt with flames erupting from both port Gnome-Rhône engines. These quickly engulfed the whole front of the aircraft. We had trouble getting out of the fuselage as the door at the back had jammed, so we exited through a window. This had been designed as a secondary escape method. To open it we had to pull a little red lever which was nearly invisible. The aircraft was completely destroyed in spite of frantic efforts by fire crews. I filmed the burning wreck with my camera which I had fetched from my room.

Following this debacle, I was given three days' leave which I spent in Munich. After returning, on 15 May, Knemeyer asked me to fly Stabsingenieur [staff engineer] Hermann of the RLM to Göttingen in our little Heinkel He 72 biplane, coded T9+IB. Because fuel supplies were becoming scarcer, there was no posh flying anymore even for the top people. Hermann wanted to assess a novel aircraft project by the Horten Brothers by looking at the progress of their Ho IX. This was an all-wing aircraft powered by two jet engines. Although they were only working in a small factory, they claimed to be the only people who would be able to penetrate the sound barrier with this design and got the go ahead for a prototype.

Arriving at Göttingen airfield I taxied to the factory complex at the southern fringe where we were greeted by the two Horten brothers. Reimar was the younger one and designer of the machine and his older brother Walter, then a Luftwaffe Hauptmann, was serving in the Jagdwaffe (Inspectorate of the Fighter Force) under Generalmajor Adolf Galland. They led us to their factory premises, a former autobahn service station with its offices and a maintenance workshop. Here we were shown the almost completely finished centre section of their all-wing twin-turbojet engine Horten IX, a new generation of fighter aircraft.

At that time, it had only mock-up BMW engines fitted, but later the whole steel pipe centre section with plywood covering had to be modified to take Junkers 004 turbojets of somewhat larger dimensions as they were the only engines then readily available.

Moving to their office, plans were shown and production figures presented. Even a project for a four-engine long-range bomber, the Ho XVIII, was examined. Then there was a detailed discussion about production methods as well as personnel and material required which went on for hours. It was interrupted only by a coffee break. Walter Horten's wife, a former secretary of the Luftwaffe General Ernst Udet, who was present most of the time, acted as hostess. She was obviously conversant with all aviation matters discussed.

As a postscript to the Horten story, the second prototype Ho IX (the first was unpowered) turned up at Oranienburg in February 1945 for testing. During its third test flight, on 18 February, it crashed and was destroyed. I heard that the pilot was rather inexperienced and this was the reason for the crash, but other reports say that he blacked out from fumes entering the cockpit. Whatever the reason, he was killed and the replacement third prototype was never completed. In spite of the boasting of the younger of the brothers, Reimar, who went to Argentina after the war, the aircraft was unable to prove his claims. Looking back, I think today that they were out of touch with reality and could never have got through Mach 1 with a thick wing like that. His claim that he was ordered to design an aircraft to carry an atom bomb across the Atlantic by Knemeyer I consider nonsense. No one in Germany had got anywhere near building a nuclear weapon. At this time Germany did not have the industrial capacity to even contemplate building such a weapon.

A possible Horten supersonic aircraft would have upstaged all other jets in development in Germany, Britain and the USA at this time. I was really looking forward to test flying the Ho IX, which was intended to be carried out by our Versuchsverband OKL at Oranienburg, but the Arado Ar 234 programme took precedence.

CHAPTER 11

A WASTED OPPORTUNITY

During the late spring of 1944 there was constant talk about a probable landing of Allied forces somewhere in the west, but to establish where, our reconnaissance capability was at a dismal level. Nothing that we had was capable of penetrating the Allied fighter screen. There was the Messerschmitt Me 262 jet fighter but Hitler had ordered this to undertake bombing attacks to destroy the invaders on the beachhead. Lacking adequate range and proper bomb-aiming capability, this was a pipe dream. Then there was the Dornier Do 335 with the radical push-pull propeller configuration, but it was not ready for operations.

A close-up of the jettisonable take-off trolley fitted to the Ar 234 V5, GK+IV. The box at the rear of the trolley, between the main wheels, contained the parachute which was deployed to return the trolley to the ground.

Our one hope was the jet-propelled Arado Ar 234 which had been designed for the dual role of reconnaissance and bombing. The first prototype in the so-called Versuchsmustern [experimental model] series, the Ar 234 V1, had flown almost a year earlier but had suffered problems with its Jumo 004 turbojets and was written off. The second prototype had also crashed, killing the test pilot, Horst Selle, its destruction being attributed to an engine fire. Three further prototypes, the V3, V4 and V5, followed and these were successfully tested together with two experimental aircraft, the V6 and V8, powered by four BMW 003 engines.

With the need to alleviate the Luftwaffe's reconnaissance problems, the Ar 234 V5, which was then at Rechlin for evaluation, was taken out of the test programme and fitted with two aerial cameras in the rear fuselage. At the same time, the V7, which had not yet flown, was similarly modified. This despite a new version with a retractable undercarriage, the Ar 234 B, having been put into series production at the Alt-Lönnewitz plant near Kottbus south-east of Berlin.

Both aircraft were then handed over to the 1./Versuchsverband OKL as it was to be known from now on. Horst had been promoted to lead our squadron and he and I were to pilot the two prototype aircraft in readiness for the invasion. While the V5 and V7 were being modified, we were provided with the V4, located at Alt-Lönnewitz, for training. I went over there to prepare accommodation and the organisation of our new Kommando. Horst soon joined me and made his first flight in the Ar 234 V4 on 1 June. I followed this, four days later, with my first jet flight in the same aircraft.

It was an exhilarating experience to fly nearly vibration free with only the noise over the fully glazed cabin and flying fast, even in throttled-back circuit. It was easy to lose sight of the airfield in bad weather conditions.

None of these prototypes had a conventional undercarriage. For take-off they were mounted on a three-wheel trolley which was released as soon as the aircraft left the ground. The trolley was then brought to a halt by a braking parachute which opened automatically the moment the aircraft separated from it. To assist take-off from the grass airstrip, we were provided with liquid-fuelled Walter rocket engines of 500 kg (1,102 lbs) thrust. One of these was mounted beneath each wing and was jettisoned following the end of its thirty-second

Horst and I pictured in Berlin during the summer of 1944. Both of us are wearing the Narvik shield on our left sleeves awarded for operations over that town in 1940.

burn period. The rockets came down after release on automatically actuated parachutes. They were then refuelled with *T* and *Z-Stoff* which ignited on contact and gave us a good push. So take-off was a dramatic event, with the jet engines screaming, and then the roar of the rockets with their smoke and stink. Peace then followed with parachutes weaving in the air: that is when they opened, which was not always the case. But we never lost our trolleys as we had only one for each aircraft which was, so to speak, dedicated to that machine. For landing, the aircraft was provided with a main ski in the centre of the fuselage, with little balancing skis under the engine nacelles. After coming to a halt, it was raised up on three spiral-type jacks which were placed beneath each wing and under the rear fuselage. The aircraft was then lowered back onto the three-wheeled trolley and locked down.

I made my second flight in the V4 on 6 June 1944, the day on which Allied forces landed on the Normandy beaches. Horst's V5 had meanwhile turned up with cameras fitted on 1 June.

On 8 June I was present when the Arado test pilot, Flugkapitän Joachim Carl, demonstrated the first production Ar 234 in front of a group of Nazi Party, RLM and Luftwaffe officials. Carl told me that he had pushed the aircraft to 1,050 km/h (652 mph) in a dive. It surprised me, however, that he told me that no camera, flight endurance or other performance flights under simulated mission condition had been undertaken. Even more amazingly, no high-altitude flights up to 11,000 metres or endurance flights had been conducted by Arado. When I said this to Carl, he replied that this was a matter for the Luftwaffe experimental establishment at Rechlin. "We test pilots don't want our flying careers shortened by high-altitude flying in unpressurised aircraft because arthritis will result," was his reply.

On 22 June, after I made two more familiarisation flights in the V4, the newly completed V7 was delivered to us at Alt-Lönnewitz from the Brandenburg factory by test pilot Walter Kröger. Four days later I carried out a

The fourth prototype, the Ar 234 V4 coded DP+AV. Horst and I both made familiarisation flights in this aircraft.

simulated photographic-reconnaissance flight in the aircraft up to 11,000 metres (36,000 feet) and attained a speed of 950 km/h (590 mph) in a dive. The flight proceeded without difficulty except that the aft skid support collapsed on landing due to loss of hydraulic pressure. During my next flight, on 29 June, at a height of 10,000 metres, I covered a distance of 1,650 kilometres (1,025 miles) over a triangular course. This was the first high-altitude endurance flight of a jet aircraft ever done anywhere in the world. The Me 262 had little endurance and rarely went above 8,000 metres anyway for tactical reasons.

When I returned after two hours and twenty minutes, the data was evaluated by the factory engineers – they were jubilant. My flight data had even slightly exceeded their pre-calculations as submitted to the RLM.

On 7 July, Horst flew the V5, now coded T9+LH, from Alt-Lönnewitz to Oranienburg and I joined him next day in the V7, T9+MH. We were now ready for action, but for reasons inexplicable to us, nothing happened and valuable time was lost. It had been mooted at this time that the Versuchsverband should have two Ar 234s, two Me 262s and two Do 335s, but only the former arrived.

To overcome my nerves Horst let me have 'his' Bf 109 G-6 fighter which the squadron had used for GM 1 tests. Horst told me of one of the experiences he had had previously with the aircraft.

> 'The climbing ability of this aircraft was incredible from 0 to 12,000 metres in twelve minutes. This was a tremendous accomplishment for those days. It was impossible to enter the data by hand, on the knee board, while climbing. I could only record the performance with an automatic camera every 1,000 metres. I had to photograph the instrument panel and hereby brought all technical data to the ground with me. On 23 September 1943 I flew with such a Bf 109 at 11,000 metres when the engine seized up with a loud bang. The airframe was intact and since I had enough altitude I was able to glide the aircraft to Werneuchen. I then managed to lower the landing gear and made a good "dead stick" landing. Typical for the Rowehl outfit. It was accepted as a matter of course that I landed an aircraft with a dead engine, for not a word was mentioned about the incident.'

Our 109 had recently been equipped with 'bulletproof' tyres for testing. Too many pilots got incinerated on account of shot and deflated tyres causing somersaults on landing. Our new tyres were filled with foam rubber. So I took off to test the machine, tossing it around for some time but when I began my landing

I felt heavy vibrations after the wheels first touched the ground. So I lifted her off again, climbed away, and asked Horst, who was in the control tower, if he could see anything wrong underneath. He said that there was nothing evident, so I came in again for a careful landing. Meanwhile the vibrations had stopped. I settled the Messerschmitt down softly but the vibrations began again. All of a sudden she tipped over on her nose and flipped upside down with my cabin ploughing through the ground with an agonising grinding noise.

Then there was dead silence. No stink of petrol, only the crackling of the hot engine cooling and the smell of hot steel and oil. There was not much room in the cabin. I was hanging upside down only inches from the armoured glass windscreen in front, the armour plate behind my head and the side windows. One of the take-off crew came running with an axe to break the side windows but fearing that he would smash my precious head too I yelled to warn him off.

It was a least ten minutes before enough people gathered around to lift one side of the Messerschmitt by its starboard wing so that I could open the canopy and release my harness and drop out on to the ground. My previous view of this had been from underneath in the furrow the cabin had cut. The reason for the mishap was clearly evident. During my second touchdown the port tyre had turned sideways on the wheel rim due to a broken rim wire. The vibrations had come from the tyre's eccentric shape after the first touch, which of course ceased as soon as I stepped on the brakes, but which was not visible from the tower. Yet again, I walked away without a scratch.

How our family fared at this time is highlighted by a letter I received from my brother Walter which luckily has survived. He wrote on 5 August from somewhere in Belgium or Holland where he was with a reserve infantry regiment. He wrote in response to my letter from Oranienburg which he had just received after a four-week delay.

His division was apparently preparing to move, to the west I supposed. This spoilt his

My Messerschmitt Bf 109 G-6, T9+CL, after it overturned on landing in July 1944. As can be seen, the tyre had completely detached itself from the port main wheel.

chance of being sent to the long promised reserve officer's course. He had just received news from Helmuth who was 'revelling' in the South of France. He had already been promoted to the rank of corporal and was enjoying life on the Mediterranean coast. Helmuth enjoyed life most of the time, anywhere. He had a knack for making the best out of any situation. Walter continued by reporting that Paul was still a civilian at Ingolstadt, but he did not know what he did with the Deutsche Werke complex. Father had sent a couple of *Eilnachrichten* [express communications] to him which, in a brief sentence, told him that they were safe after terror bombing attacks. I received similar messages (they are still in my box) but they were dated a month later. He had received father's full report of what happened during the bombing attacks in July. He wrote:

> 'It shows what a blessing it was for our home that they stayed in Munich. Otherwise their house would have burned down like all the others in the street except for theirs and those on either side. Just imagine that our parents (then seventy-three and sixty-four) together with Paul later went over to Aunt Toni (in Agnesstrasse) and put out a fire there. That they managed to save part of her furniture shows their toughness and determination of which we should be proud. What father writes about Munich otherwise is utterly sad, not only what he writes but how he writes. It sounds like an epilogue for a once beautiful city and of a world which has sunk into the grave.'

Then, in the manner of a typical architect, Walter imagined how all this could be reconstructed in a more modern and healthy way. He hoped that history would not be repeated as after the big fire of Hamburg 300 years earlier. But then he fell back into lamenting the destruction of all this beauty and historical cultural heritage. From Inge (his wife) he received reports that her two sisters (the twins Gerda and Edda) had fled to Stuttgart in the middle of a firestorm. They had both studied there. Eventually they turned up safely at Hildesheim. It was not long after that Hildesheim, a beautiful medieval town without any strategic significance, was destroyed in a single night. Our Rothermund relations lost everything. A short time later brother Walter went missing. We later found out he was trapped at the battle for Falaise and had been taken prisoner by the Americans.

Brother Helmuth and his wife Hed had obtained a small flat for themselves in Duisburg. It was frugally furnished but Hed lived there on her own in Helmuth's absence. Their flat was later destroyed in a night raid, together with that of Hed's parents (her father was a high school master). They lost everything. Both were evacuated to Weinheim/Bergstrasse in Baden, southern Germany.

Later father told me, during a short visit home during the winter of 1944-45, what had happened in July in Munich. The alert was still on and bombs were heard exploding when they realised from crackling noises coming down the stairwell that the house had been hit by incendiaries. Father, followed by mother, raced out of the cellar despite their housemates imploring them not to go. When they came to the second landing a bomb was spluttering and father took a shovel and threw it out through the shattered window. Just afterwards they found another just in front of our apartment door which he disposed of in the same way. At the same time mother covered the burning timbers with sand and splashed them with water. In our living room, near the big window, the curtains were alight above another spluttering bomb which he threw out onto the road below. Fires were everywhere along the street and glass was strewn over the floors inside.

On the day of my visit they had had another attack just the night before and were forced to pick the glass splinters out of our beds. The cold wind blew through the windowless apartment. Still they decided to stay on to the end of the war when the American soldiers came through to look for valuables.

Meanwhile, back at Oranienburg, Horst and I were idle with our precious equipment. The German military was apparently blind to the situation. Panzer divisions, located on the Belgian coast in readiness for a further invasion which never happened, were unavailable to the Normandy front. They were held there because of an anticipated second landing, which turned out to be a well-executed feint by the Allies. This error could have easily been discovered by letting Horst or me loose. But no! Even our fast transfer plan to Juvincourt was denied.

We had already made trial loadings of all our support gear into our Ju 352 three-engine transport which had a large downwards-hinging ramp at the rear. This was so we could transfer our equipment to our designated operational base at Juvincourt near Reims in France. All was ready when we were told that we could not use this aircraft and were ordered to employ rail transport. We were furious about this order which smelled like sabotage by somebody up there as the situation at the front grew worse by the day. We were originally supposed to take off on 10 July with our support gear, with the trolleys transported by rail, but the network was under constant attack by bombers and the French underground.

Finally, on 21 July 1944, we took off from Oranienburg to land on our skids at Juvincourt about forty minutes later. Horst did not arrive. As the trolleys had not arrived either, they lifted my Arado onto a low loader and put it into the first hangar on the right on the road to Soissons. There it was left idle for another week until the ground crew and equipment arrived. Even then it was without some gear destroyed in an air attack, but fortunately not the trolleys.

I discovered that Horst had to turn back because of a faulty engine. For security's sake I had the data in the tower logbook erased immediately so nobody could identify the type of aircraft, where it had come from and the transfer time from which its speed could be guessed. A special guard was put in front of the hangar and nobody, not even a visiting general, was allowed to even look at the plane. I thought I had stopped the babbling and leaks. But a couple of days later when having my breakfast at the officer's mess an engineer sitting by my side told me with a malicious grin, that he was yesterday in Reims and while having a haircut the non-stop talking French Figaro told him, by the by, that there was a new aircraft without propellers at Juvincourt which flew from Berlin to its destination in just forty minutes.

I was staggered. But the intriguing matter was that after the war, when I tried to find out what was known about our jet operations, nothing in British or American intelligence could be found by researchers. Somewhere there should be something about this. In Adelaide in 1955, I was told by a man, claiming to be a former member of a secret British commando, that their task had been to recover a film made by a member of the French resistance at Juvincourt of a jet aircraft. This film, he said, was at the War Memorial Library in Canberra. I was never able to verify his story, in spite of several attempts. Later, in 1989, I got a first indication of what was really known to the Allies about our jet aircraft operations at the time. A friend of mine, Nick Beale, who spends a lot of time researching documents now at the National Archives in London, was able to supply me with copies of documents and decoded German wireless messages. But he found no details of our Juvincourt operations.

At last, on 2 August 1944, I took off for our first operational sortie. After completing my take-off checks, I started the turbojets, released the brakes and pushed open the throttles. After taxiing for about 200 metres (650 feet) I pushed the button to fire the rockets and felt the reassuring push against my back as acceleration increased. Just as the aircraft lifted off, I released the trolley and soared into the air with smoke trailing from my rockets. After they exhausted, I jettisoned them and climbed away at about 13 metres per second (2,500 feet per minute) with an initial forward speed of 410 km/h (256 mph).

As I climbed higher and entered the thinner air my speed increased. It took about twenty minutes to reach my operational altitude of 10,500 metres (34,000 feet), by which time I was over the Allied beachhead. I jinked my aircraft occasionally, glancing through my periscope to see whether I was leaving any condensation trails but there were none. High above the Cherbourg Peninsula I turned my Arado in an easterly direction putting her into a gentle dive to build up my speed to 740 km/h (460 mph). I levelled out and concentrated on flying straight and level to commence my photograph run. I'd already opened the doors which covered the lenses and I set my cameras running. They took a picture every eleven seconds.

Smoke streams from the assisted take-off rockets as the Ar 234 leaves its trolley which is slowed down by its braking parachute.

It was a beautifully clear summer day with hardly a cloud in the sky. From my altitude I could see nothing of the titanic struggle that was going on below. I concentrated on flying straight so that my cameras could take in as much as possible with the limited amount of film I had in my magazines. My first photographic run, which lasted about ten minutes, took in the coastal strip. I then turned back through 180 degrees and followed a course parallel with the one I'd flown before but 10 kilometres (6 miles) further inland. A third run followed before my film ran out.

My mission complete, I continued eastwards heading for Juvincourt in a high-speed descent. As I neared the runway, and turned in to approach, I saw our Ju 352 on the airfield and Horst's Ar 234 V5 being winched up on its trolley. Turning onto the final approach, my aircraft, which had its flaps in the take-off position, the skids lowered and the

I took this photograph from my Ar 234 V7 while flying at 10,000 metres (33,000 feet) over the Normandy beachhead on 2 August 1944. This was the world's first jet-reconnaissance sortie.

engines practically idling, wanted to turn turtle. Despite my utilising full ailerons, I only got her back into an upright position by applying full power and inching the trim forward. As this happened just above the ground it was frightening and couldn't be explained later. I made a report and as a result we always avoided flight situations like that with power off. Gratefully, I landed safely and, within seconds the ground crew converged on my aircraft to collect the two camera magazines and take them to be developed.

Two days later I was called to the IC (intelli-

Top: When I returned from the sortie I saw from my cockpit that Horst's Ar 234 V5 had just arrived at Juvincourt.
Bottom: Equipment being unloaded from our Junkers Ju 352 three-engine transport coded T9+AB. I am walking away to the right of the photograph.

gence department) of Luftflotte 3 headquarters in Paris. There I ran into the staff I had first met in 1942 such as Hauptmann Bernhard Ahlers. He told me of the sensation my film had produced. In this single sortie I had been able to achieve more than all other German reconnaissance units in the west put together had done during the previous two months. In a flight lasting less than an hour-and-a-half, I had photographed almost all the Allied beachhead. I had taken a total of 380 photographs. We found that the Allies had landed one-and-a-half million men, one-and-a-half tons of supplies and nearly a third of a million vehicles in France. It took a twelve-man team of German photographic interpreters working day and night for two days just to do the rough checking of all the Allied troops and gear and installations in the landing zone. The detailed examination of the photographs took weeks. After the sortie, lots of

senior officers came round wanting
to look over the Arado, but the whole
thing was kept very secret and they
were not allowed to see it.

By that time Allied forces had
begun to break out from the beachhead and fan out into France. During
the bitter fighting that ensued, Horst
and I made exploratory flights as often
as the preparedness of the aircraft
allowed. Not only did we cover the
landing areas but on two occasions I
covered the south of England with its
incredible array of airfields. I think
the first of these took place on 8 or 11
August. I found that the island was
literally packed with airfields and all
had proper landing strips, mostly laid
out in a triangular arrangement.

*One of the photographs I took of the Allied
beachhead near Asnelles-sur-Mer.*

During this time our unit, now designated Kommando Götz,[20] was placed
under direct command of Luftflotte 3 in Paris with us operating under the
control of the reconnaissance squadron 1.(F)/123. While at the base, Horst
and I were worried about our ability to maintain the secrecy of our aircraft
design and the possibility of one of them falling into enemy hands. There was
a self-destruction device installed with an electric switch to detonate an explosive pack. But did it work? So one afternoon Horst and I decided to take a
spare pack and put it in a bomb crater in an open area and trigger it. Nothing
happened! We waited for some time and then decided to blow it up in the
crater with a hand grenade. We threw the grenade in and ran fifty yards and
dived for cover together. Up went the hand grenade and propelled the infamous
thing right in front of our noses.

By now we had had enough, and asked the bomb disposal people to look
after it. We then thought up another way to destroy the aircraft in an emergency.
The aprons in front of our hangars, each of which contained only one aircraft,

---

20. This was the second Kommando Götz, the first operating from Sarabus in 1943, having
been dissolved in May of that year.

sloped downwards towards the doors. We deposited a 200-litre (44-gallon) drum of *T-Stoff*, [hydrogen peroxide] rocket fuel on one side at the top of the apron and on the other side a small drum of *Z-Stoff* [sodium permanganate], the detonating liquid. *T-Stoff* was the highly volatile propelling liquid of the Walter-type liquid rockets, while *Z-Stoff* was the catalyst of which only a small amount was required to ignite the *T-Stoff* on contact. The mixing of the fuels in our rocket-assisted take-off engines was normally achieved by pressing a button on the instrument panel in the cockpit. In case of a surprise attack by American armour, somebody was to roll the unfastened containers down the aprons into the open hangar which would create an inferno down there. We did not try to test this system!

My last flight from Juvincourt was on 24 August when Paris was already in American hands. I was ordered to cover the city but, by then, the pressure in our area was increasing as German troops and panzers raced through the nearby village of Guignicourt at night. At the same time, we received signals that we were to immediately evacuate the area.

Two weeks before that I had met a girl working in Juvincourt village in a house occupied by a Luftwaffe communication unit. They were operating the Enigma, our secret telex machine. As she was tremendously attractive to me, and willing to accompany me on evening strolls, we rapidly took to one another. Her name was Elfriede 'Friedl' Sachert. One day after a daylight bombing attack on our airfield I drove up to the house on a motorbike and stopped at the girls' office. I initially found it deserted, but then Elfriede, who had been on duty with her Enigma machine, emerged from an earth bunker behind the house. She was covered in dust from the nearby bomb explosions. I took her home that evening to Guignicourt

My wife-to-be, Elfriede 'Friedl' Sachert, at Juvincourt.

where she was billeted. Normally the girls had to walk on foot the five kilometres through partisan-infested country, unprotected.

Friedl and I decided that we were right for each other, and on 22 August 1944, Horst and our Kommando arranged an engagement party. It was a great

evening at our little hotel in which the whole Kommando lived. Then, on the
night of the 27th, the signal came to break camp and all was prepared during
the night to load stuff on trucks and for the aircraft to take off at dawn. I went
to the big house where Friedl and her unit were living and told her and her
superior to immediately collect all their belongings and come with us. Only
a small number turned up, including Friedl, as American tanks were already
rumbling towards us.

It was not until 1035 hours the next day that both aircraft were ready. I
took off for Chièvres in Belgium and Horst followed suit. Our ground-support
convoys got away unscathed too together with the evacuated girls. The rest of
their detachment got caught by the Americans. Arriving over Chièvres airfield
I was shot at by our medium flak. I immediately fired the recognition signal
of the day, but it continued for over half a circuit until I joined up with incoming Bf 109s. Their pilots looked at me with astonishment, having never seen
a thing without propellers before. Their remarks afterwards were bitingly
envious of my superior speed, to which they thought they should have been
entitled to before me.

I landed the Arado in a safe corner of the big field and waited for Horst, but
he never arrived. So I organised all the facilities during the afternoon, like living
quarters and support systems for the ground crew who would arrive shortly.
They actually appeared well after dark and immediately lifted the V7 onto its
tricycle. The girls got separate quarters and were put on a special train to
Brussels next morning. I
scarcely had time to greet
Friedl and have a talk. The next
time I saw her was on a visit
near Hamburg in December,
but a lot of letter writing kept
us in touch.

By midnight a lengthy telex
reached me telling me of
Horst's fate. The date of 28
August had not been good to
him. After a satisfactory take-
off he flew at low level. When
crossing the Belgian border
near Mons he was fired on
without warning by German

*The remains of Horst's Ar 234 V5 after the Fw 190
crashed into it on 28 August 1944 at Oranienburg.*

light flak and hit in the fuselage just behind the cockpit. The flaps and skis dropped immediately and he realised that he was hit in the hydraulic system. As repairs would have been impossible, and as we were cautioned not to let the aircraft fall into enemy hands under pain of severe penalties, he decided to go straight for Germany. This is what he told me later:

'I decided to fly to Arado at Brandenburg for repairs. Upon arrival I noticed that the area had been carpet bombed and that everything was burning. My fuel tanks were showing empty and the red warning

Horst with his eyes bandaged after they were damaged in the belly-landing of the Ar 234 V5.

light was on. I decided on impulse to fly on to Oranienburg. I barely made it, going for a direct approach without flaps or the benefit of the skid at 300 km/h. Sand and stones hit my face. Like an idiot I had forgotten to put on my safety glasses, which we always carried with us. The aircraft had stopped and had no damage other than the hit received by the anti-aircraft fire. I was well except I could not see. The corneas of both eyes had some damage. I crawled out of the cockpit and lay down in the grass next to the aircraft. The medical orderlies collected me and I was treated by a doctor. Shortly after my emergency landing, a transfer pilot crashed his Fw 190 into my beautiful V5 and totally destroyed the aircraft and himself. After four weeks my eyes had healed and I received permission to fly again.'

The end of the V5 left me as the sole effective reconnaissance pilot in the west. Next morning, I received a message that Friedl and her colleagues were already boarding a train to Brussels on their way to Hamburg. That evening my men presented me with an engagement ring for Friedl which they had made from a piece of aluminium piping. I was very touched. I sent the ring on in a sealed package destined for her Feldpost number. She would receive this wherever she ended up.

CHAPTER 12

KOMMANDO SPERLING

As the Allies advanced further into France I was ordered to transfer back to Volkel in Holland on 30 August 1944. On arrival there we put the Ar 234 V7 into a hangar in the far south-east of the airfield. Despite the fact that the whole of the Western Front was now collapsing, no order came for sorties. Consequently, we used the days to replenish our equipment from Luftgau supply depots before they were to be blown up as there was no time to evacuate their material.

One of our urgent requirements was for a low-loading trailer to enable the collection of our spent take-off rockets from the fields where they came down. For its construction we needed two small wheels and I was told the best way to get a set was to go to the concentration camp at Vucht near 's-Hertogenbosch, not too far away. On arrival there I was told by the SS officers that they collected the remains of shot-down enemy aircraft. As prisoners they had some engineers from amongst the mainly Dutch intelligentsia. They had put together a collection of electrically-operated machine-gun turrets from shot-down Allied bombers which they invited me to inspect.

It was an astonishing display of all sorts of paraphernalia standing on trestles and hanging from the high roof of a large hall. You could even sit inside the stands and operate them. I noticed that the communication between SS guards and inmates was very polite. I even observed an apparently friendly joking conversation between a prisoner and an unarmed SS man. Everything in the camp was spotlessly clean. I collected two nose wheels from Liberator bombers which we judged suitable, thanked them and left.

On 3 September I was riding my motorbike in the afternoon, in sunny but very windy weather to the airfield. I had 'borrowed' the bike at Chièvres and had been unable to return it due to our rapid retreat. As my aircraft was safe I knew that nobody was working there. I just wanted to check that everything was all right. When about a kilometre short of the boundary, a sonorous sound superimposed itself over the rattle of my bike. When I looked up over my shoulder I saw to my amazement masses of Lancaster bombers overtaking me and going for the airfield. I counted about 130 of them. Jumping off my bike, I dived into a ditch beside the road and waited to see what happened. The whole of the airfield in front of me erupted in dust and smoke with dirt thrown sky high. The noise was unbelievable. After about five minutes there was silence.

When the bombers had disappeared, I rode straight through a field of craters and past shattered hangars with wrecked aircraft inside. Reaching the hangar housing my Ar 234, which my men had preferred as it had the number seven painted on its sliding doors, I saw that it was the only one which was undamaged. There were craters all around it.

As a result, the order finally came saying that we were to transfer to Rheine, 41 kilometres (25 miles) west of Osnabrück in Westphalia, during the following evening. The outlook for getting the aircraft out of this devastated field was bleak. The only possible stretch of ground for a take-off was the relatively narrow taxiway at the southern side of the field. This had only a couple of craters at the eastern end near to our hangar and to taxi to it we would only have to fill in a few craters.

There was a certain risk considering the narrowness of the taxiway, however. The uneven thrust of the engines or the rockets and the bad taxiing quality of the tricycle undercarriage with its miserable brakes could still cause a problem. The slightest deviation from a straight take-off run could push me into one of the craters on either side and destroy the aircraft – and me too. Still, I didn't want to lose the only effective reconnaissance aircraft in the west by blowing it up.

On the morning of 5 September I took off and all went well. Even the trolley survived undamaged and after a short flight I landed at Rheine, our future base. Our unit had now been redesignated Kommando Sperling [sparrow] following Horst's injury. It would remain at Rheine for the winter of 1944-45. For the men's quarters I could get only temporary billets for all of us together in a former Kindergarten. We moved into there after the men had rigged up the V7 again on arrival.

During the night something happened that angered us very much. Just after midnight, with us all bedded down in a big room (we were about three dozen men of all ranks), a loud knocking and shouting came at the door. Someone flung it open and infantry with guns at the ready stormed in led by a Leutnant. He demanded that we hand over all our weapons, showing us a typed order from the local commander. We were furious but had to accede to the request, the seriousness of which there was no doubt.

Next morning, as soon as I could, I drove to see the infantry battalion's commander, a colonel, and demanded an explanation, the immediate return of our weapons and an apology. He told me that he had acted on an order issued by Himmler. In the confusion of the collapse of the Western Front Himmler had taken over command of the whole of German armed forces in the west on Hitler's order. That idiot Himmler considered Luftwaffe units retreating from France were a rebellious element ready to mutiny. When I explained our past activities and imminent tasks to the colonel, and that in my opinion the assessment of the situation was without the slightest fact, we agreed wholeheartedly.

He apologised profusely, cursing the political interference of the uninformed. We had a short drink while our weapons were handed back at our barracks. Nevertheless, the sting in our side remained and we never lost sight of this splitting of the armed forces and the strengthening of SS influence in all fields. There was no unity anymore at home and this had clearly come out into the open in the way the air situation developed. With the retreat of German troops on all fronts we lost hope for a decent end for Germany. But still we battled on. You can't desert your mates in a desperate situation but just do your best to the bitter end. Everybody thought this but never admitted it openly. The rot had already set in with the distrust generated by the attempt to assassinate Hitler in July and its aftermath.

Late in September 1944, the Allied advance forced our main headquarters in the west, Luftflotte 3, to move from France to a big castle at Limburg east of Koblenz. It was reduced in size at the same time and reorganised as Luftwaffen Kommando West. Our photograph processing still came through the remnants of the non-operational 1.(F)/123 which were based in the same area. Meanwhile, back in Oranienburg, a battle began regarding from where our Versuchsverband OKL should receive its orders. Its independence was threatened by the demands of the inspector of reconnaissance units, Generalmajor Karl

Generalmajor Karl Henning von Barsewisch who commanded Luftwaffe reconnaissance forces between 1 November 1943 and 8 May 1945 when he was taken into western Allied captivity. He died on 19 November 1981.

Henning von Barsewisch. Because of the failure of his own reconnaissance squadrons, he wanted to take us over so that he had something to boast about. His plan was strongly resisted by our Oberstleutnant Knemeyer, who up to then had our achievements as his trump card at top level conferences.

Friedl was now in Hamburg Blankenese where the communication helpers were redistributed and trained for further duties. She didn't like it there at all. Of brother Walter there was no news. Helmuth was with a pioneer unit in the south of France but they were having to implement an orderly retreat owing to the Allied landings on the Mediterranean coast. A constant stream of post-cards came from my father stating that they were unhurt by the latest terror attacks. I had to keep pretty silent at the time because of the secrecy of my task. Everyone complained about that but I couldn't explain why.

You may remember that I had met a number of Arado personnel during my visit to Brandenburg in 1943.[21] Sometime later I again met the Arado weapons specialist, Kurt Bornemann, on the tarmac at Oranienburg. He now told me that my suggestion regarding using the Lotfe bombsight had been taken up and the device was installed in the production Ar 234 B-2 bomber in addition to the dive-bombing system originally intended. The Lotfe sight was installed and the control column so designed that the pilot could fold it away for the attack. He could then engage the PDS three-axes auto-pilot, crouch in the nose of the aircraft and use the sight to hit the target. The periscope, which I had suggested, was also mounted above the cockpit. It could look to the rear in reconnaissance aircraft while the bomber version could also turn it forward for diving attacks. The only problem was that the image was upside down, but you soon adjusted to that. It allowed us to see behind 60 degrees upwards and 15 degrees downwards. As it was my idea to install the periscope and everybody knew it, he asked me why I didn't have this system registered for an *Ideenschutz* [patent]. "Everybody does that," he said. I never followed his advice.

When at Alt-Lönnewitz, while beginning my training on the Ar 234 V4 in June 1944, I met Oberst Walter Storp in the mess, an old acquaintance from 1942. He was now commander of K.G. 6 to which we had been briefly seconded. We began a long conversation over the table about what we had done since and what we were up to now. He had been given the task of re-establishing K.G. 76 which had been virtually wiped out in air battles over France. The unit was to be re-equipped with the Ar 234 bomber. I knew him as a

---

21. See Chapter Ten.

An official photograph of Walter Storp when he was still a Major. Around his neck is the Ritterkreuz (Knight's Cross) with Eichenlaub (oak leaves).

dive-bomber man and so we discussed the ways in which he intended to use this new weapon system tactically. We did not agree.

At the end of my discussion with Storp, I realised that all the industrial effort and research and testing was wasted as the Lotfe system would never be used by the new units. It was a clash of thinking, so to speak. Hauptmann Diether Lukesch, who led the first operational bomber sorties with the Ar 234 recently gave me his opinion about bombing with the Ar 234.

'It would have been irresponsible to order horizontal bombing without any possibility of being able to see what was happening behind us. After only a few operations enemy fighters were prepared for our speed and had a good chance of a successful attack from above and behind, particularly with the Tempest. Only when the attack was recognised early did we have a good chance of evasion. By this time enemy air superiority was such that flights without fighter interception were rare and 6,000 metres (19,685 feet) was an ideal attack altitude. On the other hand, the Ar 234 B-2 was an ideal long-range reconnaissance aircraft. It could operate singly at 10,000 metres without enemy opposition and was difficult to locate on their bases due to their small numbers.

'Apart from this the conversion of the Ar 234 to the PDS auto-pilot delayed the bomber version's introduction to the front by some three months. By October 1944, fifty-seven aircraft had been delivered to III./K.G. 76, but fifty-four of these were then withdrawn for PDS installation, testing and training. As we predicted these tests were never satisfactorily concluded.'

Reading about comparable bomb tests at Rechlin at the time, my system came out far ahead of the dive-bomber idea and, in addition, there would be no problems with flak. After leadership of K.G. 76 was taken over by Oberst Robert Kowalewski, he thought my idea excellent but, by then, it was far too late for the units to train on it properly. There was not even fuel left for them to fly. To prove the safety of the high-altitude and high-speed approach I pointed to my own experience of flying approximately seventy such missions in straight lines for photography at longish distances. I was never intercepted by enemy fighters as long as I stayed at high altitude and travelled fast. There is no doubt that K.G. 76's hit rate was abysmal.

This still taken from a cine film shows the rocket-assisted take-off units being jettisoned from an Ar 234 after take-off. The Walter 109-500 rocket-assisted take-off units were mounted beneath each wing, outboard of the turbojets. Each unit was capable of delivering a thrust of 500 kg (1,102 lbs) for thirty seconds.

This exposé serves only to demonstrate the effective use or misuse of a planned idea by its getting into the right or wrong hands. The superiority of a weapon comes to nought when the right people are not selected to implement its use. It's the same in politics and business.

After two days in Rheine, on 7 September 1944, an officer from Oranienburg, Oberleutnant Wolf Loah, arrived to assist in ground operations. He was a grounded pilot, having been badly burned in a crash in Horst's former Ar 240 in Russia (as related earlier). I knew him already and got on rather well with him. He brought three letters from Friedl which she had written to Oranienburg. In these she let me know that she was safe, if not very happy with the situation in Pinneberg where the girls, besides updating their skills, had to sew leather belts for military stores. The food was lousy too.

On the night of 9 September an order by phone from Luftwaffen Kommando West in Limburg reached me at Bentlage Castle, which we now occupied as permanent quarters. It set out the next day's mission which was to cover the Thames Estuary, looking in particular for ship concentrations in preparation for another landing operation. I asked if I should also take a look at London, just a couple of kilometres upstream, but the reply was non-committal. I suppose they have left it to my judgement, I thought.

I climbed out over the German Bight towards Heligoland on the following morning. In clear blue skies, I met an aircraft coming the other way with an endless contrail stretching back to the English coast. It was a Mosquito, like myself probably unarmed and doing the same job. We passed at a distance and, both being unarmed, all we could do was to wave to one another. Approaching the shore from the west, visibility became a bit blurred because of the mist which extended right up to my height of about 11,500 metres. Nevertheless, vertical photography was still acceptable. The Thames Estuary, including London, looked like a mushroom farm from the masses of barrage balloons which were up protecting against V-1 flying bombs. As my counter showed that I still had plenty of film left, I photographed the city right across and then turned for home. Horst then described what happened next:

'Erich didn't know then that this was the time when the V-2 rocket had been let loose over London. The evaluation of the photographs showed that the V-2 was unreliable and militarily useless. A 500-kg bomb placed correctly could do more damage. We rather enjoyed this coincidental result as did the Staffel but then I received a telegram addressed to me. "The flight over London did not take place. The pictures are to be destroyed. Charges are to be filed against the pilot. Military judges are on the way." I was dumbfounded. This could not be true and even if this flight had not been ordered this negative proof of the ineffectiveness of the V-2 attacks should be of paramount importance to the High Command of the Luftwaffe and the V-2 programme. I did not want to hand over my good friend Sommer to the bloodhounds nor did I want to file charges against him without good cause. Adolf and Fatso Göring were unreachable so I decided to look up Goebbels at the propaganda ministry in Berlin. I did not think much about the risks that I was taking. I was fully aware that it was risky for a unit commander to leave his unit without orders. The Staffel knew nothing about my intentions nor did anybody know that I was about to visit Dr Goebbels. I flew to Berlin and marched into the propaganda ministry. They treated this rather obscure Hauptmann and Staffelkapitän in a friendly way and assured me that I could see Dr Goebbels the next day since he was out of town. I did not want to leave my unit for more than a day and was happy to speak to his adjutant. Everything was discussed and official minutes of my complaint were kept. I gave a copy of the minutes to my wife for security reasons in case there were any difficulties. The next day I was back with my Staffel at Rheine.'

My first inkling that this was happening occurred on 11 September, just before I left for another early morning sortie, this time over to the Wash area of eastern England. I received a call from 1.(F)/123 in Limburg. A rather posh voice told me that I had exceeded my instructions in filming London. Somebody high up was upset and a 'blood judge' was on his way to court martial me. I immediately got Horst at Oranienburg on the blower and heard that he already knew of the threat. He was most upset and was threatening to chuck everything in, which of course would have had catastrophic consequences for us. He told me he

Top: A close-up of the take-off trolley with my Ar 234 V7 in the background. A special protective cover had been placed over the glazed nose.

Bottom: Ground crew jacking up the rear fuselage of the Ar 234 V7, T9+MH, prior to its return to the take-off trolley. This procedure took approximately 20 minutes during which the aircraft was vulnerable to air attack.

was going to Luftwaffen Kommando West's Limburg headquarters to pound the table to complain of their lack of support for us. He had already been to the propaganda ministry to see Goebbels, the minister, whom he had met during the 1920s in Berlin. He told me that he had been welcomed with open arms, and asked to supply more, not less, photographs of London. His guess was that Goebbels was trying to discredit somebody else in the Nazi hierarchy. He thought that the situation was getting a trifle dangerous and Goebbels had promised to help, but did nothing of course.

Meanwhile I carried on as usual. No 'blood judge', as we called them, arrived. Someone must have recalled him. After the war Horst suggested to me that SS

A German propaganda leaflet apparently showing that the V-1 missile had virtually destroyed London.

Obergruppenführer Hans Kammler, who had been put in charge of the V-2 missile programme, was behind the threatened court martial. But I have two different explanations which could be more likely.

Around 1965, when Horst was with the new German Bundeswehr [armed forces], he took part in Europa flying competitions. In one of his letters he wrote that during one of these he had met a former Stabsoffizer [staff officer] in the previous Luftwaffe High Command, General Panofski. They got talking about their experiences during the Second World War, and their conversation turned to my threatened court martial. The general exclaimed with some surprise: "So, this was the man who caused us so much trouble at the time." The mention of the general's exclamation in Horst's letter stuck in my mind. I concluded that it may have been that the driving force to court martial me over the London incident had come from the Luftwaffe Führungsstab [headquarters staff] in Berlin. They probably had the wind up, fearing Himmler's wrath and his executioners. They were always ready to pounce and to send some supposed wrongdoer to the Eastern Front or put him before a firing squad.

My other explanation came about after I visited the Bundesarchiv [Federal Archives] at Freiburg in 1986. While there, I discovered the original order in the diaries of the Luftwaffen Kommando West. These clearly stated, in a separate section after the order of the day for Kommando Götz, 'London ist nicht aufzuklaren', which meant 'no taking photographs of', or 'flying over London'. Why this order was not transmitted to me directly, and why it was given at all, is still unclear to me. The same order had applied to our operations with Höhenkommando Beauvais in 1942 with the Junkers Ju 86 R.

I did not like these high-ranking officers and their, in my perception, incompetent arrogance. To give an example: when I visited their lair in Berlin, in the autumn of 1944, a high-ranking officer showed me the results of my reconnaissance flights in Normandy and southern England which he had proudly assembled. I realised from his remarks that all my efforts had achieved was for him to take them under his wing and go to his superior officers and show them what 'he' had done. This would reinforce the importance of his office and escape the tendency to dissolve it and send him to the Eastern Front. Thus he would escape the '*Heldenklau*' (hero pinchers) as we called the Nazi hierarchy. They were like a gang of thugs.

My conclusion now is that with the threat to court martial me, our general staff was prepared to sacrifice me to save their necks. My reconnaissance over London showed that it was in fact intact – only a fraction of the city was destroyed in contrast to Himmler's boasting. By this time the SS leader had taken over the command of all army divisions in the east in an attempt to stem the Russian advance. He even stopped the civilian population from running away from the front line by blocking the roads. He told us in a loud-mouthed fashion that by the action of our V-weapons (the so-called *Wunderwaffen*) on London the city would be annihilated in a short time and the Allies would be forced to capitulate and end the war. With my photographs I had exposed the fabrication. We trusted none of them anymore.

As I mentioned previously, my telephone call with Horst brought him to Rheine by rail on 12 September. He had with him another letter from Friedl. I then tried to pull some strings to get her posted to Oranienburg or somewhere nearby and waited for the opportunity to get to the base to achieve that. At this time Friedl was on leave with her mother at Demmin in north Germany, east of Rostock. Meanwhile our Kommando had settled in Bentlage Castle three kilometres west of Rheine on the River Ems. It had ample space. The mail from home gave no news of brother Walter. Helmuth, who had been with his engineering unit near

the Spanish border, was now somewhere in the Reich, and Paul had to temporarily cease his studies.

The weather was mostly foul around that time and not conducive to reconnaissance. In the evening I sometimes went for a walk along the River Ems in the park behind our castle. One evening I came across a

Bentlage Castle which was our billet when we were based at Rheine. Nowadays the castle is used as a hotel.

dugout on the western embankment and had a conversation with its occupants. They were a middle-aged married couple from the township who told me that their nights were constantly disrupted by air raid alerts. So they built this hideout for themselves and their two teenage daughters to be safe.

A few nights later I heard a single British heavy bomber rumbling low over the castle. He was probably in trouble as the main force was already well clear into the eastern Reich and he had broken off the mission. Seconds later bombs exploded in the pitch dark down by the river.

Next day at noon I heard that six people had been killed in an earth bunker by the river. When I went to the site later I found an immense crater where the dugout had been. Of course nobody could have survived such a disaster. The victims were the middle-aged couple, their two daughters and two young Luftwaffe soldiers who occasionally used to visit the lonely dwellers for a game of cards. It was useless to contemplate if they all would have survived in the endangered township. Death strikes sometimes in the most unusual circumstances. Like the poor woman found dead in a foxhole at the entrance to our park – hit by a stray cannon shell from a dogfight in the sky high above her during a bombing raid.

On 27 September 1944 a fully fit Horst finally arrived with his new Arado 234 B-2 coded T9+GH. This was the first Ar 234 we had received with a fully retractable undercarriage which was to prove a great advantage. Just before he received this aircraft he wrote asking for another crate of red wine for the 1st Staffel and saying *'Flieg nicht soviel – Hals und Beinbruch – Dien Horst'* ('Don't fly so much – broken legs and necks – your Horst'). His arrival left me free to go to Oranienburg for discussion with the Führungsstab and the propaganda ministry as well as to visit Friedl in Pinneberg.

So I left Rheine on 6 October by rail for Oranienburg, and visited the Führungsstab the next day with the disappointing result already mentioned. At the propaganda ministry there was no special interest in my case anymore, but everybody was exceptionally friendly. "As you are here do you want to see a movie?" they asked. "There is one just started in the

Horst's Ar 234 B with a wheeled undercarriage arrives at Rheine. The aircraft was coded T9+GH.

second theatre for screening and censuring." It was *Freiheit No. 7* with Hans Albers; a story about a sailor and whores in Hamburg. Eventually they decided it was not suitable for the war effort and was not shown until after the war.

Next day I went by rail to Pinneberg and found Friedl healthy and we were overjoyed to meet again. We went on a walk along the River Elbe and then to Hamburg for a meagre lunch. Then we discussed her immediate future. I would try again to get her a transfer to Oranienburg.

By the evening I was back in Oranienburg. From my letter from there to Friedl I seemed to have had a disagreement with the establishment there, which went deep enough for me to contemplate a transfer. The Versuchsverband now had a new commander, Major Wolfgang Heese. I was not very happy when he took over as I felt that he lacked combat experience. Anyway, whatever the reason for my disagreement, I seemed to have calmed down after a couple of days, though I thought it wise to call off Friedl's transfer to Oranienburg until another opportunity would arise.

While at Oranienburg I picked up my new Ar 234 B with its retractable undercarriage. Following some test flights with the aircraft, coded T9+IH, I flew back to Rheine on 16 October, making my first operational flights in the aircraft shortly afterwards. Meanwhile I had received a radio message that Horst had sent to Oranienburg that 'your missing brother has reported here (Rheine) by phone'. This turned out to my brother Paul who was now in Gütersloh, from where he was shortly to transfer to Berlin as an inspector of motor transport.

When I flew back to Rheine, I found that Horst had been joined by Leutnant Wolfgang Ziese who had arrived on 11 October with a third Ar 234 B, T9+HH. Ziese had been a test pilot with the Siebel company in Halle before joining us. His first job with us had been to fly the 'push-pull' Do 335 V3, T9+ZH, which had been experimentally fitted with a photographic-reconnaissance camera. He made a few test flights with the aircraft, but constant serviceability problems prevented any of these being extended to cover the British Isles. Its proposed 'target' was the port of Scapa Flow in the Orkneys.

At the end of the war Ziese returned to the Siebel plant in Halle which fell into Soviet hands. Here he was forced to help continue the development of the DFS 346 supersonic research aircraft. On 22 October 1946 the majority of specialists were forced 'voluntarily' to be 'guests' of the USSR and were taken by train to Podberesje east of Moscow. While he was there, Ziese sent me several enigmatic letters describing the test flights which he had carried out

The remarkable Dornier Do 335 V3, coded T9+ZH, which was experimentally flown by Wolfgang Ziese. The aircraft had a unique back-to-back engine layout which gave it the remarkable top speed of 760 km/h (472 mph).

with the second DFS 346 launched from a captured B-29 bomber. During one of these flights, he crashed, following which he wrote on 7 December 1949:

> '...I could not write for some time because I fell on my nose and had to be repaired. There was not much broken. ... I had taken up our old hobby again this summer. At the last one, a beautiful pike, just before I had it, I fell down a steep embankment and broke my nose and got some cuts. In the spring I will do some more work...'

Sadly, this was the last letter I received from Ziese. He refused to be operated on in Russia for stomach cancer and died there in 1950. It is doubtful whether he ever broke the sound barrier.

Following my arrival with the Ar 234 B, two other pilots were assigned to Kommando Sperling. The first to join us was Feldwebel Walter Wendt who, like Horst, had come from the Telefunken electronics company and had been with us in the Crimea in 1943. Wendt immediately began his training on 'my' old Ar 234 V7. The fifth pilot was Oberleutnant Werner Muffey who had entered the Luftwaffe early in 1939. His flying training began with the Luftkriegschule [air warfare school] at Dresden in November of that year. He learnt to fly a large number of aircraft types and, during the summer of 1942, he piloted General Albert Kesselring around the Mediterranean. There he had the disagreeable experience of having his He 111, P4+AA, shot down by a 'friendly' Messerschmitt 109. Only he and Willy Mensching of the crew of five survived. In 1943 he was transferred to our Versuchsverband and flew operations in a GM 1-equipped Ju 88 from Riga. Muffey brought with him a fourth Ar 234 B, coded T9+KH. Muffey's training on the Ar 234 was rather rudimentary as he later wrote.

The pilots of Kommando Sperling just after I left. From left to right: Wolfgang Ziese, Walter Wendt, Horst Götz, Oberleutnant zur See Böhmer and Werner Muffey. Böhmer was to advise us on cooperating with U-boat operations.

'When I was told by Major Heese that I was shortly to join Kommando Sperling, I was surprised when he told me that I would only need about a day to familiarise myself with the Ar 234. Nevertheless, I said "Jawohl, Herr Major" and went into the officer's mess to try and speak to someone who had flown the aircraft before. I think I ran into Josef Bisping, who I had last seen in Warsaw with his Ar 240, and we chatted about the differences between prop and jet aircraft.

'The weather was dreadful the next morning when I had my first flight in T9+KH. It was raining and the cloud ceiling was about 200 metres (650 feet), so I had a near miss when I passed the high masts of the transcontinental radio station at Nauen. I soon became disorientated and, heading west, mistook the Weser for the Elbe. Remembering what I had been told about the aircraft's short endurance at low altitude, I made a 180 and fortunately recognised familiar ground after a while. Going straight into Oranienburg I forgot about all the supposedly difficult things when making the landing approach, and completed a marvellously smooth touchdown, not even bothering to use the braking parachute. This filled me full of praise for the amiable behaviour of the kite, and, losing all inhibitions, I wanted to transfer to Rheine as soon as possible.

'A cable was then sent indicating my intention to join the unit and back came very precise instructions on how to go about approaching areas threatened by enemy attacks. These included the FuG 16 radio frequencies to be used, the appropriate time schedule, auxiliary frequencies in case of emergencies, what to do when contact proved difficult, the beams available for the FuG 25 I.F.F. and the appropriate codes. I thought everything looked very professional and reassuring, especially for a greenhorn under western skies. That the Kommando operated so safely was due, in no small manner, to Götz's leadership.'

Walter Wendt watches from the radio van as one of my rocket units releases prematurely and bounces along the ground.

After the war, Muffey became director of the Esso oil company in Hamburg.

By this time the strength of our Kommando had been expanded to thirty-two technicians with a small increase in servicing vehicles. One of the most important of these was the radio van which served as a mobile command post. It was situated near the end of the runway in order to cover the take-off and landing manoeuvres when the aircraft was at its most vulnerable. As we approached the airfield we developed a technique of switching on our transmitters for two seconds without speaking as we returned from a mission. The resultant burst of 'static' informed the listeners on the ground that the Arado was nearing the airfield, but did not give away our position. On top of that we organised a direct telephone line from the local radar station to the contact on the airfield to give him a wider field of warnings. During this time, we had no losses.

To defend the airfield itself, our take-off and landing lanes were covered by a large numbers of guns, although there were never enough of these to deter a really determined attacker. We also expressed some misgivings about the usefulness of the old men of the Volkssturm [home guard] who were guarding our aircraft.

One evening, to check on their effectiveness, we put on disguises and drove a jeep to the airfield. We were not surprised to discover that they let us through unchallenged. They even helped us push the aircraft from their hardstands

Ar 234 B, T9+HH, being refuelled prior to a sortie. This aircraft was usually flown by Werner Muffey. The rocket-assisted take-off units are in place and Willi Mensching is laying on top of the aircraft. Note the ground crew member standing by on the right with a fire extinguisher to deal with any fires caused by fuel spillage.

before we started the engines and created a lot of noise in the otherwise quiet airfield. Horst next asked one of them to show him his rifle. He handed it over without a murmur. Then we drew our pistols and screamed "hands up" at them. We disarmed them all and kept them covered. Horst next went with Werner Muffey to the guard house, shot out the lamps and told them to come out with their hands up. They grumbled at this but were quickly disarmed and stood against a wall. One complained that he had a wife and kids and that we should spare him. We took all the weapons with us to our quarters and called their commander. We told him that if his men were missing anything they could come to our quarters and pick it up. He snorted at this but did not dare do anything to us because he then would have had to admit that our aircraft were left unguarded.

Despite this we had a great group of competent pilots. We refined our air safety technique as we were constantly molested by enemy fighters and light bombers as well as suffering heavy-bomber attacks. Nobody was allowed to take off without ground radio support from beginning to end of his mission or flight. So there was an immediate warning to the pilot in the event of an enemy fighter being around. Despite the Arado's excellent performance we were still vulnerable at low take-off and landing speed. The Messerschmitt 109s of J.G. 27 which were stationed on our field 'for our protection' suffered frightful casualties as they didn't take these precautions.

The emblem of Kommando Sperling. The motto
can be loosely translated as: 'Off to the west or the
UK, the sparrow fast is on its way, and at
anything he pleases, he clicks his camera releases.'

While I was with Kommando Sperling we only had two mechanical problems that I can remember. On one occasion Horst was forced to land with the trolley of his V5 still attached. He managed to do this without damaging the aircraft, but without brakes it was a tricky proposition. The other problem was when one of the rocket-assisted take-off units on my aircraft released prematurely and cavorted across the airfield causing considerable alarm.

A year earlier, I had been promoted to the rank of Oberleutnant and now received the Frontflugspange for reconnaissance pilots with the 200 bar (for 200 missions) There was even talk that Horst and I had been nominated for the Ritterkreuz [Knight's Cross]. We heard later that General Karl Henning von Barsewisch, our envious top boss, had turned this proposal down. We didn't do anything for which he could boast, you see. He was still fighting to get control of us.

CHAPTER 13

KOMMANDO HECHT

Although Kommando Sperling was performing excellent service over the northern part of the Western Front, the range of our Arados was not sufficient to cover the south. Consequently, during my visit to Oranienburg, I had received an order to form a second Arado Kommando at Biblis, 8 kilometres (5 miles) north-east of Worms. I decided to call it Kommando Hecht (*Hecht* meaning pike due to the likeness of the Arado's fuselage to the fish).[22] The unit was only to have me as pilot with one aircraft, but with a full complement of service personnel.

Late in October, I visited Limburg by car to discuss with Luftwaffen Kommando West the role of the new unit. Then I went on to Biblis, but why this airfield was selected for these operations I could not understand then, and still can't today. It was situated in the Rhine Valley, near a big industrial centre between the Odenwald forest to the east and the Harz mountains to the west and north. This meant that it trapped a large amount of condensation in the average winter weather conditions of westerly and south-westerly air streams, and that resulted in fogs under the slightest provocation. Secondly, there was no hard runway of any kind and only one hard taxi track leading from the rain-sodden, grassed airfield deep into the pine forest beneath whose cover I had to park my aircraft. Thirdly, there was no maintenance hangar or technical equipment beyond that found on any tactical airfield. On top of that the normal east-west approach led over tall fir trees, and the northern flank of the airfield was bounded by another formidable bank of forest. This meant that any bad weather landing had to be dead accurate.

Shortly before my final transfer to Biblis I flew the film, which I had taken during a mission, to Limburg in a Fieseler Storch for processing. While there

---

22. I learned after the war that *Hecht* was also one of the code names for the Ar 234.

I was to receive further instructions and discuss what photographs my future Kommando should take. It was a very stormy afternoon with considerable turbulence as I skipped and hopped over the landscape to avoid enemy fighters. Several times I hit my head on the roof of the Storch, despite being well strapped in. With daylight almost gone I landed back at Rheine. I had to apply considerable throttle to land against the storm. The Fieseler almost hovered like a helicopter but I managed to taxi to the splinter box area of Kommando Sperling in the adjacent forest. The airfield seemed deserted: no assistance was to be seen and as I taxied carefully into a right-angle turn, a sudden squall tipped the Storch over on its nose into a shallow ditch, damaging the propeller.

On 3 November I had news from Friedl that she had finally been transferred to the Jüterbog-based staff of my top boss, General von Barsewisch. Here she served as a cipher clerk and enigma machine operator. This proved very convenient as she was able to follow my progress from the incoming communications.

Meanwhile our preliminary equipment was on its way to Biblis. One of the trucks was shot-up by a night raider in spite of it travelling in the dark with its lights dimmed. The driver and my chief mechanic, Feldwebel Albert, were killed. When all was ready, I flew my Ar 234, T9+IH, to Biblis on 10 November. Despite all the bad points with the airfield there were some good ones. Firstly, I was greeted by the airfield commander, Major Roman Dawczynski, a former leader of IV.(Erg)/K.G. 40. He was a very nice officer who promised everything I demanded. The only electronic equipment we had was a VHF Tornado Peiler, which worked to my FuG 16 transceiver and a UHF Funk Bake [radio beacon] landing aid. The former could home on to ground stations when landing, and the latter allowed for east-west approach with pre- and main signals. This was most important for descending over the Odenwald mountains and high forest just before touchdown. One final advantage was that Biblis was relatively unimportant and therefore mainly free from Allied air attack.

As you can imagine we had a lot of bad weather at this time of year. Heavy rain often led to the grassed runway becoming sodden. The only firm taxiway was to the east leading into the forest. On either side of this were parked about a dozen Fw 190 night fighters. I left my aircraft further down and to the right, on rather muddy ground. There were no solid platforms of any kind. The mechanics had to work in the mud which made things very difficult considering the painstakingly clean work which had to be done to keep the sophisticated mechanics of the fuselage and engines in top condition, or even get them airworthy. We did manage to erect a Nissen hut nearby for them to shelter in and

At Rheine we took turns to man the radio van. Here Wolfgang Ziese officiates. At Biblis, Wolf Loah did the job on his own.

warm themselves. In spite of all that, we kept up a regular photographic service for the army. Oberleutnant Wolf Loah, our ground-support officer, had his wireless post in a farmhouse at the forested edge of the field from where he could see me and listen for enemy aircraft. More than once he had to warn me off just before touch-down as Thunderbolts were ready to pounce.

For the first operational flights, the aircraft often had to be towed out of the mud into which it had sunk. For this we had a powerful bulldozer which we attached to the main-wheel legs by steel cables. Then we were supplied with steel mesh which we placed on the ground to support the wheels. The mechanics still had to work in wind, rain and snow without any cover until the New Year when a hangar was finally erected.

As I mentioned previously we were rarely troubled by strafing enemy aircraft as the airfield was not prominent. One day, however, a group of Thunderbolts came in at low level opening fire at anything that they thought worthwhile. Most of them quickly disappeared apart from one who was game enough to try it a second time. He shot-up one of the Fw 190s parked on the taxi strip. As it burned (recorded by my bad colour film) he circled over the western area and was hit by our 20-mm flak guns. The suicidal pilot still kept attacking, or at least tried to, but then his aircraft caught fire and went straight into the ground. No parachute. A mad fellow I thought.

A letter from Friedl spoke of the fear in her home town of Demmin because of the Russian advance. She was very depressed by the current situation. I visited Weinheim to where Hedwig, Helmuth's wife, had been evacuated with her parents. Here I met brother Helmuth on 25 November when he was on leave before going to Berlin on an officer's training course.

The situation in the air was getting worse with frequent mass bombing raids into south-west Germany by the Americans during fine weather. That same fine weather was ideal for us too. On more than one occasion I had to take off during air raid warnings and climb through what seemed like screens of ground-attack fighters. At lower altitudes these were mostly Thunderbolts, then at about 5,000 metres there were Lightnings up to the level of the B-17 bombers at about 7,000 metres (23,000 feet). Above them again was a protective screen of Mustangs.

I received my orders directly from Luftwaffen Kommando West at Limburg. Its requests soon filled my order book, but I had only been away from Horst at Rheine for a few days when he let me know that I was not forgotten. He had so many requests for reconnaissance that he could hardly fulfil them with his four aircraft and pilots. He had authority from the top to call on me for assistance, as if I hadn't got enough to do! Consequently, I often landed at Rheine after sorties in the north-west. I then took off again, flew another sortie, and returned to Biblis.

Sometimes I stowed two halves of a slaughtered piglet behind the armour plate at my back. The Rheine area had surplus farm production due to them being cut off from transport into the Reich owing to interruption of railways and roads by Allied bombing and strafing. The arrival of this treat at Biblis gave my ground crew an additional incentive to keep my aircraft serviceable and, a few hours after landing, the forest around Biblis was permeated by the lovely fragrance of a roast. Imagine, however, what Allied propaganda would have made of it if I had been shot down: 'Hitler is so desperate that he is forcing pigs to fly his latest planes!'

By November 1944 the Western Front had stabilized at a line through Saarbrücken-Monschau-Venlo-Arnhem. While the Allies prepared for winter, our army had managed to collect together a new group from the tattered remnants of the units which had fought, lost, and become scattered in Normandy, France and Belgium. This prompted Hitler to propose that these troops should be hurled against the weakest part of the American lines, breaking through the densely forested Ardennes region of Wallonia in Belgium, France and Luxembourg. The objective was to retake the vitally important port of Antwerp which was being used to supply the Allies, and recapture the Belgian capital of Brussels.

Early in the morning of 3 December, a radio message came directly from Luftwaffen Kommando West ordering the reconnoitering of the River Maas crossing between Dinant and Liège at all costs. The problem was that the end of November is notorious all over Europe for its bad weather and 1944 was no exception. The fog hung over the moist fields and paddocks and the fir trees were dripping. This had prevented aerial photography for weeks. The *Wetterfrosch* [meteorologists] gave me a chance in the target area between 1000 hours and midday with broken cloud between 1,000 and 3,500 metres. The problem was that they had to rely on meteorological reports coming in from the Channel port of Brest. This was still in German hands and we also received regular reports from submarines operating in the Atlantic. The trouble was that these were general in character and often not much use when considering areas influenced by local conditions.

I joined my aircraft by 0800 hours, having picked up Wolf Loah, my operations controller, in my Citroen car. After Oberfeldwebel Schmidt, my chief mechanic, and Stabsfeldwebel Darr, who supervised the photographic equipment, reported that everything was okay, the engines were tested, after which the fuel tanks were topped up.

It was a frosty morning. Visibility was bad, about one kilometre at ground level, with the tops of the tall fir trees disappearing into the mist. Because it hadn't been moved for a week, the wheels of my aircraft had sunk a little into the soft ground, and when we tried to move her with the six-wheel fire truck, she wouldn't budge. In the end we got our big Lanz Bulldog tractor with its immense power, and by attaching two tow ropes to the main-wheel legs, managed to pull her free. She was then towed to the take-off point at the rain-sodden eastern limit of the airfield. It was still too early for take-off, so I quietly went through my pre-flight checks. Meanwhile, Loah had taken up his

Top: Film cassettes being removed from the rear fuselage of the Ar 234 by ground crew.
Bottom: The Zeiss Reihenbilder or sequence camera Rb 50/30 with its film magazine mounted at the top. The designation indicated that the camera had a focal length of 50 cm with a film size of 30 cm x 30 cm.

position in the command room of the airfield administration building. Equipped with a FuG 16 radio and telephone lines to the Jägerleitstab [fighter control staff] he could see me and cover my take-off point.

Finally, at 1000 hours, I got a green flare. Easing the throttles forward, my Arado began to move slowly and heavily over the uneven paddock. Even with full power on she accelerated sluggishly so that after a 200-metre run I gave her the gun and pushed the assisted take-off button. I felt the reassuring push in the back and the trees began to blur. Gradually, the rumbling diminished and I lifted the nose wheel and came free, holding the variometer at a steady 5 m/sec climb until the speed increased. Then I pulled her up faster and jettisoned the spent rocket boosters.

With my wheels up and flaps in, I began climbing through the dark grey soup at a steady 8 m/sec and about 450 km/h (280 mph) with full throttle to gain my anticipated operational altitude of 10,000 metres as quickly as possible. I kept an eye out for ice forming on the wings but, as usual, there was no sign of it. It felt like being wrapped in cotton wool inside the heated glasshouse, with no vibration and only the air whistling past the Plexiglas.

About eight minutes later bright flashes of sunlight began to flick past and soon afterward I broke through the cloud. I could see for many kilometres in front of me over a wavy white ocean, but to my dismay, there was no indication of a break below. I climbed on until I was halfway to Dinant on the River Maas, but again there was no break in the clouds. Therefore, I decided to throttle back and stay at 5,000 metres for a time, but still no hope!

After recalculating my time of arrival over the target, at an average speed of 450 km/h, I descended after reaching a point 80 kilometres (50 miles) short. As I dived into the grey soup, I kept a careful watch on the variometer and airspeed indicator. Too fast a descent and I would hit the Ardennes mountains before I came out of the clouds. There was no reliable cross check with the Tornado Peiler, so my calculations had to be right. I was a bit uneasy when the altimeter dropped below 650 metres (2,000 feet) – the highest peak of the Ardennes, but there was no hope of coming out of the clouds above 300 metres (1,000 feet). It became darker and darker in the cockpit with blackish spots racing past beneath. Then, thank God, some cultivated land appeared with no forests. My altimeter showed 250 metres and I had the Maas in front of me, with Dinant slightly to the left. Visibility was about 6 kilometres (3¾ miles).

I had already throttled back during descent to the minimum injection pressure of 5 psi and kept it that way to save fuel. Then I turned the crank which opened the sliding gates covering the camera lenses, and set the shutter interval regulator to its highest speed. As I had no hope at this altitude of getting any overlapping pictures with my 75-cm cameras, at least they would prove I was there.

With the heater turned off, I shivered with tension, feeling terribly alone above hostile territory and fearing tracers might hit me at any moment, but nothing happened. I saw no movement on the ground and when I reached the river I turned right to follow its course north. I noted small road crossings together with some more important ones and some blown-up bridges with temporary structures replacing them. Other roads ended at the river with nothing beyond and still not a soul in sight!

I calmed down, but stayed alert in case someone might open up from an unexpected direction. Round the bend of the river, to the east of Charleroi, was a tricky spot, but all was quiet. Still flying at a leisurely pace just below the clouds at 250 metres, I saw a small twin-engine plane approaching from the north. It crossed under me without any reaction, obviously feeling completely safe on its home ground.

So far I had my mental notes right, but a change was to come. About ten kilometres short of Liège four spots appeared from the far north-east like flies or ducks in echelon, and this forced me to keep one eye on them and one on the ground. When the spots came nearer I recognized them as American C-47 Dakotas, probably a transport unit. Having reached the river, the leader turned eastward toward Liège and the rest duly followed. I strained my eyes to detect any weaponry sticking out from the big fuselages, but couldn't see any. Also being unarmed, I decided to join them on their flight toward Liège. The river was obviously the best navigational aid for the lazy American flyers.

I was now about 2,000 metres behind and gaining on them, and thought that if I had a gun or a ton of bricks, I could have sunk the unsuspecting string one by one. About four minutes later they turned left over the outskirts of Liège and I began to overtake them on the right. There were definitely no guns sticking out, in fact all I could see were the astonished faces of the men in the cockpits. Suddenly the leader broke away and I realised that I had lost my protection from ground fire. Now speed was the only hope. So I had to beat it. I opened up the throttle and dived down the short distance to the roof tops and roared over the city till I had enough speed to shoot up into the clouds and into the safety of the grey soup. Once inside the cloud again, I felt safe.

Setting course for home, I climbed to 5,000 metres and throttled back. The Biblis Tornado transmitter, to which I had switched, gave me the correct course. After twenty-five minutes I was above its position. I then began my bad weather approach which I had worked out previously with the courses and times noted on a pad. Over the Tornado transmitter, I clicked my stop-watch and changed course to fly off in a parallel direction to the approach course plus 30 degrees for three minutes. Then I went back on to the parallel course for another five minutes after which I began the standard blind flying turn to port of two degrees per second. After one-and-a-half minutes and completion of a 180-degree turn I was well within the Funk Bake vector and about 3,000 metres above the Odenwald. I corrected onto the equi-signal beam and after two minutes (about five minutes and 25 kilometres away from Biblis), lowered the undercarriage and flaps to 15 degrees. I then descended steadily toward the Funk Bake pre-signal which was about 5 kilometres from the airfield perimeter. Reaching that point at about 1,000 metres, I throttled back to near idling speed until I reached the main signal. Although still in the clouds, I knew it was safe to lower the flaps to 45 degrees and let the aircraft down.

On the ground I found it just as dark, chilly and unfriendly as before I took off. I reported the few notes and sightings I had made by telex and telephone before submitting a written report to Luftwaffen Kommando West. None of the pictures I had taken showed anything of importance, although there were two interesting pictures of V-1 hits. They clearly depicted the enormous impact of the weapon, with blocks of buildings flattened, and views through the shattered windows around the fringe. In the afternoon I was informed by phone that an aircraft of Kommando Sperling had taken some pictures of the target through the very thin holes in the cloud cover that I had been promised. In his memoirs, SS Colonel Otto Skorzeny, who led the 150th Panzer Brigade in the Ardennes offensive, reported that he had complained bitterly to Göring that the information on the Maas crossings never reached him. So what happened to our photos?

Next morning, I received a letter from Horst Götz, which he had written the day before just after returning from the funeral of Walter Wendt. He told me that Wendt had picked up a new Ar 234 B to replace the V7 which had been written off after being damaged. As Wendt took off from Oranienburg to fly to Rheine, on 25 November, those on the ground saw that his starboard turbojet was on fire. They tried to warn him but, for some reason, his radio was either switched off or not working. Using rocket assistance, the aircraft took off normally, but as soon as these cut it was left flying on the full power of one engine. To aggravate matters the starboard rocket unit did not release and within seconds the Arado flipped over and dived into the ground behind the Heinkel factory. Wendt was killed instantly. In his letter, Horst also warned me not to risk my aircraft in a fruitless operation at the whim of the top brass.

As the Americans retreated, they positioned heavy flak around the Ardennes area and, as soon as I poked my nose out of the clouds at 4,000 metres, to watch their retreat from the German offensive on 16 December, they let fly at me.

Generally, my aircraft had sufficient speed in normal flight to easily outpace the average enemy fighter of the time. This gave me confidence, although I still had to calculate all risks in certain situations, such as climbing and coming in for landing. In addition, our mechanics had to rectify a lot of the sloppy work that had been done on the factory assembly line. Apart from the badly finished fuselage the engines had to be regularly stripped down by us before being

Feldwebel Walter Wendt who was killed on 25 November 1944.

installed even though they were brand new. The specified life of each 900 kg (1,980 lbs) thrust Jumo 004 engine was only twenty hours, enough for just ten sorties before overhaul. I tried to stretch the time once by flying them over forty-five hours, but then the starboard one gave out during a V-2 calibration sortie over Amsterdam. It shed disintegrating turbine blades through the fuselage behind me. Fortunately, I managed to return safely on one engine to Rheine from where I had taken off on that day.

Safely? Not quite, because when I descended on one engine towards the east over solid cloud cover I switched the radio direction finder to the frequency of the Rheine Tornado beacon. Diving through the clouds and turning southwards, I listened for the signal in the turn until I heard the constant tone. This prompted me to head towards the Tornado beacon. Still turning, and breaking clear below the clouds at about 1,000 metres, I found myself above a vast stretch of water instead of land west of the River Rhine. Perplexed, I checked the radio compass and found that I was heading north in the opposite direction and following the wrong radio beacon constant tone. I then realised that I was over the vast flooded Dutch lowlands (the land below sea level flooded by British bombs which breached the sea dams) with nothing but water in sight. After performing a proper check, I turned into the right signal zone. I had not done this check while turning within the clouds but I still had enough fuel reserve to see me home safely. The landing with one dead engine was uneventful. Both engines were then exchanged and from then on I stuck to the recommended twenty hours between engine overhauls.

We flew several sorties to calibrate the aiming of the V-2 missile against the port of Antwerp which was then in Allied hands. On this particular occasion I was positioned near the battery which was based between Aachen and the Rhine. I had just crossed the river when a rocket came up in front of my nose and for which Ziese was already waiting over Antwerp. He had received a warning five minutes before the launch. We were of the opinion that the high penetration of the V-2 was a disadvantage as our pictures of the Antwerp run showed wastefully deep craters.

In spite of my vulnerable situation on take-off, climbing at about 450 km/h (280 mph), I was only attacked once, probably on 21 December. This was on a day when the B-17 Fortresses with their massive contrails clouded my target area and I had to throttle back to conserve fuel during my reconnaissance run at 7,000 metres. As I turned for home I saw, high above me, four Mustangs diving towards my Arado. The first one made a half-roll, followed by the second and then the third. The fourth Mustang hesitated. When I had first spotted them I had pushed the throttle to full power and dipped the nose to pick up speed. I knew by then that the first three would have no chance of catching up, but the fourth was in a critical position for me. In the rear-view periscope, I saw him levelling off behind me from his dive at a distance of about 1,000 metres, but by then I was at full speed and he had no chance of catching me.

Unfortunately, that was not the end of my troubles. I had pushed the Arado through its critical Mach number and the controls began to jerk and my buffeted aircraft went into a still faster dive. I could not pull her up with the normal controls. My only recourse was to cut the engines to the minimum before they flamed out and apply the ratchet trim wheel carefully. To my relief smooth control gradually came back. My actual airspeed, which I calculated afterwards from the indicated one adjusted for height and temperature, was 950 km/h (590 mph). That was considerably less than the 1,030 km/h (640 mph) at 8,000 metres which I had previously registered in the V7 without buffeting. I filed a report about that experience.

I survived this, but on Christmas Eve 1944 I had a close shave. It was a frosty day. Snow covered the airfield. The sky was clear and pale blue. Again I had to climb through flocks of fighters, low and high and then the bombers, to do my unmolested photographic runs between Saarbrücken and Luxembourg. No high-altitude fighters were about. Having finished the run and turning for home I noticed occasional white cotton wool-like things flick past. It was 'window' – which were aluminium strips dropped by the B-17s to confuse our radar.

As I returned, I was surprised to find that no air situation information was being broadcast by Loah in the communications room. I decided to call him on my FuG 16 radio, which I rarely did, but got no reply. Approaching Biblis I saw the reason. The previously pure white snow-covered field had been transformed into a dirty mess of craters. As I flew over the airfield, a red signal flare shot up in front of me. I immediately throttled to idling and made for Darmstadt, a short distance away to the east. As this airfield came into view, heavy flak came up in spite of me firing the recognition flare of the day. They had been bombed too and had fires burning. The same happened at Frankfurt/Rhein-Main and then Frankfurt/Hochheim. Go to Limburg I thought, but I

Horst watching anxiously for a returning Ar 234.

could see in the far distance the typical smoke bomb falling, the sign of a bombing attack in progress. It was now Wiesbaden/Erbenheim or bust, a small airfield not designed for a jet, about 50 kilometres to the west.

Flying over the field at 1,000 metres and firing my last recognition flare, I saw that this runway was also full of craters. Searching desperately, I noticed a strip of grass which had been marked out with fir tree twigs. The craters in between had been filled in but spray painted to simulate craters with shadows. That must have been from a bombing a week ago I thought. With little fuel left I decided to land. I lowered my flaps and undercarriage and turned for final. All of a sudden tracers came up as if from a watering can. I had no time or speed left to avoid the fire but just concentrated on landing at near stalling speed. I touched down behind the fence and had enough room before reaching a concrete taxi way which I followed in the direction of two hangars to the left. The one to the right was closed but the left one had no doors and a Fieseler Storch was parked inside. I taxied straight in to hide from possible strafing enemy fighters. While still rolling forwards with engines running, I opened the cockpit hatch, when ouch! I felt a painful burning at the back of my neck and, looking round, saw flames and smoke rising to the hangar roof. I quickly jumped out and down. As the aircraft was still crawling forwards towards the rear wall I had to grab the chocks from under the Storch and block the Arado's wheels. I was perplexed. What had happened?

Now on the floor of the hangar I saw that the forward fuel tank of my Arado was on fire with the top cover already burned away. Red flames and black smoke rose vertically from the bathtub-size tank to the hangar roof with a loud roaring noise. My immediate concern was to save the film cassettes still clipped to the top of the cameras only about two metres to the rear of the burning tank. In addition, the other near-empty tank in between could also catch fire at any moment. I dashed to the front of the hangar to wait for the fire fighters.

Then a man I had previously seen running across the airfield approached. He had a Luger in his right hand and was puffing heavily. He was still running towards me when I threw my flying cap to the ground in a rage and let out a stream of Bavarian swear words. All of a sudden the man stopped, startled, then ran towards me again and to my astonishment threw his arms around my neck. When I asked him what the pistol was for he said, embarrassed, that he had orders to arrest or shoot the kamikaze American pilot. The man was a sergeant. I asked him to help me up on the port wing to cut the engines. I had just got up there when he came too close to the hot engine exhaust, burned his hair and disappeared at high speed. The fire engine then arrived and I directed them to let the foam fall from above into the forward fuel tank. With a little pressure and in a gentle arc the fire was quickly extinguished. Then I asked for a screwdriver to open the camera compartment to lift out the film cassettes.

A crowd had meanwhile assembled and amongst them was the Oberst and Fliegerhorstkommandant [airfield commanding officer] who had personally ordered the flak crew to fire on me. Still full of rage over the loss of my aircraft and the order he had given to fire on my aircraft while landing and taxiing, I let the gentleman have it with a vengeance, so much so that he put his heels together and saluted! But then, when I took off my flying jacket to cool off, he saw my rank badges and pointed out in accusatory terms that he would have me reported for insubordination and court martialled. My only answer was that it would most probably be he who would appear before a court following my report. With that, he turned red and pissed off with his entourage. Later, on inspection, I found that a single incendiary bullet had hit the fuel tank from below through the undercarriage compartment. As the tank was pretty empty the vapour on top of the diesel fuel had exploded spontaneously. Ground witnesses told me that my Arado trailed a 150-metre-long flame on approach and while landing and taxiing.

After talking the event over with a young flak officer I told him that a bottle of Cognac would settle the score and organised a car to get me and the film cassettes to Luftwaffen Kommando West headquarters at Limburg. I then telephoned Horst at Rheine who suggested that I drive there after dropping off my film at Limburg. He would see to it that a new Ar 234 was delivered from Oranienburg for me. I also spoke to Wolf Loah at Biblis before I left and discussed with him and the ground crew what could be done. I asked him to pick up my toiletries and other things which I needed from my billet in the private villa. I also gave him instructions on what to salvage from the burned aircraft. This included the instrument panels which I had personally laid out to give me an unimpeded forward view. This made accurate parallel running of photographic sorties over a given area much easier.

When I arrived at Limburg at 2300 hours I found that a Christmas party was in full swing. The commander of Luftwaffen Kommando West, Generalleutnant 'Beppo' Schmid, offered me a glass of hot punch and asked whose head I wanted for the destruction of my Arado. I said none and that I had settled the matter. This seemed to satisfy him. I wrote my report after sending the telex for Oranienburg and the General der Aufklärer (von Barsewisch) at Jüterbog where Friedl was now stationed. In this way Friedl, who I knew would get the secret telex through her fingers, would be informed that I was unhurt. I rang Horst again who had promised to send me his car to get to Rheine. The first car returned to Wiesbaden from where I had borrowed it.

It was a cold drive in the pitch-dark night with Gefreiter Kraus as driver. The route went through completely devastated townships, the worst being Münster, with virtually no indication of how to navigate through the rubble. We nearly toppled into a huge crater which had opened up the road during the night and was unmarked. It was filled with water from the Dortmund-Ems canal which ran parallel with the road.

Finally, I arrived at Rheine. I had a talk with Horst and then a long sleep. As Horst had his birthday the next day we had a fried goose for dinner. Boy, what a grandfather of a goose he must have been. Knife and fork made hardly an impression on him, not to mention our teeth. But the potatoes and sauce were fine!

After a couple of days Hauptmann Josef Bisping, who was flying experimental night-fighter sorties with the Ar 234 at Oranienburg, brought my new aircraft, coded T9+EH, to Rheine. Next day, New Year's Eve, I transferred the aircraft to Biblis. As I was flying at our prescribed height of 800 metres for a transfer flight over the Reich and approaching the Wiesbaden flak position which was on my

Although of poor quality, this is one of the few photographs of my new Arado, coded T9+EH, taking off under rocket-assistance from Biblis.

flight course, I dived on the flak crew responsible for the destruction of my previous aircraft at full power and shot over their guns at 800 km/h (500 mph) at almost zero altitude. This scattered them and sent them all flying!

When I arrived at Biblis we found that the hydraulics of the new machine were a shambles. I often had to manually pump out the undercarriage before landing and the flaps would often not operate without much coaxing. Although this problem was partially fixed it was to recur as you will see.

Early in January 1945 an order came from the General der Aufklärer that the inactive reconnaissance Staffel, 1.(F)/100, would re-equip with the Ar 234 and transfer to Biblis where they were to undergo training with my Kommando. After this was completed, I was to transfer to Italy. At the same time Horst's Kommando Sperling at Rheine would train the newly reformed 1.(F)/123 under Hauptmann Hans Felde. This unit, which had been inactive since May 1944, was also to be equipped with the Ar 234. In von Barsewisch's diary entry, dated 2 January, he recorded the Führungsstab's decision that these two new Staffeln would support Army Groups B and G on the Western Front. One of the advantages of this was that I had now a film-processing unit at my base, but it took a long time until this unit got into shape. When I left for Italy on 14 March 1945 1.(F)/100 still had to fly its first operational sortie. I went on with my own business independently, flying whenever the weather was acceptable and my aircraft serviceable. My order book was always full.

Meanwhile Friedl was aware of the Christmas Eve debacle from my telexed report which had passed through her friend's hands during the night. Shortly afterwards she moved to Würzburg where a part of the staff of the General der Aufklärer had moved. I determined to visit her there before going to Italy.

When I think back on this winter of despair I find there is a big gap in my memory. I can only remember a few distinct events, despite racking my brain. Some of these are from other people who I met subsequently. The date when visiting our parents in Munich where there were no window panes left in our apartment I cannot remember, nor why I had the opportunity to visit.

Brother Paul told me long after the war that we met in Berlin during the winter of 1944-45, together with brother Helmuth. He had been moved to the Eastern Front which, by then, was pretty close to the German border. Paul was a technical supply inspector with a Luftwaffe truck manufacturer in Berlin. He told me that I mentioned at that time my encounter with Kraus 'Wiggerl', my former classmate in Ingolstadt. He was later to be with Mercedes-Benz as boss of the racing team and the father of the Volkswagen Golf car with Audi at Ingolstadt, his home town. I wrote to him later but he never answered.

Why I can't bring these important events to life again worries me constantly. Perhaps temporary amnesia? Brother Helmuth, who later took part in the battle on the River Oder in which they reoccupied a section, told me later that he had witnessed unbelievable cruelty by the Russians against the occupied German population.

On 11 February, Horst had the misfortune to witness the death of Hans Felde, Kapitän of 1.(F)/123. Returning to Rheine from a reconnaissance mission over Hull on the English east coast, Felde's aircraft, coded 4U+DH, was chased by an RAF Tempest and shot down. Long after the war I read the report by the British pilot, Squadron Leader David C Fairbanks of 274 Squadron who wrote:

> 'As I came through a small patch of cloud I saw the enemy aircraft about 800 yards dead ahead at approximately 1,500 feet above Rheine airfield. He was just dropping his nose wheel and started to turn to starboard. I dropped my tanks on seeing the airfield and closed to approximately 250-300 yards and placed the bead on his starboard turbo and slightly above, firing a half-second burst to test my deflection. I saw little puffs of smoke on the fuselage and then a great burst of flame. The enemy went straight down immediately and blew up in the centre of Rheine airfield.'

Following this Horst was appointed the new commander of 1.(F)/123 and I was ordered to report to Oranienburg to take over his squadron (1./Versuchsverband OKL). I flew over straight away in my Arado. It was late in the afternoon and there was scarcely a man in sight. I rolled my aircraft to a standstill in front of the main hangar. Only the chief engineer, Arno Trebs, greeted me. We talked and he told me the sad news that in the past week there had been four tragic deaths. Following the loss of Felde mentioned earlier, Josef Bisping

Erwin Ziller in the cockpit of the Ho IX V2 being instructed on the Jumo 004 engines by a Junkers engineer. I had hoped to fly this revolutionary all-wing aircraft but it was too late to see service.

and his radar operator, Hauptmann Albert Vogl, were killed on 13 November. During one of their night take-offs someone had inadvertently switched off the airfield lights, causing Bisping to pull the Arado up too steeply with the result that it stalled and smashed into the ground. Five days later Leutnant Erwin Ziller was killed when the Horten Ho IX V2 which he was testing, hit the ground at a steep angle following an engine failure. The resultant crash threw him and both engines into an embankment. The destruction of the Horten IX signalled the end of my hope of flying this exciting revolutionary aircraft.

What took my interest at that moment were two weapon packs on the floor at the right-hand side of the open hangar. Trebs told me that these were two of the three 20-mm gun packs intended for the night-fighter version, but their use was now in doubt following Bisping's crash. I pleaded with him to give me one of these so-called Magirus bombs as I could now scarcely land without enemy fighters attempting to intercept. After thinking it over for a few moments he agreed that he would give me one without consulting his superiors. He kept his word. During the night he had it installed in the recess in the belly of the fuselage originally designed to carry a bomb. The electrical connections were added and a gunsight was installed. I didn't mention it to anyone during the night's talks. The Magirus bomb comprised two 20-mm cannons with 150 rounds of ammunition each. Trebs told me that all I needed to do was to get the gunsight calibrated when I returned to Biblis. So, at the break of dawn next morning, I duly returned to Biblis where the gunsight was adjusted.

On the night of 22-23 February, British and American aircraft bombed the city of Worms, 11 kilometres south-west of Biblis. Within twenty minutes two thousand years of history was destroyed as the medieval centre caught fire and burned. Many civilians were wounded and killed and two thirds of all houses were ruined. From where I was I could see the bloody red glow of the flames and hear the explosions.

I immediately got on my motorbike and rode south to see what help could be organised. Crossing the bridge over the River Rhine, with billowing smoke coming from the burning town beyond, I saw a shadow of a vehicle coming my way. I swerved slightly to the right and the shadow whizzed past but not without it catching my left little finger on the handlebars. It was cold and my hands were numb. At the end of the bridge, in the dim light of the red-coloured clouds of smoke and fire, I propped my bike against a low wall and went down into the old city. It was quite eerie. Nobody in sight as if all had fled. The only noise was the crackling flames from the burning houses and falling timber and walls.

As I moved further into the city, the road turned to the right and I came into a narrower street in which visibility was a little better. The smoke had been lifted by the heat of the fires. Then I saw a movement beyond the burning timber lying across the pavement. When I ran over I found an old woman in extreme distress waving to me. She pointed to the steps of a burning three-storey house which made up the whole street. Approaching nearer, I saw an old man sitting on the stone steps. He mumbled something to me but I could not understand what he said due to the howling noise of the flames. I immediately lifted him up over my shoulder and carried him out of the city to the bridge to where my bike was stowed. The wailing woman followed. I understood that she said that there was nobody down there anymore. Eventually I handed the old man to some helpers who had arrived out of the smoke.

It was only then that I realised that my little finger was dangling in a way it shouldn't and discovered that it was broken. This probably happened when it was caught earlier as I rode over the bridge. It began to hurt badly and I went home and to bed in Biblis. In the morning somebody from 1.(F)/100 drove me to a small country military hospital nearby and the finger was bandaged under a dreadful Formalin anaesthetic. During the next day's mission, the bandage slipped off my finger and had to be set again, this time under more comfortable ether anaesthetic. Nevertheless, it slipped off again during the next day when I landed in Rheine following a mission. It was set again and this time put in a stretch bandage. As I was ordered to Oranienburg for instructions relating to the Italian commando, Horst flew me over in a Fieseler Storch.

Würzburg following the RAF bombing attack which took place on 16 March 1945. Approximately 5,000 civilians were killed and the historic old city almost completely destroyed.

On the way I had to cut the plaster off my finger as a sort of gangrene had set in beneath. I decided to leave it in the shape it was by then and as it still is today.

Not long before my transfer to Italy, I drove to Würzburg by car with Wolf Loah to see Friedl. I had a good excuse for the trip: being called to receive detailed orders. The first person we met in the officer's mess was my old rowing club trainer from Ingolstadt/Donau, Gustl Suttor. He was now a major in my commander's office and we had a great chat. At noon Friedl came off duty and it was wonderful to see her again. We went to town in the afternoon and up to Marienburg Castle and enjoyed the beautiful peaceful day with the view over the old bishop's town and the wide River Main. It was the last time that we would enjoy this city as it was on that day. Several days later the old baroque township was turned to rubble and completely and senselessly destroyed. Fortunately, Friedl was not hurt. The airfield was up in the hills and nothing of military importance was damaged. It was sheer vandalising terror as with Dresden four weeks earlier. With hindsight I can find no excuse for destroying a whole cultural heritage for the deeds of a madman. The British have to be as responsible for this just as we Germans are held accountable for this dreadful time.

Returning to Biblis, after my visit to Würzburg, our road transport to Italy was ready but then we were ordered to transfer it to a train to save petrol. We knew that it was sheer madness to do this. The train left, still in daylight, against my protests. I had just returned to my room in the house where I was billeted, when I heard the commotion to the south. There was a noise of howling aircraft engines and gunfire and I saw smoke rising. After driving to the spot in a borrowed car I found the train, with most of our vehicles on it, in flames. The locomotive had been badly holed and was blowing steam. Luckily the engine driver had managed to stop instantly and all personnel had leapt behind the carriages and the embankment and miraculously nobody was hurt. But most of our equipment was gone.

Our rail transport to Italy burning after the Allied ground attack.

This debacle led me to send urgent messages for immediate replacements, which Horst promised to organise. Almost immediately he sent them by road to Italy under the command of Oberleutnant Manfred Mänhardt and Feldwebel Pösch, his sergeant, both very competent men. Mänhardt I knew from Sarabus in the Crimea as a very clever technician. On 9 June 1944 he had been awarded the Ritterkreuz for completing 300 missions with 4.(F)/122, but later managed to get a transfer to our establishment in Oranienburg. Pösch I knew as our resourceful NCO at Juvincourt. He always found a way to organise something, quietly, modestly but always successfully. No wonder he became a prosperous man later as an insurance broker.

The remnants of Kommando Hecht under Wolf Loah finally left for Italy by road early in March 1945. I then waited for their report after they had arrived in Italy. Two further pilots with new Arados were also promised for the new Kommando and dispatched from Oranienburg.

CHAPTER 14

KOMMANDO SOMMER

As I mentioned in the previous chapter I received orders at the beginning of February 1945 to transfer to north-east Italy. There I was to establish a new Kommando at Udine/Campoformido. At this time Germany lacked any effective aerial reconnaissance of the Italian front. As soon as 1.(F)/100 was ready for operations I should leave.

Eventually, on 14 March, both sets of our road transport reached their destination at Udine. I then took off from Biblis assisted by the ground staff of 1.(F)/100. Refuelling at Lechfeld, I arrived at Udine in beautiful spring weather. My reception committee consisted, in addition to all the ground crew, of Manfred Mänhardt, Wolf Loah and the two new pilots, Leutnant Günther Gniesmer and Stabsfeldwebel Walter Arnold, both of whom I had never met before. I heard from Horst that Gniesmer had flown his first Ar 234 operation with 1.(F)/123 at Rheine early in January. He transferred to Udine via Lechfeld on 24 February and was followed by Arnold a day before me.

Udine was a big airfield with a bitumen runway orientated east to west. Dispersal splinter boxes were some distance away and connected to the runway by hard-rolled taxiways. All looked good. Manfred had organised our head-quarters in a large country house at Ceresetto six kilometres to the north on the slopes rising from the plain. The only other unit based on the airfield was the short-range reconnaissance squadron, NAG 11 equipped with Bf 109s.

As the runway was long and the countryside level beyond it, I didn't need liquid fuel rockets for take-off. My first missions took me over the whole front line from east to west and proved uneventful. I just let the cameras run the whole way and the only thing I noticed was that the old towns down there were badly ravaged by Allied bombing. On almost every second day I flew a route from Ancona to Livorno which at last gave the German army an idea of what was going on behind the enemy lines.

We had a ground wireless station serving the aircraft mounted on top of an earth bunker

Our billet at Ceresetto in northern Italy.

not too far from the runway. I had a camouflaged cover erected just off the eastern end of the runway over the taxiway to slip under after landing. This hid my Arado from strafing fighter-bombers which were as thick as mosquito swarms and attacking anything that moved. Our recent presence was of course known to the enemy as soon as we arrived because of the unusual sound of our jet engines and the numerous spies. Many Italians from the surrounding villages and the town of Udine were passing on information to the Allies at this time. We had been made aware of Italian partisan sympathisers all over the place. For this reason, we avoided using the Italian telephone system as much as we could.

Otherwise I remember the location and the Italian spring with great affection. Most days we were greeted with clear blue skies. Behind our white-painted three-storey country house were green rolling hills with vineyards and white villages with red roofs in front of the majestic background of the towering Alps. These often shimmered in the far distance in the bluish light of the warm spring sun. Just to sit in the garden in the warmth and let our eyes sweep over the vast plain below to the horizon was soothing – if there just had not been a war on.

Usually our headquarters were as busy as a beehive with men working on vehicles or repairing instruments or all of us having lunch or dinner at long tables in the shade of trees and under camouflage nets. There was only an occasional alarm when fighter-bombers swooped along the road below and our machine-gun post at the air situation watch let loose a rattle.

Our emergency airfield was to be Osoppo just 25 km to the north in the Tagliamento valley. We officers made an excursion the day after my arrival to familiarise ourselves with its location and facilities. It really looked like an emergency field, as the runway was still not sealed and taxiways with splinter boxes were under construction. This work was guarded by Tartars from the Crimea under General Pyotr Krasnov.[23] His men made an imposing impression with their broad shoulders, tall figures, handlebar moustaches and fur caps with flashing eyes beneath. They were trustworthy and tough fighters in the partisan guerrilla war going on in the hills.

On this occasion we arranged a meeting with officers of the Luftnachrichten [air signals] units operating the Jagerleit radar stations in our area and we discussed our cooperation. A direct telephone link to our men on the airfield was organised in order to give us warnings of air movements right on the spot. It was to be a godsend for our activities and probably saved my life on more than one occasion. The day ended with a fine meal at a village inn in the mountains where I got my first taste of polenta.

My initial operational sortie took place on 15 March, a two-hour flight over the Ancona and San Benedetto areas of the Italian Adriatic coast. This was followed by a mission to Pisa, Livorno (Leghorn) and Elba along the Italian east coast on 17 March, over the Apennines two days later, over Ancona on 21 March and another two-hour sortie over Livorno, Perugia and Ancona on 23 March. Two days later I undertook the first of two extreme-range missions, transferring to Lonate in north-west Italy for a flight over Marseille, Toulon and the Côte d'Azur in southern France and the island of Corsica. This was three minutes short of a two-hour sortie. In order to have enough fuel to return I touched down at Lonate, north of Milan, on the outward journey to have the aircraft refuelled. To my amusement the ground crew there fitted dummy propellers to the jet engines to disguise them.

On 26 March I flew a sortie over Ancona, Firenze [Florence] and Livorno and covered the Apennine passes next day. For three weeks I had decided to keep my other two pilots on the ground to familiarise themselves with our operational procedure. Günther Gniesmer was an eager young man. Born in Buenos Aires in Argentina of German parents he had come to Germany on a visit with his mother and younger brother just before the war broke out. While he joined the Luftwaffe, his brother went to the army in the east. Walter Arnold was an older pilot who had joined the Luftwaffe early as a professional soldier.

---

23. Krasnov was a Russian who had defected to the Nazis taking with him a group of Cossacks. At the end of the war, he and his men voluntarily surrendered to British forces in Austria with the promise that they would not be repatriated to the Soviets. Despite this he was handed over to the Soviets and hanged in 1947.

He was a quiet man who told me that he was not too sure about the aircraft and that his confidence in it was not high. No eagerness to fly missions was apparent. I had sympathy for his attitude as I had experienced this type of pilot who considered the profession as a soldier as a lifelong occupation rather than a means to a hero's death.

During my operational flights both pilots were to man the microphone of the wireless station next to the runway. This was to give them an idea of how we did things from the beginning in addition to flight planning and final debriefing. All of my flights, except two long-range sorties to the west, were uneventful and went without a hiccup. Our one problem was having to be constantly aware of the reconnaissance Lightnings which covered our airfield and subsequent fighter-bomber attacks.

When refuelling at Lonate I was invited to have a snack in the mess where I met Italian officers who wanted to know all about my aircraft. My reaction was, of course, quite evasive. There was already too much talk going on. One pretty warm afternoon at Lonate I had difficulty lifting off at take-off in spite of the long runway and just made it at the end as the ground dipped slightly away. I had to pull it up 'by the toes' so to speak. The reason for this may have been my full fuel load plus the relatively high temperature, or perhaps because of the infamous airstreams known south of the Alps for their violent downdrafts.

One fine morning, I think it was 5 April, we could see and hear from Ceresetto some commotion going on at the south end of the airfield. We drove there in Mänhardt's rattling old Fiat 1500 Special which he had requisitioned. On arrival we found that there were constant fighter-bomber attacks going on at half-hourly intervals by all types of enemy fighters. Just as we were driving onto the taxi strip and into the splinter box, a group of Thunderbolts attacked the western side of the airfield with gunfire and napalm bombs.

As I was going to fly an operational sortie, and seeing that an attack took place at regular intervals of about twenty-five minutes, I took off after an attack by Lightnings and made a photographic run over the western part of the front.

As my sortie continued I received reports from the radio operator on the ground that the attacks on our airfield were still continuing at regular intervals. Returning from my operation I descended to the south of Udine to come in a wide sweep from the east. I never did a circuit anyway. A big cumulus cloud had built up over the Udine area from the bomb explosions and, as I passed it from high above to the south, a dark spot came around its top followed at a greater distance by a bunch of about twelve others. The first spot materialised into an

One of our Ar 234s being towed by a Kettenkrad-tracked motorcycle. This is actually Muffey's T9+KH photographed at Rheine.

enemy fighter which I identified as a Spitfire. As it would cross my bow well in front of me on its way south I decided to have a go at it. I flipped the safety catch off my cannon, throttled back and got behind it. Of course the pilot saw me or was warned by his mates and started to turn to starboard while I let the cannon blast away. But hard as I might pull, the shots went past his tail. Realising that if I continued I would be in a dangerous position, I broke off, pushing down and opening the throttle to gain speed. Having achieved that, I pulled hard on the stick so that the Arado shot up vertically, a manoeuvre which no eggbeater could follow.

Looking down from above I saw that all these fighters were combining in formation, meaning that none of them was going back to interfere with my landing. After receiving clearance from the ground, I touched down, taxied into the shelter on the taxiway off the runway, and waited for the tractor to tow me into the splinter box about one kilometre to the south. We had scarcely pushed the Arado, tail first, into the corner of the square earth embankment splinter box and thrown the netting over when the sirens wailed again. The tractor disappeared in a moment while I waited for my car to collect me and my films. No car came. Then I realised why. High in the east a squadron of Spitfires were diving straight towards me and the splinter box. All I could do was run and look for any available shelter. Finding no foxhole within reach I just dropped down and laid myself as flat as I could. This left me staring straight into the muzzles of their guns with the flashes appearing from their wings as they fired. Then the rockets came in. I counted four from each aircraft and the noise was dreadful with dirt flying everywhere.

When it was over I was completely unhurt. I got up and raced for the splinter box. Rounding the corner of the earth wall, I saw burning oil drop from the belly of a NAG 11 Bf 109 which was standing opposite my Arado. There was nothing I could do without help, so I watched intently. Then flames spewed from the cowlings and grew rapidly, enveloping the whole aircraft. Then its ammunition started to explode with coloured tracers flying and popping in all directions. I noticed two incendiary bullets got caught in the camouflage netting of my Arado with tiny flames licking up from the ground. I went over to try and save my aircraft, hopping from leg to leg in the naive belief that in this way I wouldn't be hit by the bullets spraying from the Bf 109 close to the ground. Anyway, it worked!

Without being hit I stamped the fires out. Seconds later cars and trucks arrived and the fires from the burning Bf 109 were extinguished with foam. The films were then recovered from my Arado and home we went. It was the penultimate attack of the day. The Arado had some damage from bullet holes through the cabin and fuselage but these were not serious and were repaired within a couple of days.

With my aircraft temporarily out of action it was time to get Leutnant Gniesmer into action. He flew his first sortie in T9+DH on 10 April 1945, following one of my regular routes by covering the Livorno sector again. For the first time it was me that was standing on the earth bunker together with Mänhardt, the wireless operator and the Luftlage [air situation] man. Beside us we had a MG 15 aircraft machine gun mounted on a tripod.

After a good hour I noticed a blue and red line together forming a wide half circle to the north-east on the chart recording the air situation. Querying this on the phone we were told the traces related to one twin-engine and two single-engine aircraft flying together. The lines were drawn by the Luftlage man who got direct air situation messages from our fighter control radar station. We found this strange but Manfred suggested that it could only mean that two fighters were waiting to intercept Gniesmer as he returned. These were being directed, he thought, by a radio operator aboard a twin-engine aircraft listening on our frequency, possibly using a captured Funkgerät 16 (FuG 16) radio set. The enemy certainly had our frequencies by now in spite of us never talking on our radios from the air but only on the ground. I usually indicated my arrival by pressing the transmitter button in a certain sequence, but never spoke anything in reply to a message from the ground.

To test this theory, I took over the microphone to impersonate the incoming pilot (Gniesmer) and the tower was instructed to take over our ground station procedure, with which it was by now familiar, with their transmitter.

So, at the time of Gniesmer's estimated return, but before we received his signal, I imitated it, whereupon the tower began to give the ground station report to my 'aircraft'. I simulated its receipt and waited the usual five minutes, then gave the approach signal with my transmitter signalling 'dash, dot, dash', which usually came about one to one-and-a-half minutes before touchdown. We were all anxious to discover what would happen.

All of a sudden two dots appeared from the east at low altitude, rapidly becoming two Spitfires shooting over the runway with their guns blazing. I dashed for the machine gun on the tripod and tried to return fire at the fighters. But, swinging round in an attempt to keep the gun trained on them, I was thrown off balance and toppled down the embankment with the whole thing! Somewhat embarrassed, I scrambled back to the top of the bank. As nobody was hurt in the noisy affair everybody laughed. Soon afterwards we got Gniesmer down safely, with him wondering why he received an air situation report twice.

Following the successful outcome of this mission, Gniesmer undertook a long-distance flight along the southern coast of France. He was to refuel at Lonate as I had done previously. At Lonate he was redirected by a telephone call from our superior command at Vicenza to reconnoitre the eastern sector of the front rather than the west. He was not so lucky this time. He never returned. Late in the afternoon a phone call informed us that he landed by parachute near Ferrara in no man's land. Although he bailed out, he struck the horizontal stabilizer which fractured his skull. His aircraft crashed nearby which resulted in an order that it 'was to be destroyed without fail because it is a new type'. Nevertheless, the British Eighth Army captured the aircraft next day but it was reported that the

The remnants of Gniesmer's Ar 234 after it had been set on fire by retreating German troops.

Germans had 'set fire to the fuselage which was burnt out from nose to within a few feet of the tail. One jet unit had been scraped off a hundred yards before the aircraft came to rest.'

Although rescued, Gniesmer was unconscious and in a hospital at Ferrara. There was no way we could find out what happened because of his injuries. He died two days later without recovering consciousness. For a long time afterwards I was inclined to think that it was the open telephone call at Lonate that had led to his demise. Some years ago I got the American report of the interception which indicated that it was Gniesmer's tactical error when confronted by the two Mustangs on patrol, that led to his getting shot down. I had repeatedly warned him never to risk the situation in which he had found himself. I felt very sorry as did everyone, about the death of this nice young chap. To compound matters his brother, so his mother informed me later, was killed on the Eastern Front. This is the combat report from the pilots of the two Mustangs, Lieutenants Hall and Cooper of the US 52nd Fighter Group:

> 'While escorting a lone Fortress at 22,000 feet (6,700 m) in the Bologna area at 1300 hours, two Mustangs saw an Ar 234 at the same altitude approaching a group of bombers from 4 o'clock level. The Mustangs being about two miles away and at 11 o'clock to the enemy, turned and headed it away from the Fortress. When the enemy saw the Mustangs, he turned north, flying straight and level at about 400 mph (644 km/h). Attacking from dead astern, one Mustang set the left turbojet on fire and the Ar 234 went into a gentle dive and finally crashed into the ground south-east of Ferrara.'

For years afterwards I felt somewhat responsible for Gniesmer's death. In 1976, when my daughter Renate and I travelled through Italy, we visited Ferrara and enquired of the whereabouts of the German war grave. Unfortunately, we were directed to the wrong one which only contained four dilapidated German graves from the First World War. The *Cimitero Centrale* was closed on the weekend. His grave is supposed to be in there. I never understood what made him act in this way, to bring on this disaster. He was certainly not stupid – maybe just youthfully reckless. The feeling of smooth speed in the Arado could easily give you a false sense of security, I admit. It had to be consciously overcome to enable one to run for it, the only way to survive in this nasty climate.

By this time, the middle of April 1945, we were becoming increasingly aware of the growing activity of Italian partisan units in the vicinity and of our

Due to the fact that many of my photographs were lost while retreating from Italy, there are no pictures of my Ar 234 at Udine. This shows another Arado 234, T9+KH, being towed at Rheine which would have looked similar to my T9+EH.

vulnerability at Ceresetto. This led Mänhardt to gather together some weapons for our defence just in case, but he could only find some old long-barrelled rifles and hand grenades and a couple of machine pistols. We trained on them in our spare time and I found that I was now a very bad shot compared with my earlier achievements in target shooting. I thought perhaps I was getting jittery, but couldn't find any other sign of this. In fact, I felt extremely confident, calm, and had lost any sense of fear, which had sometimes plagued me in earlier times. I only realised this later.

Our airfield was now under constant surveillance by high-flying aircraft of No. 60 Squadron of the South African Air Force and No. 682 Squadron of the RAF. They came over at least twice a day. One time, during a run over the eastern Adriatic coast, I saw amphibian vehicles in the area of Lake Comacchio, cruising in the shallow waters and made a mental note. After half an hour, when returning from the south and still at a height of about 8,500 metres in clear sky, I saw a Lightning higher up also going north.

I'll let him have it, I thought, and flicking the gun switch on, I dipped down slightly to increase my speed and then climbed from below to get under him. But then I saw, glancing left towards Lake Comacchio, that the amphibians had turned into a distinct channel. Following my orders, I reluctantly turned to port to photograph this happening with the remainder of the film in my cassettes. By that time the Lightning had disappeared. About five minutes later

I got an air situation report that there was a Lightning over Udine. I wondered if he was ever warned by his own radar or ground stations. Some years ago (in 1979) I had one of the pilots (Gordon Jack) of a Florence-based mixed American-British reconnaissance unit visiting me here, but he didn't know of the Udine operations. I have now some of their aerial photographs (taken on 4 and 16 April) of Campoformido in my photograph album.

One day, while my Arado was undergoing maintenance, I decided to let Arnold loose with his T9+FH which had not yet undertaken any operational flights. He was towed by the tractor to the western end of the runway, started his engines and was already beginning his take-off run when, seemingly out of nowhere, two Spitfires came in low from the west towards the runway with their guns blazing. We had no warning whatsoever and were completely surprised. Arnold stopped immediately and jumped from his aircraft to run for cover, but the spectacle was already over. The front fuel tank of his machine was holed as well as his cabin. He was not hurt, but visibly shaken. It was to be Arnold's only operational attempt.

On 15 April 1945 (as I know now from the official history of the US 15th Air Force) the Americans staged their last great bombing attack on targets behind the German lines in Italy and in southern Germany and Austria. During the morning I flew as usual but when I returned at noon and put the Arado under the camouflage tent on the taxi way, I got a warning of the approach of enemy bombers. I cut the engines, but no towing tractor arrived. When I opened the canopy I could already hear the droning of masses of aircraft high up. After climbing down, I could see four waves of Liberators of about thirty aircraft each in echelon formation jockeying for position. They were at about 5,000 metres and were coming from the north towards the airfield.

I calculated that their present course was not directly aimed in my direction and waited. The four waves were flying some distance apart but in echelon. The first wave let their bombs go like rain under a thunderstorm cloud. They hit the western edge of the airfield in a two-kilometre-long trail of fire, dirt and incredible noise and I pitied anybody possibly caught in this holocaust of anti-personnel bombs.

As the second wave edged nearer to my position I bolted and ran for the safety, or so I thought, of a village cemetery bordering the airfield. This stretched far into the countryside. I was not quite at the cemetery wall when the wave of destruction raced past the camouflage tent and my Arado disappeared in a cloud of dust. Seeing that the third wave was now coming straight for me I ran in the direction of our earth bunker back on the field to my right in which the ground staff was sheltering.

I came to a barbed-wire fenced area which was so low that I could jump over it although I tore my trousers in the process. Behind me a wall of fire went beyond the cemetery and into the village. Constantly looking up I saw that the fourth wave had shifted to the right and that it would hit our bunker head on. I nearly gave up hope of escape but finally, now completely out of breath and sweating profusely, I raced around the corner of the bunker. Leaning against it was a bicycle which I grabbed and shot head first down into the sloping entrance and rolled around a corner with the inferno directly overhead. The earth wall held as the bombs were only small though countless in number.

I was the first to surface again, but in a cloud of dust. What I saw initially was that the bicycle had no tyres left and our Mercedes car had two flat tyres and splinter holes. When the dirt had settled I saw a two-wheeled cart 300 metres away standing on the road to the south-west. One of the two mules harnessed to it was down but the other still stood on spread legs. It was dreadfully mutilated, with part of its belly open and blood streaming down its eyes, its body shaking. An immense pity overcame me and I shot the poor animal to put it out of its misery. It fell immediately. The look in that poor mule's eyes, as if sad and not understanding, haunts me to this day.

In no time at all the flak soldiers, to whose batteries the mule transport belonged, arrived and the corpses were quickly carved up for provisions. Our car was still drivable after a tyre change so we went to where my Arado was parked to find it only slightly damaged with a flat tyre and two holes through the Plexiglas canopy. This damage was repaired or patched up next day for me to undertake another mission.

Then, on 20 April, the end came to my T9+EH which had served me well since the beginning of the year. I returned from a sortie and tried to lower the undercarriage but the main wheels wouldn't extend. Approaching the airfield from the west, I managed to pump out the flaps by hand but the indicator lamps for the main wheels stayed red. I tried every trick in the book by repeating all orders electrically and manually plus chucking the aircraft about in an attempt to loosen any mechanical obstruction, but to no avail. I warned the ground crew that I would have to make a belly landing. I decided at the last moment to try to save my precious Magirus bomb, again by pumping out the nose wheel manually. The grass area was full of bomb holes, so I had to bring her down, despite the cross wind, on the repaired runway. All went well until, at about 70 km/h, I couldn't hold her level anymore and the starboard wing started to scrape the ground. This caused her to flip over to port and then bounce back onto the starboard wing, which broke off completely. Finally, she flipped back to port which broke off the nose wheel, cracked the wing causing the throttle linkages to break and the turbojet to run at full power. As it was now exhausting towards the fuselage it burned a hole in it and up went the nearly empty fuel tanks. I stepped from the total wreckage fully intact apart from scraping my knuckles in my haste to get out.

Afterwards the mechanics put the remains on stilts and tried to release the undercarriage but it still wouldn't budge. Eventually we decided to blow it up before we left the airfield a week later. Well not quite. The tyres still came in handy as I had lost a lot of them on the steel splinter spiked runway on touchdown. On one occasion we had been supplied with a spare set of wheels by a pilot of a Bf 109. I never found out how he managed to do this although he took off at the crack of dawn which gave him the only chance of getting through to München/Riem and back.

CHAPTER 15

THE END AND
A NEW BEGINNING

By the middle of April 1945 the whole of the Italian front had collapsed. The only serious fighting reported was against Yugoslavian partisans. Orders came to send soldiers from our unit to this front. Then a second demand came for me to send Manfred Mänhardt and Wolf Loah to the same area. I disregarded both orders as we were still an operational unit.

During the last four weeks no mail had reached me from home. I did not know of either Friedl's whereabouts or how our parents fared. American troops had penetrated the western part of Germany. The end of our fighting was near and with it the unconditional surrender as demanded by the Western Allies and the Russians at the Yalta conference. Yet the telexed Wehrmacht situation reports continued to arrive every day informing us of what was happening on all fronts. They were always stamped top secret.

I remember one day that the telex concluded with the air situation on the Italian front, spelling out enemy plane movements at more than 3,000 against the German air activity of one single aircraft – my Arado of course. There was no fuel left for piston-engine aircraft except what was left in their tanks, and most of those were empty. Our unit still had an adequate supply of J2 kerosene fuel for the jet engines and some B2 and C3 petrol for their Riedel starter motors. We guarded this jealously.

On 22 April our troops were beginning to flood back over the River Po and I covered the retreat with flights in weather unfavourable to the mission until, two days later, I carried out my last flights, completing both missions with Arnold's T9+FH. I noted in my logbook, that '*Alles läuft*' (everybody's running). By then I had flown just over fifty operational flights in the Ar 234, none of which had been aborted due to bad weather. Further orders to dissolve our

Allied troops crossing the River Po in pursuit of our forces.

unit and go into guerrilla war fighting failed to reach us, even if they were issued. Another order, which asked us to transfer to Bozen (Bolzano) in southern Tyrol, did arrive, however.

On 26 April, one of our trucks had an unfortunate incident. In a narrow village street on the way to Udine to collect supplies, it was hit by strafing fighters and the guard, Obergefreiter Gerhard Liepelt, was killed. The truck in the incident was now at Udine for repair. Next day, while we were in front of our house, a squadron of Mustangs came patrolling at low level, shooting up anything they could see down on the road. Our machine-gun post was too late to open fire on them. They were nearly at our height (60 metres or 200 feet above the plain below) but then they turned back along the same stretch and we opened fire together with a 20-mm flak gun down on the road. We saw how the last of the string of Mustangs was hit and saw him diving into the ground and blow up. We drove to the site of the crash and found that the pilot had been thrown clear but torn in half. Somehow it was established that he was an Australian.

During the night of 27-28 April, one of our flak detachments of four soldiers together with their gun had been overpowered by partisans not far from Ceresetto, in the hills behind our billet. With this report by our neighbouring unit of NAG 11 came news that an Italian Major had been shot dead in the next village in the direction of Udine. I was with Mänhardt at the airfield early to see that all was cleared and the wreckage demolished and the men with equipment ready for the retreat. I picked up my motorbike there and went back alone. My order to demolish the remnants of my T9+EH was never carried out as I discovered sometime later.

Passing the hangars, I saw some Bf 109s circling low to the south. Asking an engineer what this was all about he said they were Italian – 'good men' he called them. So I thought too, when I saw them attacking a squadron of Thunderbolts, dogfighting wildly and a Thunderbolt falling out of the sky burning.

What puzzled me, however, was that when the gunfire stopped, both groups flew south, more or less together. Recently, I discovered from an Italian aviation historian that no Italian unit equipped with the Bf 109 existed by this time. He said that there were Germans in these machines but, if so, why did they fly southwards afterwards?

It was about 3 p.m. when I arrived at Ceresetto and after half an hour the driver of the truck in repair in Udine, Gefreiter Flasdiek, arrived on his bicycle and reported that he was riding it up the hill, coming from Udine, to the next village to ours (Torreano) when he was overtaken by some lads who pushed him off his bike and disarmed him. They took his pistol, belt and cap and then let him go. This was bad news. We could be in serious trouble before leaving the area next morning.

I decided to try to resolve the situation. As the light truck had just arrived from the airfield I told Feldwebel Schmidt and about ten men to arm themselves and follow me in the truck at a distance. I would precede them on a pushbike while I rode, apparently oblivious of anything, towards the village across a wide valley. Before mounting I took the safety catch off my pistol and pushed the barrel into the index finger of my leather glove. So, with outstretched fingers (and the right index finger on the trigger) I pedalled up the slope with both hands on the handlebars. Reaching the entrance to the village I saw a dozen or so young and middle-aged men, standing in civilian clothes, blocking the road. I waved to them to make way, which they did with some hesitation and I was through. Nothing had happened. The road led into the village flanked by high walls with vines hanging over and round vaulted gateways leading into houses. About sixty metres on I noticed a shadow crouching in one of the doorways to the left and was ready. "Don't look there" I told myself. Then the shadow sprang up and brandished an enormous revolver ready to fire. As he jumped at me I swung my right arm across, fired and let myself fall onto the road against the wall. There was silence at first, with both of us on the ground. Then gun shots rattled from where my men came up, still not in sight. But the assembly of men stampeded and fled in all directions. Only one came along the lane and seeing that his mate was down, he tried to get something out of his trouser pocket. I pulled off my glove and pointed my exposed pistol at him. He bolted and was lucky as my pistol had jammed – the spent cartridge could not be ejected after the first shot because of the glove encasing the barrel.

My men came racing up and found that I was safe. The partisan had been shot through the mouth but was not critically injured apparently. He had a cap with a red star in his pocket and identification papers belonging to the Garibaldi Partisans, *Divisione Osoppo*. After searching the village and threatening the frightened peasants with dire consequences if this interference didn't stop, we loaded the man onto the truck and brought him to NAG 11's hospital where the doctor took care of him. His large-calibre revolver had two empty cartridges in the full chamber.

I had little sympathy for partisans or any armed civilians with their aim of shooting me in the back – me as a clearly defined uniformed target. They were hiding behind women's skirts and so endangered the life of any civilian. I would have had no hesitation in shooting first before asking questions given the necessary circumstances which a civilian had created. Too many soldiers had died while hesitating or were slaughtered in the dark by throat cutters. I felt entitled to do what I did but I still feel sad at its necessity.

Of course the news went through the whole area like wildfire and, around 10 p.m., I was called over to NAG 11's headquarters as a delegation of the partisans had arrived to begin truce talks. We came to the agreement that if they returned the flak soldiers immediately with all their weapons and kept out of our way, we would take no further action.

I had not mentioned till now, that the country house we were occupying was owned by a banker who usually lived in Trieste but preferred to inhabit the domestic quarters of his country estate rather than expose himself and his family to the dangers of guerrilla warfare and bombing in that city. He had a wife of imposing features, a daughter in her late teens and a son of about seventeen. With them lived the banker's father, the only one to speak German as he was an old Imperial Austrian engineer (Trieste was Austrian till 1918). The banker and his French-educated wife both spoke French and so we could communicate with them. The youngsters smiled only obligingly when spoken to. We were sometimes invited by them for an evening glass of wine and conversation. Grandfather told me humorously of his experiences as an engineer in the Austrian empire and how they blasted the Simplon Tunnel through the Alps.

We kept tight lipped about our military affairs as their national interest necessarily conflicted with our own. They had to extricate themselves from a situation into which Mussolini, with or without their cooperation, had put them. They were almost overpoweringly friendly with "Yes", or *"Certainement Signore commandante"* at every opportunity. When one night I found our telephone operator, a young student, not at his desk but in an embrace with the still attractive and voluptuous lady of the house in the dark passage, I knew what she was up to with this young chap. Her young son I had not seen for a couple of days and I suspected him to have joined the partisans. And his mother was trying to get information about our intended movements.

We finally decided to break camp on 28 April and left Udine at noon the next day. Just before that I sent Arnold off with the one remaining Arado, T9+FH, to fly to Bolzano in the Dolomites as ordered. I decided to travel with my Kommando. The repaired truck returned and was loaded and we were ready to leave. Then an extraordinary thing happened. Part of our Kommando had already left the yard of the country house through the arched gate when the lady of the house accompanied by her daughter and some village women came into the yard carrying trays with glasses of Slivovitz (plum liquor) and offered the drinks as a farewell gift. The men didn't appear for this ceremony. With smiles on all sides we left, not without having incapacitated the gear we left behind, like the wretched little French car. No partisans attacked us on our way to Udine and beyond.

It was 30 April and the weather cleared as our convoy of twelve vehicles stopped some kilometres north of Udine. A military supply depot there was to be abandoned and blown up. Before that took place I sent two of our trucks over to collect what was necessary to sustain us for four weeks. Nobody knew what would happen once we got to the Alps. It was said that our forces were to make a last stand there in what was to be known as the *Festung Alpen* [Alpine

fortress]. It was hoped that a clash between the Americans and Russians would take place with the hoped for result of us getting better surrender conditions. Our only danger was from SS units bent on executing retreating soldiers. We had no weapons against their armoured cars, only our legitimate transfer order to Bolzano and the equipment we still had on board.

There was still no armistice and we travelled with our blacked-out vehicles deeper into the Tagliamento valley in eerie moonlight and then to

On our way home from northern Italy to Austria on 1 May 1945.

Friaul with Toblach (Tobiaco) as our target. There were still reports of road transports and trains getting shot-up at night by Black Widows (night strafers) on the passes. Next morning, we were in clouds with snow falling and freezing cold. We reached Toblach, the Austrian-Italian border town, at noon, where all traffic stopped.

All sorts of rumours circulated as we met other retreating convoys. The Americans had taken Bolzano already and were on the move to the north. No Arado had landed there which meant that Arnold had gone straight through to Holzkirchen near Munich. That meant we were free in our movements to reach safety and home.

While at Toblach, an army administration officer approached me as we were talking our situation over and surveying our convoys, and made a suggestion. He had a safe with a lot of money belonging to a defunct division on an unreliable truck which contained millions of Reichsmarks and Lire. Could I help him? I felt instinctively uneasy, anticipating a certain danger about carrying a cargo like this. I made an excuse and declined and he disappeared. I never regretted the decision. Then I met Hauptmann Arno Kötzting, leader of 2./NAG 11 with his convoy. He told me that he had news that Hitler had committed suicide and that he would be travelling back to Lienz, some short distance to the east, which had an escape route to the north. We turned and aimed for there too.

Reaching Lienz, we settled down in the gymnasium hall of a barracks, glad to be out of the freezing weather. An instruction sifted through the melee the next morning that all units should assemble on the parade ground and as Hitler was dead they should swear an oath of allegiance to his successor Admiral Karl Dönitz, which we did. That was the last act of military discipline we were to witness. No further instructions or orders of any kind were given or received. We decided to travel a couple of kilometres towards Villach along the River Drau (Drava) until we reached a spot where the valley widened and we could park off the road under trees. There was a village up the mountain to the south, called Berg ob der Drau and we investigated and found it quite capable of accommodating fifty or so men plus our two female cooks, young Italian women who decided to come with us from Ceresetto for fear of partisan retaliation.

We were now between the pincers of the British coming from Villach in the east and the Americans coming from Toblach in the west, so we carried out regular patrols with my motorbike in both directions to pick the right moment to escape to the north over the snaking Katschberg pass. The two advancing forces had halted now and so we bided our time until the armistice was declared. Of course we had the radio, but our Radione UHF receiver had been silent for a long time as the Russians had menaced Oranienburg long ago. After some days we found out that the railway station near our convoy park still had communication with Villach via the telephone and so could warn us about any movement from there.

One afternoon I was on a patrol ride on my motorbike in this direction when coming back in the dark with lights dimmed the road turned to the right around a rocky precipice. Without warning I was confronted by a lowered railway crossing barrier just metres ahead. I had not anticipated that the railways would still be running. I braked hard, swerved and slid under the boom gate hitting it with my right cheek. I was lying there stunned when big locomotive wheels went by only centimetres past the rear wheel of the bike lying just beyond me.

With a pounding head I lifted the bike up after the train had gone, but could not start it again. After leaning it against a tree I went for help to the next house back on the road which had a light shining through a slit in the curtains and knocked on the door. The door opened only a fraction and when I tried to explain my situation it was slammed shut on me. Very angry, I went back to the bike and sat there and waited. I don't know how long it was, but finally a truck came along with men from our Kommando searching for me and they got me home to Berg. When I looked in the mirror I saw that I had a very swollen head. Maybe that had frightened the people in the house, I thought.

Now there was a partial truce on the southern front signed by General von Vietinghoff, Oberbefelshaber Süd-West (commander-in-chief south-west) in Italy. A general armistice was to be effective during the night of 7-8 May 1945 and that was the signal for us to bolt as all military movements were ordered to cease. We did not feel bound by the order due to lack of controlling powers and just wanted to get home. During our time at Berg, Loah and Mänhardt had had a serious disagreement concerning politics past and present. Despite this, they both advanced to the turn-off to the north, just before Lienz, and waited for my signal from Berg railway station, where I monitored their progress using the telephone in the building. The following morning Loah came with my bike and told me that everybody had started moving towards the north and that we should not wait any longer.

So we joined the long trek of vehicles worming its way towards the mountains into the Katschberg pass, moving haltingly in a stop-go fashion. Some vehicles could not make the steep turns (the steepest was about 30 degrees) and were pushed out of the way, sometimes toppling over the edge of the narrow road. As my motorbike allowed for easier movement, I constantly ran backwards and forwards along our convoy to check that they were all safe. They were now split into several groups. By about midnight most of our vehicles had passed over the summit while I waited for the remainder. When the last of our trucks arrived, the crew in the cab told me that they had got stuck on a very steep bend and could only continue by abandoning the trailer and pushing it down the embankment into a rocky creek. They were urged to do this by the drivers of the following vehicles.

I asked where the luggage was which I had put into this trailer and they shrugged their shoulders. They had nothing on their truck they said. It was my larger suitcase with all my papers and logbooks and my little radio in it that I was worried about. My smaller suitcase was on an earlier truck, I knew. Furiously, I turned my bike and went down the pass between the trucks until I came to the bend which they had described. Down there I found the trailer in the creek, still on its wheels. Opening the door of the enclosed trailer, which was used for spare clothing, I found the clothing was still packed tightly about 30 centimetres (inches) deep. It was evenly distributed but there was no hump (indicating my suitcase) visible.

I wondered if it had been used as sleeping quarters. I could find no trace of my luggage after going through the contents of the trailer and I thought that some marauders must have taken it. Forced labour men and inmates from concentration camps were already filtering back south and may have pinched my case. But why was the clothing not disturbed? The suitcase had not been there after our unit had set up night camp I later concluded. Nobody offered an explanation the next day when I enquired. In the cab of our last truck were, besides the older and reliable driver, two non-commissioned officers, Feldwebel Schmidt and Oberfeldwebel Darr. They were both Berliners who came from the seedy part of the capital. They were excellent mechanics but otherwise shady figures. The loss of my logbooks, notebooks and letters upset me badly, especially later when I began to reconstruct these times after thirty-five years.

In the morning the stop-go progress of the snake of vehicles continued towards Radstadt. Using a side track, we came to the point where the road junction led eastwards in the direction of Bischofshofen. A couple of cars in front of ours had stopped. The reason for that was a tall Austrian Major standing at the crossing, halting all traffic. I asked him why and on what authority he was doing this. He answered that the armistice articles forbade all military movement as from this day. Then an army general came up from our direction and after a short discussion we made the grandstander jump out of our way by drawing our pistols. This Major was of course part of the plot by the 'Austrian Resistance' which tried to rake as much of the German goodies off the road for possible use by the Austrian economy after the war.

We didn't play the game with him, but shortly afterwards we came to a complete halt. It was getting dark, when a rumour drifted through the column that an American officer was stationed at Bischofshofen just ahead. He was able to give authority for convoys to travel on and direct them to certain destinations. The problem was how to get to him? The narrow road was completely blocked. However, I managed with my motorbike, sometimes pushing it underneath vehicles to get it to the other side, and squeeze through. It was now near midnight.

In the centre of the small township, one of four young officers riding inside a *Kübelsitzer* (a four-wheel-drive Mercedes army vehicle) hailed me. I recognised him immediately as the photographic officer with 1.(F)/100 from Biblis, Oberleutnant Hans Meyer zur Heyde. They were on the run from the north, we from the south and we exchanged news. He already knew where this American officer was and directed me to his jeep waiting in a triangular town square. When my turn came this major just asked my name and rank, number of men and vehicles and where we wanted to go. "Munich," I said of course. He wrote all down on a piece of paper with a pencil, signed it and tore it off his pad, saying "next please". Back at the convoy we read that he had written Zell am See instead of Munich. It didn't worry us unduly.

I had picked up two important pieces of intelligence during the night. The first was that General Eisenhower was on his way to Zell am See and the roads would be cleared for him. Secondly, that a camp for German army personnel was established just before Kitzbühl and to the left of the road in a mountain valley. Conditions were cramped and bad with no facilities at all. Ten thousand were already in it. Another thing I saw was that some officers in German uniform had white armbands and were said to be armistice assistants.

Salzburg and Zell am See were to be avoided. In the morning, when the column moved again, we reached the River Salzach and followed it upstream and as most of the vehicles had turned towards Salzburg, we had a relatively free road ahead to Mittersill. No patrols stopped us. The weather became fine and warm and we were in good spirits. Just before Mittersill we stopped for lunch and altered our passport to read 'Zell am See and Munich'. White armbands were made for Mänhardt, Loah and me and duly stamped with our squadron seal. Nobody can understand that anyway, we thought.

An example of overcrowding in an Allied internment camp for German military personnel.

From here our road turned north in the desired direction. I was hanging back a bit on my motorbike and passed that infamous turn-off to the previously mentioned internment camp and found that our convoy had stopped a kilometre further on. I was told that our last truck had suddenly hung back and turned off onto the side track and they were waiting for its return. My God, I thought, they have been caught and put in the internment camp. I turned back and followed the turn-off for about five kilometres until I came to a closed boom gate with a black American soldier on guard with his gun at the ready. There stood our truck with three disconsolate men beside it inside the compound. They were the non-commissioned officers mentioned earlier and the driver. We spoke a few words then I told the American soldier that this was my truck, showed our authorisation and pointed to my armband. He told the truck to turn and out we went through the opened boom gate.

Why these men should have tried to go their own way, even taking their comrade's luggage with them, I never got satisfactorily answered. They told me that they thought this would be a safer way over to the German border. I didn't believe them. This was pure treachery I told them and cut them dead from then on, as did most of the others. I suspect now that they were involved in the disappearance of my luggage three nights before and embarrassment or a bad conscience had hit them.

At Siegsdorf (now on German soil) we got onto the autobahn and tried to travel on it but were immediately pushed off by American troops coming towards us. Beforehand we had been relieved of all valuables, such as medals, pistols and other easy pickings by foot soldiers with guns at the ready. I did however manage to hide my treasured wrist watch from them. We camped near Traunstein and in the morning a jeep with a major came up and directed us to travel to a collection camp near Holzkirchen. There I met my old commander Major Kurd Aschenbrenner of K.Gr. 100 from Vannes as well as others I knew. It was there that I lost my camera to pilfering Americans. They sold it to another of my comrades for a bottle of brandy, but this eagle-eyed soldier found where it was and stole it back again but it was lost to me.

After a few days our convoy was moved to the concentration area for Luftwaffe men in the Heiligenkreuz forest and from there I sent my first message home since we left Udine. Our trucks were now used for supply runs for the camp as authorised by the Americans. The camp remained under German command, however. We were to be dismissed from the armed forces after being sifted through for special interrogation as to war crimes or belonging to special organisations. As we thought that our technical involvement could be of interest to them we forged our *Sold Bucher*[24] to show something else besides the interesting Versuchsverband O.K.L. Being sent to the French coal mines was not a very nice prospect. It happened to some innocents or people who just got into the wrong queue in front of the interrogator's tent in Bad Aibling, our final demobilisation camp. Mänhardt nearly copped it that way but was only behind barbed wire for a couple of days before our men managed to get him released.

During my stay in this holding camp, Stabsfeldwebel Walter Arnold, the pilot of our last Arado T9+FH, turned up. As he was unable to touch down at Bolzano because of bad weather, he told us that he had landed at Holzkirchen south-east of Munich where he blew up his aircraft just before the arrival of the Americans.

During 1985, I received a copy of four logbook pages purporting to be those compiled by Arnold. In these it was claimed that he had carried out 'my' sortie on 15 March and at least one other flight which he could not possibly have done. It was also recorded that he flew from Osoppo, but this airfield was never used by us because it had no hard runway and no take-off rockets were stored there. The confirmation of the flights at the end was absent which I, as his boss, could have done during our time in camp. Secondly the writing was too constant for having been done at the time.

When I think of him, it all looks nearly impossible. He was a quiet, inoffensive, almost shy person, but reliable and honest. Sure, he was not an eager beaver to fly the Arado which he didn't quite trust and did not hesitate to tell me so openly. This was the reason I let him loose only late after my machine was out of action and Gniesmer lost. If he did write these pages the only reason

---

24. A booklet accompanying a soldier and containing dates of commissions, pay, holidays, medals and names of units he served in.

that I can guess is that he needed them to support an application to get into the post-war Luftwaffe but it's a mystery I am still trying to resolve, but with little hope after forty-five years. I wrote to Arnold immediately but the letter was returned unopened after some protracted delay with a message scribbled on the back that the recipient had died in 1985, just before I wrote the letter.

Friedl.

One day, while still at the camp, I was overjoyed to see Friedl standing at the boom gate near our tents. I had not thought to see her again so soon due to the turbulence of the dislocated millions of people. She had come from Munich and was able to tell me that my parents were safe and that she was staying with them. What a joy and relief that was. They had got my message. Unfortunately, she had no news of my brothers. Friedl returned again later and was able to stay with a farmer before going back the next day. She took some of my last possessions with her as I didn't know if I would get them through. Friedl wasn't sure herself as there were constant inspections on the road and the Americans just took what they liked, declaring it army property.

After six weeks it was my turn too as most of my unit had already been dismissed and I was finally home and the war was over. It was 29 June 1945 and what an end it was for this long-suffering nation and for Europe.

Home at last I found my parents and Friedl together with our old maid, Marie. They were in good health, but thin through lack of food. Marie had managed to scavenge supplies left from abandoned army warehouses. Our apartment was habitable but with cardboard covering most of the windows, the glass of which had been blown out during bombing raids. What had happened to our evacuated paintings and other valuables was then still unknown as communications had broken down completely. The first thing was to get a ration card which didn't entitle one to much food – about 800 calories a day. It was at least something. A condition for it was that you had to be legally dismissed from the armed forces and that you had a job or were looking for one.

Meanwhile we didn't know what had happened to other family members and relatives. We were told later that my brother Helmuth had retreated from the front east of Berlin towards the British army in the north and had been taken prisoner there. The same fate befell brother Paul, who left Berlin just in time and headed west in order not to be captured by the Russians. For some time, the Soviets had the reputation of retaliating against Germans with much cruelty, whipped up in their hatred by their political commissars. My brother Walter's fate remained unknown.

As for Friedl, she had moved after the destruction of Würzburg with her staff to Herzogenaurach near Nürnberg [Nuremberg] where the staff of the general of reconnaissance was discharged. Everyone then had to find his or her own way home. So Friedl, with some friends, naturally tried to go home to Demmin where her mother was still living with her grandchild Rosi, daughter of Friedl's sister Hilde. In Plauen in Saxony they were overrun by the advancing American troops and she was put into a camp, dismissed from the Luftwaffe and given an American pass. Her sister Hilde escaped from Berlin too, just in time, and travelled towards the British sector.

Friedl next went to see her older sister Herta who lived nearby. The news about Demmin was bad, with the town destroyed in the fighting or shortly afterwards for alleged resistance. Many women had been raped and all the houses had been looted.[25] Her mother's fate was unknown. So she decided to look for me. She knew that I was in Italy and still alive at the time of receiving my last telexes. She had my home address in Munich and after an adventurous journey she knocked on the door of our parents who, of course, took her in. There she was, in good shape and reasonable spirits until she got the joyous news that although her mother and her niece, Rosi, had been thrown out of her apartment in Demmin by the Russians they were otherwise safe and unharmed.

Uncle Karl and Aunt Gretl lived up in the Alps at Hundham, where I had visited him around 1943 while on leave. I also saw Aunt Mary (Uncle Jus' widow) who

---

25. On 1 May 1945, hundreds of people committed suicide in Demmin induced by the atrocities committed by Soviet army soldiers the day before. As the Wehrmacht had retreated they had blown up bridges over the Peene and Tollense rivers near the town, thus blocking the Red Army's advance and trapping the remaining civilians. In retaliation, Soviet units then looted and burned the town, and raped and murdered many of the people, mostly women and children. Renate Sommer told me recently that her cousin, Helga, who was aged ten at the time, managed to hide from the Russian troops. This incident is now acknowledged to be the largest mass suicide ever recorded in Germany. After the war, discussion of the mass suicide was forbidden by the East German Communist Government. [Ed.]

Munich as I remembered it when I returned after the end of the war.

lived further up on the Dandlberg in a rented farmhouse at that time. They were all fine. The young Karl, who lived in Zehlendorf in Berlin had fled to Hamburg with his wife Lore while the sons Peter and Michael were in children's evacuation locations near their grandfather on the Samerberg.

Cousin Hans had been with a Luftwaffe unit somewhere in Austria and at the end had made his way home on foot, in civilian clothes, to Wertheim. He had his notary office there where his wife Margaret lived with their daughter Ingeborg. Those who lived in the countryside were of course better provided with provisions. Munich was the worst spot to be at this time. It was the reverse situation from the First World War when my parents were nearer the honey pot in Griesbach and all the relatives came to visit us to stock up their larders. This time there was probably not much of the larder left in the countryside either, as I can't remember that any help came from there. But we managed, in spite of all of us getting thinner and thinner.

Brother Walter's wife, Inge, lived with her parents and sisters in Hildesheim. They had lost everything during the Allied destruction of that city. The bombing left Helmuth and Hed destitute. She and her family were evacuated to Weinheim an der Bergstrasse and were living there while I was flying in Biblis. Hed had had a baby son, Axel, on 8 October 1944 and I had often visited them in the evenings on my motorbike as Weinheim was not far from Biblis. One day during the winter of 1944-45, Axel was to be baptised and I was to be his godfather. Of course I intended to be present at the church ceremony, but a special request ordered me on a mission. To telephone was not possible, but just to show them that I was prevented from coming, I decided to buzz the town on my way back. This sort of thing can have a very bad effect as I learned on the evening of my visit when I was received with some coolness.

The town had just had an air raid warning. Then came terrible swishing sounds like a stick of bombs was falling and everybody ran for shelter. Hed, with Axel in her arms, raced for the cellar and crashed heavily into an open door, fearing that this might have given Axel a bad head injury. The pastor at the church told them that he had crawled under the font which he happened to be passing. Fortunately, Axel was not hurt as everybody can now see. But sister-in-law Hed's eyes still become steely when she recounts the tale to me.

Uncle Heinrich Jolas was in Kaiserslautern where his daughter, Lisbeth Kessler, had lost most of her possessions when their house was burned out. Her husband was killed in another bombing attack on the town. However, the damage our wider family suffered during the war was mostly material. We were lucky in that nothing was stolen from our evacuated properties in Landsberg and only a few of my photos at Weinheim disappeared. My uncle's properties were not touched and neither were those of cousin Hans. About cousin Karl in Hamburg I am not sure. But Uncle Jus' villa in Rosenheim was occupied by American officers and Hans' office in Wertingen was closed to him. He was not allowed in there as he had at one time joined the Nazi party, he who was anti-Hitler, because he was more or less compelled into this action. So for the time being he was forced to sew flour bags for a local miller. In the First World War the loss of life had been far greater. Nearly all families lost a son then, except the Sommer's, who were spared again in this conflict.

The family had to rebuild again practically from nothing – to house, clothe and feed itself – but first to find each other again and start life anew.

AFTERWORD

I typed up Dad's memoirs some years ago, correcting some of his grammar and slightly altering sentences for better readability on occasions but was always careful not to change the meaning of his words. In this time of social media, which my father missed out on, I am so tempted to put a smiley face after some of his rather pompous-sounding sentences as I know that most of them are tongue-in-cheek.

The Erich Sommer I knew was a gentle man. He would avoid stepping on an ant if he knew it was there. Cockroaches and spiders were carefully removed from the house and all creatures great and small (except journalists who were criticised relentlessly) were to be cared for and protected. I'm sure he would even have saved a journalist in trouble.

My father was much more than just a Luftwaffe man with an interesting war experience. He was also a builder, a photographer, an amateur geologist, a faceter of gemstones, an opal miner, a rock hound and a man with a deep interest in the history of his adopted country Australia. He built a small inboard motorboat and had solo adventures in that to rival those of his Luftwaffe days. He bought a VW Kombi van which gave the opportunity for more adventures. Mother and I frequently joined him on these and witnessed first-hand his cleverness at getting out of sticky situations though the getting into the situations in the first place were often inevitable as no outback creek bed, muddy or sandy road or sandstorm was enough to deter him from continuing in the direction he had planned.

As for J Richard Smith; I am most grateful for his taking these 'memoirs' in hand and thinking they were worth sharing. He has done a wonderful job of picking the best bits and making them more readable, while keeping to the intended spirit of my father's story.

Renate Sommer
Encounter Bay, South Australia
October 2017

MEMORIES
OF HORST GÖTZ

Horst was born on 25 December 1911 at Beuthen, West Prussia, Southern Silesia which is today named Bytom in Poland. He began his flying career with the Deutsche Verkehrsflieger Schule [German commercial pilots' school] in 1933. Two years later he joined the Telefunken electronics company as a test pilot, avoiding being inducted into the Luftwaffe. Pulling strings with the aid of Oberst Wilfried von Cornberg, head of the Luftwaffe personnel department, he managed to get himself transferred to Kampfgruppe 100 in December 1939 where I first met him. We became firm friends and when I was reassigned to the Dresden Air War Academy in late November 1940 he managed to get himself transferred back to Telefunken. In March 1941 we both returned to Kampfgruppe 100, again courtesy of von Cornberg.

When I was transferred to the Ergänzungsstaffel[26] in June 1941, Horst also left the Gruppe, first to re-join Telefunken and then to the Luftnachrichten-schule at Strausberg near Berlin. (I was later to do a course of astronomical navigation there.) Early in 1942 he was transferred to Casablanca where he managed to get me to join him in May. For the next few months much of Horst's war history followed a similar path to mine but, following our transfer back to Oranienburg in a He 111 coded T9+EL on 14 May 1943, I left to begin training as a pilot. On 15 June Horst went to Budapest in another He 111, T9+HH, to undertake the training of Hungarian pilots loaned to Rowehl by Oberst Keks, inspector general of their reconnaissance forces. He returned to Oranienburg on 18 August 1943 by which time he had been promoted to Oberleutnant and had become the Staffelführer of the first Staffel of the Ver-

---

26. See Chapter Six.

suchsverband experimental unit. Horst now takes up the story:

'I had tested various types of aircraft including the new Bf 109 with the G-supercharger. During this period American bombers were already flying missions against Berlin. I had often observed aircraft with various amounts of damage fly westwards at low altitude. Fighters did not attack them. I suddenly decided to try and be a fighter pilot. I got hold of an armed Bf 109 and took off after some of these sick American birds returning home after a raid on Berlin. Near Nauen I managed to get one in my sights but, just as I wanted to open up, the crew abandoned the aircraft by parachute as it crashed and exploded. A miracle had occurred. There were still German fighters near Berlin and one of them had got my prize. I had no luck as a fighter pilot!

'On 15 September 1943 another segment of my career began with a new adventure. Regular reconnaissance aircraft were then unable to bring back many pictures from England. The defences were too strong. It fell upon the Rowehl outfit to fly unusual aircraft on surveillance missions over England. We had the altitude champion, the Ju 86 R, now without a bomb, the Arado Ar 240 and later the Do 335 with an engine in front and one in the rear each driving a separate propeller. Our home base was now Orly near Paris. I flew the two-seater Ar 240, which was partially pressurised, equipped with GM 1 power boosting and very fast. Its working altitude was 10,000 metres (33,000 ft) and in a shallow dive I could reach 700 km/h (435 mph). For transport I had arranged for a captured four-engine French Bloch 161 to be used.

'We tried to fly over England with the Ar 240, but I always had to turn back because of the strong fighter defences. As we approached our "colleagues" were always waiting for us at a higher altitude. I finally realised why this was happening. The French resistance radioed every one of our take-offs to England since it was customary to announce every flight with time and point of take-off. Now we only announced "main-tenance" flights and we got through. We even used the vapour trails of outgoing bomber formations as cover. It was also difficult for our recon-naissance aircraft in the Mediterranean theatre. We also had to help out there. We took off from Orly, re-fuelled in St Martin (southern France) and flew missions over the Mediterranean and the Southern Front.

'We often listened to the prohibited radio station "Calais" which was located somewhere in England. The announcers, German turncoats, asked us to come over and approach certain airfields on a given heading and a certain altitude, waggling our wings. We would be treated as guests. None of us accepted the friendly invitation!

'During one routine flight from Orly to Berlin in a Ju 88 something unusual happened. We received a warning of enemy fighters in our vicinity. Suddenly we had an English escort. To the left and right and behind us were three English fighters. None of them opened up on us. They flew peacefully next to us and so close that we could see their faces. The natural reaction was to dive toward the ground and weave around at treetop level but none of them followed us. My hair stood on end unnecessarily. After the war I asked my English NATO friends why they did not shoot us down. Nobody could answer that question. It was probably my guardian angel's doing.

'Following a reconnaissance mission over London I had to land in Brussels because enemy fighters were near Orly. Brussels refused me permission to land because of an enemy aircraft in the vicinity. But I had to land because my fuel was low. While we were still in the air we saw that everybody in Brussels was heading for the air raid shelters. Once on the ground I headed immediately to ground control and found out that they had warned us that we were the cause of the air alarm in Brussels. A single unidentified German aircraft had caused all this trouble. On another occasion I tried to land at Orly and received good radio instructions to land. As I broke through the cloud cover near the field I found myself in the middle of the barrage balloons. Either I was the idiot and had over corrected to the wrong side or the radio beacon I had received was incorrect. I was able to pull the heavy aircraft into a near vertical side slip and eluded the heavy steel cables. From then on I insisted on receiving radio approach instructions twice and I did my own calculations with more care.

'Leave was hard to come by especially after I became Staffel commander. Now and then I did get home and celebrated "birthdays". An excuse was always there since one escaped again and again from fighters and flak. A proper holiday however was not to be had during the war. The Americans were rotated after twenty-five missions but we had to fly until somebody did us in. My friend, Hans-Georg Bätcher, flew 600 missions. Hans-Ulrich Rudel flew many more but those were exceptions.

'During leave in Berlin we practically had an air raid every night. We helped put out fires in our neighbourhood and assisted people as best we could and damned the noble British who strafed us while we were doing this work. In our house these heroes managed to put a bullet hole into the children's room.

There was Nuremberg and only German war criminals, but of the war crimes of the Allies nobody spoke or speaks of today. Here people are still being re-educated and the past is being dealt with in a one-sided way – *Vae Victis* (woe to the vanquished)!

'A positive and humanitarian story should be related here: One day a young Dutch woman came looking for help to my wife. She had travelled illegally and without papers to Berlin in order to find her husband who was a forced labourer. It needs to be added that the "forced" was more or less voluntary since the Dutch could pick where they wanted to work. The poor young woman did not even have a ration card. My wife found the husband in a worker's quarter and arranged with the bureaucrats that he could move with his wife into our home. A resident permit was also procured for the young wife. Jaap and Cora DeWitt Havers became part of our family. They helped to put out fires and put back roof tiles that had been blown away by bombs on our house. At times Jaap brought along some of his French co-workers to help. They always muttered, "War no good!" Everything was shared in a brotherly way with the Dutch – even our last cigarette. That is how badly foreign workers had it, at least with us.

'When we met them in Amsterdam after the war for the first time, they embraced us with tears in their eyes in front of pedestrians. Not too long ago the DeWitt Havers' family in Amsterdam did invite us to a party and the now greying couple assured us that the best time of their life was that they had spent in Berlin with us during the war. Now they were spoiling us, a great pleasure indeed in return. Many times they spent their holidays with us here in Nieby; a friendship of members of two nations that has lasted a lifetime.

'We flew with our varied reconnaissance aircraft from Orly until April 1944 and then came the order to return to Oranienburg. We had no idea of what was waiting for us. The reason for our return to Oranienburg soon became clear enough. The invasion was on the horizon. Our few crates in the west were barely able to leave the ground. A successful reconnaissance of the island was out of the question. Siegfried Knemeyer, now an Oberst and chief of the TLR (Technische Luftrüstung/Technical Air Armament) had an idea. Two Ar 234s, the V5 and V7, pure prototypes were fitted with aerial cameras and I was going to get them. I did not realise that a new era of military aviation was about to dawn. I had heard of jets but did not know any details. I flew to Alt-Lönnewitz and had my first look at the legendary aircraft, followed by thirty minutes' instruction. I quickly found out about the landing and take-off speed as it related to the trolley and skid arrangement. These aircraft did not have a conventional landing gear and we had to take off with a trolley. I took the V5, my former crew member Sommer who had now become a pilot took the V7. The code letters, GK+IV, on my machine were still from the factory. Sommer and I discovered later that these were the first two jet reconnaissance aircraft to be used on a mission.

'The take-off procedure was rather complicated. First press the starter, and then inject fuel until the turbines started at around 6,000 rpm. Then J2 kerosene had to be added slowly until 9,000 rpm was reached. Only then could the engines be throttled back and idled. Once airborne there was a totally new feeling. There was a low whistling noise in the cockpit. Take-off with the trolley went without a hitch. The trolley was dropped and I was off. It was a miracle. Galland once said that it was as if angels were pushing. We had the same impression, for the Arado exhibited an incredible speed. I reached the Elbe and the Rhine very quickly and back to Alt-Lönnewitz to land on the skid. Landing was very similar to landing a glider.

'We familiarised ourselves with the aircraft and transferred the V5 and V7 to Oranienburg. The Allied invasion was running full blast. I anticipated that our Kommando Götz would soon move west and reported our two jets ready for action. I also had a Ju 352 as a transport aircraft. Nothing happened and we remained on the ground. The traitors in the highest leadership positions did not want the invasion to be interfered with.

'On 17 July we finally received permission (not orders) to fly to Juvincourt on the invasion front. No air transport of the technical equipment but movement by rail, which was a very dangerous undertaking in those days. The saboteurs or idiots were at it again. I divided our special equipment onto two freight trains. Only one arrived at the destination. We took off on 17 July for Juvincourt; Sommer in the V7 reached his destination while I had to return with a faulty turbine. On 2 August I was finally able to join Sommer after an engine change. Sommer had just returned from his first successful reconnaissance of the invasion front. Weather permitting, we flew missions over the front but it was too late. The Allies had gained a foothold in France. Reconnaissance up to our arrival was zero over the invasion front. The unarmed Arados performed very well. The Allied fighters could not touch us as we outran them in a slight dive at 900 km/h (560 mph). In those days the fighters did not attack us very often.

'We had to gain experience with the jets on a daily basis. We heard about the critical Mach numbers but what it really meant we never found out until one day it happened to me. I was on my return from the invasion front at 10,000 metres (33,000 feet). It was impossible at that time to decrease power in the turbines at this altitude and so I proceeded in the usual shallow dive towards Rheims. The true airspeed was 950 km/h (590 mph). I shall always remember the speed. Suddenly there was a jolt in the crate, followed by a shudder. The nose was down and suddenly there was no rudder response. The aircraft was uncontrollable. There was one possibility and that was to shut down both engines and hope that the air resistance would slow the aircraft down. I was very lucky again. The Arado did slow down and I was gradually able to apply a little rudder control and pull out of the dive. Now I was flying a glider without power and had to reach 2,000 metres (6,500 feet) and a speed of 500 km/h before I could restart the engines. If my adversaries had paid more attention then, it would have ended tragically for me. They did not pursue me. The engines started and I returned to base having gained another valuable experience.

'Another problem occurred when, during a rocket-assisted take-off I noticed that the trolley could not be dropped by electrical or mechanical release. An aborted take-off was impossible and I had no choice but to take the 600-kg (1,320-lb) trolley with me. This was a risky business because it just hung there by the 1,000-kg bomb-release mechanism. The smallest mistake on my part could have slammed the trolley into the aircraft, which would have been the end of me. I made a few careful turns around the airfield, and requested by radio for the ground crews to clear the airfield in order for me to come in diagonally so that I could use the longest possible landing strip. I knew that the hydraulic hoses had been torn away and that I had no brakes to land this fast bird. My radio message had been acknowledged, but the airfield was not cleared. The man in charge, Ing. Arno Trebs prohibited his men to do that and commented: "Let him try to land safely as best he can." Yes, we had characters like him too in those days. I brought the crate down with a great deal of speed (*Affenzahn* or breakneck speed) and ended up in a potato field. Mother Earth had embraced me again.

'Flying seems to be ninety-nine per cent luck and one per cent experience and skill. Nevertheless, we adjusted well to the first operational jets, which was keenly observed by the RLM. We constantly had to write reports about our operational experiences. This only took precious time away from us.

'Following my recovery from the crash of the V5 on 28 August,[27] I returned to Rheine on 14 September with a brand new Arado with a retractable undercarriage. I considered this a great leap forward. Sorties continued and, on 6 October, I was lucky again when six Thunderbolts (we called them *Trunkenbolde* – drunken bolts) came after me from altitude and tried to blast me out of the sky. First I had to get rid of the take-off rockets and disposable fuel tanks and then I had to gain airspeed. My speed increased slowly to 500 km/h and then 700 km/h (435 mph) and faster and my good little Arado made it again and put the pursuers far behind me. It had worked once more!

'One day as I was returning from London something unusual happened. One of the engines began to shake. That happened now and then when a turbine blade broke off and I did not know yet which engine had been affected since the performance was still normal. I was at an altitude of 10,000 metres, our usual operational altitude, over the North Sea. I wanted to stop the bad engine but instead picked the good one. So I was gliding again without power but this time over the North Sea. Again I slowly descended to below 2,000 metres and managed to restart the engine. I was able to reach Rheine on one engine. I was very lucky again because none of the many enemy fighters cruising over Germany at this time saw me.

'On 10 November 1944 my friend Sommer had to transfer to Biblis with two Ar 234s. I received a phone call from Erbesheim. "I had to land at Erbesheim after a mission and was set on fire by our own flak. Aircraft completely destroyed. Pilot unhurt." I drove angrily to Erbesheim to take those responsible to task. A very young Oberleutnant with his aide, a Leutnant, who both had schoolboy faces greeted me pale but ready for anything. I could not get myself to have these two sorry chaps

---

27. See Chapter Eleven.

punished. I took the only bottle of schnapps they had as payment. The four of us emptied it and the incident was settled. By this time the V7 had been retired and we were all flying Ar 234 Bs with wheeled undercarriages.

'During the winter we had trouble starting the engines because of the cold. We let a little of the starter fuel run through to the turbine and lit it with a blowtorch. A barbaric method, but it worked!

'One day I was ordered to report to the commander of the reconnaissance forces, General von Barsewisch. He told me in a cordial manner that I would be assigned another Staffel, 1.(F)/123, which was to be equipped with Ar 234s. The Staffel leader was Hauptmann Hans Felde. I was supposed to train the pilots to operational status. When I explained that training at an airfield that was constantly under enemy attack was impossible, I was curtly told: "You may be a good operational pilot but you lack leadership qualities." I was dismissed. An additional 250 men were now my responsibility. It happened just like I had predicted. Felde was shot down before my very eyes by a Tempest and his burning aircraft literally ended at my feet. It was his first and only mission with the Arado.[28] We lost many pilots of his Staffel in a similar way. The old-timers seemed to always return untouched.

'By the spring of 1945 things began to get more and more difficult and when tanks appeared near Rheine we transferred to Rheinsehlen on 23 March 1945. We were not long there before we moved again, this time to Lübeck-Blankensee and then to Höhn near Rendsburg. During these last weeks of the war, I really became acquainted with our Allied counterparts. Without much opposition these heroes of the air killed hundreds if not thousands of civilians in low-level attacks. These were mostly refugees that had escaped the Russians. Men, women and children lay dead or wounded on the roads. We could not help; there was nothing we could do. I had to watch for instance how an American Lightning targeted individual bicyclists. Once one of these heroes crashed in his burning Lightning. We found him slightly wounded and asked him why he hunted individual women in the fields. He denied it and stated he had only attacked fuel trains. For the first time I did not offer a cigarette to a prisoner. When the German jets appeared much to the chagrin of the Allies, German pilots were machine-gunned on their

---

28. See Chapter Thirteen.

parachutes after they bailed out. We received orders to reciprocate but we never carried this out. "German Huns and bandits" could not do such a thing.

'The end of the war reached us in Höhn near Rendsburg. On 7 May I was called to the Gruppe headquarters in Schleswig. I found a strange atmosphere there. High-ranking brass asked me to take a seat. All of a sudden the treatment was friendlier. It came from the very officers who, only a few weeks before the end, had ordered 1.(F)/123 to fly missions in all weather conditions and against overwhelming enemy superiority. The enemy was already in Hannover and I did not want to incur more losses. There was no point.

'First I had to drink a schnapps and then I was told that the war would be over the next day. I was also told that I could fly my aircraft wherever I wanted to and after a conference with Eisenhower there would be no more attacks. There would be no more take-offs after that. I did not imagine the end quite like that. I gathered my pilots together at Höhn and told them it was up to them to fly as close to home as possible or go wherever they wanted to. All aircraft were ready for take-off the next morning and some wanted to go to Austria, Czechoslovakia, southern Germany, Denmark and Norway.

'I had the same intentions. I had no experience with a lost war but was of the opinion that the captain should be the last to leave the ship. That is why my aircraft was the last to take off. It did not work because the left gear collapsed. As I discovered later the mechanics had opened a valve on the hydraulically operated undercarriage and made a take-off impossible. They did not want to be without their leader. I growled a bit but then understood their action. In their place I would have probably not have acted differently. With a heavy heart I blew up my own crate. Only the periscope remained. It remained intact. It is now a souvenir with my friend Sommer. It decorates his desk in Australia. I had no idea of what would come next and moved my crew into a forest south of Rendsburg. We remained there until one day an English tank appeared and the crew told us to report to an English command at an airfield in Schleswig.

'Maybe these episodes leave some impressions about the past, retold by somebody who was there. According to Churchill, the wrong pig was slaughtered. Many of my later NATO comrades later said that we fought on the wrong side. That Germany remains divided our friends will surely see to that.[29] The victors received the least because they lost their empire after they declared war on Germany. Because of their short sightedness and lack of understanding of the world situation the Western World built a more dangerous enemy than Germany ever was: the Soviet Union. One thing is sure that today's western peace goals are the same as Germany and her Allies' war goals. The fight against Communism. The wheel of History cannot be turned back, it is too late.'

---

29. Horst's memories were written sometime before German reunification on 3 October 1990.

LIST OF TERMINOLOGY

Dipl.-Ing. • Diploma Engineer

Ergänzungs • Reserve Unit

Fliegerhorstkommandant • Airfield Commanding Officer

Flugzeugführerschule • Pilot Training School

Führungsstab • Air Staff

Gefreiter • Leading Aircraftsman

Geschwader Kommodore • Wing Leader

Hauptmann • Flight Lieutenant

Kampfgeschwader (or K.G.)• Bomber Wing

Kampfgruppe (or K.Gr.) • Bomber Group

Kommandeur • Commander

Kurierstaffel • Communication Squadron

Landespolizei • Semi-Military Police

Leutnant • Pilot Officer

Luftkriegschule • Air War Academy or Air Warfare School

Luftnachrichten • Air Signals

Luftnachrichten Schule und Versuchs Regiment • Air Signals Training and Experimental Regiment

Luftnachrichtenschule • Air Signals School

Luftwaffe Führungstab • Headquarters Staff

Major - Squadron Leader (rank)

Oberfeldwebel · Flight Sergeant

Oberleutnant · Flying Officer

Oberst · Group Captain

Oberstleutnant · Wing Commander

Reichs Luftfahrt Ministerium (also RLM) · German Air Ministry

Ritterkreuz · Knight's Cross

Stabsingenieur · Staff Engineer

Stabsstaffel · Headquarters Flight

Staffelkapitän · Squadron Leader (position)

Technische Luftrüstung · Technical Air Armament

Unteroffizier · Corporal

Volkssturm · Home Guard

Waffenstillstands Kommission · Armistice Commission

INDEX